NEIGHBORHOOD
SUCCESS STORIES

NEIGHBORHOOD SUCCESS STORIES

CREATING AND SUSTAINING AFFORDABLE HOUSING IN NEW YORK

CAROL LAMBERG

Empire State Editions

An imprint of Fordham University Press

New York 2018

Visit us online:
www.empirestateeditions.com
www.fordhampress.com

Library of Congress Control Number: 2018933430

Printed in the United States of America

20 19 18 5 4 3 2 1

First edition

to Settlement Housing Fund

Contents

Foreword

Gale A. Brewer, Manhattan Borough President

Carol Lamberg knows her stuff, and she shares it all in this book. It's a testament to her decades-long struggle to create affordable housing in New York City by any means necessary—one that has great relevance today, even as federal support for housing programs has dwindled to a trickle.

Carol's tenure as executive director of Settlement Housing Fund began in 1983 and took flight with the efforts sponsored by then mayor Ed Koch to create 225,000 units of affordable housing.

The Koch administration chose Settlement Housing to manage the renovation and occupancy of a nine-hundred-apartment development in the West Bronx, eventually named New Settlement Apartments.

Settlement Housing Fund's efforts to create a thriving community from the burned-out shells of fourteen buildings constitute an object lesson in good management, as the organization took care of the tiniest details every step of the way, from construction to tenant selection to on-site community programs.

The lessons Carol learned during her journey are described in detail in these pages, and her central insight—that affordable housing developments are successful when there is sustainable maintenance funding and the people in charge are competent—could be applied to all municipal government, and in particular today's affordable housing community.

Foreword

Ruben Diaz, Jr., Bronx Borough President

On a hot day in August 2017, I had the distinct privilege of visiting the New Settlement Community Center on Jerome Avenue in the Bronx. I had been there many times before, but today was something special. My visit was part of a larger celebration of a major policy victory.

Several years earlier an advocacy group that does work in the Bronx, known as Community Action for Safe Apartments (CASA), had set its sights on passing what was known as the Right to Counsel Act. This bill, if passed, would provide vulnerable tenants with cost-free representation in housing court.

More than that, this bill would change the entire paradigm of housing court, putting tenants on a more equal footing with landlords during eviction proceedings. CASA stood strong on this issue from the first day it was proposed, and in return mayor Bill de Blasio and a host of other elected officials, myself included, would come to New Settlement that day to sign the law and celebrate its implementation.

But the day was just as much a celebration of New Settlement Apartments and the vital community space they had created on Jerome Avenue. In a traditionally underserved area we had a vibrant, active place where the community could come together to share meals, exercise, build relationships, agitate on the important issues of the day, build strength through neighborly interactions and friendships—and, on occasion, alter the shape of the city for decades to come through advocacy on important new legislation.

I have always understood the necessity of strong community spaces—the spaces we share together—especially the New Settlement Community Center. Through my own capital budget I have provided the center with $1.4 million in funding, and I frequently advise my colleagues in government all over the city and state to visit the center and see what is has to offer as a model for their own communities.

The New Settlement Community Campus , comprising three public schools and a community center, offers a model of integrated community and school programming with amenities rarely available in neighborhoods like Mount Eden. From the sixth to ninth graders who are learning to swim for the very first time, to the teens and adults who are discovering dance, yoga, and healthy eating, the students and community members and the Bronx have an outstanding new resource at the Campus.

The considerable progress seen in the Bronx today—in economic development, housing, and the overall revitalization of the borough—is no accident.

A lot has changed in the Bronx, and for the better, since I first took office. In 2016 the Bronx saw an incredible $3.27 billion in total development, 37 percent higher than 2015 and the most of any year since I've been borough president. That same year, the Bronx also saw more than 14.2 million square feet of total development, 41 percent more than 2015 and, once again, the most since I took office in 2009.

In fact, since 2009, the Bronx has been home to nearly $13 billion and 70 million square feet of total development.

We've seen incredible public investment, as well. Since coming to office in 2009, my office has provided $248.6 million in total capital funding to 725 projects. That's nearly a quarter of a billion dollars—a tremendous number.

We've reopened the historic High Bridge, connecting northern Manhattan to the West Bronx for pedestrians and cyclists alike.

We're rebuilding the Kingsbridge Armory, bringing a $350 million investment to Kingsbridge Heights.

We're expanding commuter rail service in the East Bronx, which will, for the first time, offer one-seat transportation to approximately 160,000 Bronx residents.

Thanks to a jump start of $10 million allocated from my office, we are delivering on a promise to rebuild the historic pavilion at Orchard Beach and return it to its former glory.

Following years of planning and discussions, we're replacing a portion of the Sheridan Expressway with a landscaped boulevard.

Most significantly, we have funded an incredible amount of affordable housing. My office has leveraged approximately $2.1 billion with an allocation of more than $51.9 million in capital funding to the development of eighty-six projects. This direct investment has created 7,772 units of affordable housing in every corner of the Bronx. This funding is helping us fight displacement, ensuring that those Bronx residents who fought so hard for the well-being of their communities during our most difficult times can stay in our borough and enjoy our positive transformation.

When I took office more than eight years ago, the Bronx had the highest unemployment rate in New York State. Today, we have seen some of the lowest unemployment rates in our borough's history. More Bronx residents have jobs than ever before.

We are attracting new businesses and new development. The *New York Times* said that we are one of the hottest places to visit in the world. We certainly have more work to do, and life is not perfect. But we are moving in the right direction.

These successes did not happen in a vacuum. We could not get to where we are today without the advocacy and activism of elected officials, community leaders, nonprofits, businesses, and everyday Bronxites who for so long would not take no for an answer.

We would not have seen the incredible public and private investment that has come to the Bronx in recent years without the work of earlier trailblazers, like New Settlement Apartments, a nonprofit organization that invested in our communities when it was not fashionable to do so. When our borough needed an anchor to stabilize our communities, it was organizations like New Settlement Apartments that stepped into the void, creating new housing units and community spaces.

I remember playing in rubble as a child. I remember when "The Bronx is burning" was more than a historical tagline.

But I can never forget the role New Settlement Apartments played in helping our borough rebuild. The people of the Bronx owe them a debt of gratitude.

NEIGHBORHOOD SUCCESS STORIES

PART I
Overview

1

Housing Issues and Experiences

When we think of basic human needs, food, clothing, and shelter are at the top of the list. And when we think of what constitutes acceptable shelter, we think of housing that is not only spacious enough and in good condition but also affordable, especially for families with limited incomes. And in a city like New York, where the market exerts such a powerful grip on the cost of shelter, the concept of affordable housing is not only of paramount importance but also, given current economic conditions, an increasingly elusive commodity.

Given the critical importance of affordable housing in a city like New York and similar localities around the country, it's no surprise that public and private groups have searched endlessly for the best ways to meet this need. From the public housing projects created during the Great Depression to the programs that were part of Lyndon Johnson's Great Society, from Richard Nixon's Section 8 program to the de Blasio administration's effort to put market-rate and subsidized apartments under the same roof in New York City, there have been many efforts to address this issue.

Housing programs work when resources are adequate and when competent people are in charge. This book illustrates examples of successful community development in the Bronx and on the Lower East Side of Manhattan, using seven different methods of finance, only one of which is available today. The buildings were developed between 1975 and 1997. Despite the success of these programs, developing and operating affordable housing is a challenge. Every building is something of a miracle. I think of Goldberg's law: "Murphy was an optimist." Still, when the results are good, the process is tremendously rewarding—you can go to the eighteen buildings in the Bronx and the seven sites in Lower Manhattan, look at them, and marvel at what can be accomplished with good financing and attention to management. It takes a lot of work, but the results are more than worth the effort.

All the programs that helped finance these developments should have remained on the books, and simply updated as needed. Instead, only one of the programs is still operative—the one that is extremely complex and depends on piecing together various sources of grants, equity, and debt.

Articles in the press often assume that public housing and urban renewal have failed, despite the long waiting lists for many public housing buildings and other government-financed developments. One problem is that journalists, scholars, and some attorneys can make it seem even more difficult to rebuild poor neighborhoods than it needs to be. For example, the goal, popular in 2016, is to create regulations that encourage low-income, minority families to move to "high-opportunity areas." A study at Harvard by Raj Chetty and Nathaniel Hendron has been widely cited.[1] It shows that a sample of young people increased their incomes after moving to higher-income neighborhoods. If a nine-year-old moved to a high-opportunity neighborhood, the child could be earning $14,000 in his or her twenties, as opposed to $11,000 for the young person who remained in a low-income area. The goal is admirable: encouraging low-income tenants to move to high-income communities. During the Obama administration, rules were established to allow higher rents and other preferential treatments that encourage the location of new developments in "high-opportunity areas." These policies could block efforts to improve high-poverty neighborhoods. I believe that the gains from this new approach are not sufficient to warrant the new obstacles to efforts to improve low-income areas. It is possible to convert poor areas into thriving communities by coordinating mixed-income housing with campaigns to improve schools and create neighborhood amenities. The two kinds of effort are not mutually exclusive.

Today, the public is finally aware that housing is not affordable in many big cities. In addition, foreclosures have caused lingering problems in neighborhoods around the country. In his February 3, 2015, State of the City address, mayor Bill de Blasio, a progressive leader, spoke of affordable housing as the most important way to address income inequality: "This administration is taking a fundamentally different approach—one that not only recognizes the need for more affordable housing . . . but demands it."

1. See Raj Chetty and Nathaniel Hendren's Equality of Opportunity Project, http://www.equality-of-opportunity.org/.

Although some people still think that housing problems disappeared when the economy recovered from the recession of 2008, residents of high-cost regions cannot find a home that is even remotely affordable. There is a consensus today that something should be done. However, in real dollars the federal housing budget is a fraction of what it was in the 1970s. According to the Low Income Housing Coalition advocacy group, federal budget authority for housing assistance declined 50 percent between 1976 and 2007 and since then "primarily serves to maintain existing units" instead of creating new ones.[2] In addition, hundreds of thousands of affordable units have been demolished or converted to market-rate housing.

Why Is There So Little Federal Money for Housing?

There are many reasons why this happened. Between 1975 and 1985, the increase in public housing or units with Section 8 aid was over two hundred thousand per year. Between 2010 and 2015, the annual increase was less than twenty-five thousand units.[3] Although between 1986 and 2016 approximately ninety thousand apartments a year were partially assisted through the Low-Income Housing Tax Credit Program, they met only a fraction of the need.

The public mood also changed dramatically. The reluctance of Congress during Barack Obama's second term to authorize any public expenditure for housing probably explains the federal housing and community development budget's sorry state today. The Trump administration's initial budget proposal involves deep cuts in housing assistance that would result in dramatic increases in homelessness.

In addition, the press covers failures and controversies instead of housing success stories. One potential editor who read my draft manuscript asked whether I could add some instances of failure instead of focusing

2. The Department of Housing and Urban Development budget is confusing. Until 1983, all the payment commitments for long-term contracts for Section 8 were included in the first year's budget. Afterward, contracts were usually renewed for one year at a time, thereby reducing the budgets. However, operating cost increases in later years prompted the need for more assistance per unit. The tragic bottom line is that HUD stopped committing new funds for vouchers at a time when homelessness kept increasing. The budget proposed by the Trump administration is even worse.

3. Center on Budget and Policy Priorities, Chart Book Summary, April 12, 2016, https://www.cbpp.org/. The source for the initial numbers is an older study for the Center by Edgar O. Olsen, "Affordable Housing Programs for Low-Income Households," NBER working paper 8208, April 2001.

on successes, which he did not find as interesting. I prefer emphasizing best practices.

Housing advocates are also partially to blame. Over the years many have been their own worst enemies. When it comes to housing programs, there is considerable debate about what works and what doesn't. We argue among ourselves about whether public ownership is better than private ownership, whether resources should all go to the lowest-income groups (the "truly needy") or whether middle-income families also need aid. We argue about whether tax incentives, capital subsidies, or operating subsidies are the best way to fund housing. We fight among ourselves instead of joining forces to obtain adequate resources to do the job properly. Only a few housing professionals admit that providing quality housing is mostly about money and the competence of the people in charge.

As a housing professional with a half century's worth of experience, I have visited affordable housing developments in fifteen countries and more than two dozen American cities. Many were excellent. Some were horrible.

We Could Have Kept the Old Programs

I have seen housing programs come and go, often with too little resistance. New administrations at all levels of government often want to put their stamp on a program, rather than adjusting existing frameworks to meet new conditions. Programs get trashed instead of tweaked. Although some improvements have resulted, the process often represents a waste of time. It would be easier to amend the federal programs used to develop the buildings on the Lower East Side of Manhattan than to eliminate them and start all over with "new" initiatives. In the best of times, it takes perseverance to enact new laws and then to develop and implement regulations. In addition, it also takes time and considerable political will.

One leader from the Carter administration described amendments to improve existing programs as "warmed-over toast." He thought that the Carter White House needed to create a new program that it could "own."[4] This was the beginning of a period of cutbacks in housing assistance. I once almost got fired because I circulated a press release claiming that when it came to housing, Carter was worse than Nixon had been. Luckily no one in the press paid any attention, and my job was secure.

4. This was reported by Anne H. Lindgren, who was special assistant to the secretary of the Department of Housing and Urban Development during the Carter administration. She said this to me in Washington, as I was advocating a simple amendment to a program instead of scrapping an entire older framework.

In fact, the programmatic details are much less important than are the resources devoted to construction and maintenance. Housing developments shine when enough funds are provided and when great people run the buildings. In rental housing, it is important to select tenants carefully. It is best to reject people with bad credit or very poor housekeeping skills. I know that sounds harsh, but both low- and moderate-income residents have high standards about their neighbors. For families who need help in daily living skills, supportive housing can offer an excellent environment. For home ownership, good credit is essential. It does people no favors to sell them homes they cannot afford.

When resources and management are adequate, affordable housing developments are great for residents. In addition, affordable buildings often improve the surrounding communities, as I will show in the histories of developments that I provide in the chapters that follow. It's gratifying to visit the neighborhoods where we built housing, remembering what they'd been like previously. By no means could anyone say these developments are a failure.

Despite popular perceptions, in New York City and other areas public housing was a huge success when there were excellent professionals in charge and enough government money to maintain the buildings. Sadly, these days resources for supporting and repairing public housing are minimal, and the professional staff members in many cities are less than competent, if not corrupt. Still, there are great public housing developments throughout the United States and around the world, including many in New York City.

Integration

When it comes to public housing, one example of resounding success is Singapore, a nation of more than five million people, where 82 percent of the population lives in public housing. Although the first public housing buildings were basic, over the last decades the tall public housing structures have been architecturally attractive, deserving awards and accolades. Most of their families own their units, using loans from their government retirement fund and grants for the down payments. The loans are repaid if the units are sold.[5]

In 2012 I visited the Pinnacle@Duxton, a huge complex of seven buildings in Singapore, each fifty stories high. There was a running track

5. A good description of Singapore's housing programs is provided in an article in *The Economist*, "Why 80% of Singaporeans Live in Government-Built Flats," published June 6, 2017.

on the twenty-sixth floor along the perimeter of all the buildings. A huge roof terrace connects the buildings and offers sculpture gardens, comfortable seating, and amazing views. There are 1,848 apartments, along with shops, community facilities, a food court, a childcare center, an educational complex, and more. It was incredible to see.

On August 30, 2015, the CNN TV journalist Fareed Zakaria asked Singapore's deputy prime minister, Tharman Shanmugaratnam, to name the most significant accomplishment in his government's history. Zakaria seemed to expect an answer that involved the success of the nation's economy. Instead, the official spoke of public housing policies that mandated ethnic diversity in every building through a system of quotas. The result, over decades, has been interracial harmony and respect. "You cannot simply assume that the natural workings of the market or of society will produce social harmony," said the deputy prime minister. "They won't. The government has a role to play. And it's not about speeches and symbols. It's about specific mechanisms and programs to achieve the outcomes we all seek."[6]

In the Two Bridges urban renewal area on the Lower East Side of Manhattan, the goal from 1971 until its official completion in 1997 had been to achieve a mixed population, including Asians, Latinos, African Americans, and Caucasians, reflecting the surrounding community. In the Bronx, a mix of Latinos, immigrants from Africa, and African Americans of various incomes became the residents of a reconstructed neighborhood known as New Settlement Apartments, now consisting of eighteen brick buildings developed between 1989 and 2017.

However, because of litigation against quotas that had been established in a development in Brooklyn known as Starrett City, achieving integration today is possible only through strenuous outreach efforts. I believe that the Starrett decision should be revisited to allow overt efforts to achieve racial and economic diversity in housing complexes.

The buildings in the West Bronx and the Lower East Side were developed by Settlement Housing Fund, a New York City nonprofit organization that has created more than 8,700 apartments and owns twenty-nine buildings comprising 1,676 affordable apartments.

Clara Fox, who founded the organization in 1969, served as its executive director until her retirement in 1983. I then took over her role, remaining in that role until my own retirement in 2014. I hope that the

---

6. Fareed Zakaria, "What America Can Learn from Singapore about Racial Integration," *Washington Post*, June 25, 2015.

stories of these two complexes—our showcase developments—illustrate that community development is worth the investment of money and significant effort.

New Settlement and Two Bridges

The first tenants of New Settlement Apartments, owned by a nonprofit affiliate of Settlement Housing Fund, began arriving in 1990. The New Settlement Apartments story illustrates how the project helped transform a devastated neighborhood into a thriving though still mostly lower-income community.

The development of the Two Bridges urban renewal area began over forty years ago and involved six different federal housing programs. The area, which is economically and ethnically integrated, consists of six residential sites, a running track, and a supermarket. Working with the Two Bridges Neighborhood Council, Settlement Housing Fund led development of both the housing and the supermarket.

The Two Bridges Neighborhood Council, which had been formed in 1955 to promote neighborhood integration and advocate for good public schools, was designated as an urban renewal sponsor in 1965. In those years, "maximum feasible community participation" was required for government housing programs, especially for New York City urban renewal projects in the post–Robert Moses era. After interviewing potential co-developers for the six sites, in 1971 the council chose Settlement Housing Fund.

The residential sites were developed between 1973 and 1997. One building is owned by the New York City Housing Authority, one is a condominium, two are owned by for-profit developers, and two are owned by affiliates of nonprofit organizations. Unfortunately, only one of the programs used for development remains on the books today. A luxury developer bought the supermarket site, and the building was torn down in 2013, victim of an increasingly hot local real estate market.

These two examples of neighborhood development offer concrete evidence that various kinds of government financing can be used to provide excellent and affordable communities. The investment of public funds has unquestionably paid off, making the efforts by developers and owners were well worth the trouble. While the development process was challenging and sometimes daunting, the stories of these buildings illustrate best practices that should be replicated.

Based on having helped develop more than fifty affordable housing complexes and visiting many others, I've learned a few lessons. The model used by Settlement Housing Fund involves mixed developments that integrate low- and middle-income families. However, I've also seen exclusively low-income or middle-income buildings that work as well. Good management is crucial. And while these projects may seem costly in the short run, investment in community development eventually provides an excellent return.

In the years since I joined Settlement Housing Fund, the landscape for social service programs in the United States has changed profoundly, and with it the landscape for affordable housing. The vast public housing projects that proliferated in New York City and elsewhere during the postwar years are no longer being built. Public money for affordable housing is in desperately short supply. Memories of the political goals of Franklin Roosevelt, Fiorello La Guardia, and Lyndon Johnson have long since faded. Visions of a Great Society have are largely confined to the history books. At the same time, there are men and women working in New York City and around the country to help those who need a secure and affordable roof over their head.

In its specifics, this book represents something of a time capsule because of these dramatic changes in the world of affordable housing. But for anyone concerned with housing for low- and moderate-income populations in the United States—from scholars to researchers to urban planners—the lessons learned are of great import for future generations. Housing providers to this day grapple with issues of financing, building maintenance, and income mix. The challenge of encouraging groups with disparate agendas to come together in pursuit of a single goal is even greater in an increasingly polarized society. The need for creative compromises continues as groups grow further apart. Not losing faith when trying to provide services is harder still.

Every American deserves a decent home. Housing programs should become an entitlement. I hope this book offers both lessons and encouragement toward making that happen.

2

Getting Started at Settlement Housing Fund

Settlement Housing Fund, created in 1969, was originally formed to provide technical assistance to settlement houses in New York City and to other private groups formed to create low- and middle-income housing. The organization, which started owning buildings in 1990, currently owns twenty-five buildings in Manhattan, Brooklyn, and the Bronx.

I started working in the field of affordable housing in 1959, when I was nineteen years old. During summers in college I had worked for Roger Schafer, a lawyer, financial consultant, and crazy idealist. He taught me all there was to know about housing programs, and I went to work for him full-time after college. He would bring me to community meetings in Harlem or the Lower East Side, showing up in lavish cars like a red Land Rover or a baby blue Cadillac convertible, which he borrowed from his rich friends.

Residents of Harlem would laugh because everyone knew that Roger wasn't rich. What he had was pizzazz, elegance, and great connections. His law school roommate was Elliot Richardson, the attorney general who resigned during the Nixon Watergate scandal in what became known as the Saturday Night Massacre. Roger had been a pacifist during World War II and worked as a mental health nurse overseas. He cared passionately about low-income housing.

My work involved meeting with community groups that were sponsoring housing with Roger's help. One summer I worked with a group of residents and union members who were trying to build a cooperative development in the West Village. The plan was killed by Jane Jacobs, the famous advocate of small-scale neighborhood development, who dismissed the project as an intrusion that would destroy the Village's hominess. I learned to be skeptical about famous heroes.

Eventually Roger sent me to Washington, D.C., to lobby for changes in various federal housing acts, and to my amazement I was successful. I studied all the bills, read the *Federal Register* as intensely as if it were a novel, and learned arcane details about housing policy

Roger had clients that ranged from giant private developers like Rose Associates to religious orders like the Josephite Fathers and the Episcopal Church, to community groups in Harlem. I met all of them and worked at various sites as well as directly with Roger. My best weapons in lobbying were the Episcopal ministers, some of them canons and even bishops. I had a list of five hundred religious leaders, and I would contact those whose parishes were in the districts of key congressional leaders. I was surprised by how normal they were, by their idealism, and by their willingness to use their connections to support housing programs. Most of them knew their senators and representatives personally.

I explained, for example, that the Rent Supplement Program, which helped low-income tenants pay rent in private buildings, had no federal funds appropriated in 1966. Phone calls were made. I wrote testimony for congressional hearings and accompanied the clergymen who were witnesses. Senators asked great questions and debated the issues seriously. The members of the clergy enjoyed the give and take. It was nothing like the personal diatribes one hears today. Thanks in part to their testimony, appropriated funds for the Rent Supplement Program climbed from zero to $100 million, serious money at the time.

This was the era of Lyndon Johnson's War on Poverty. Ambitious housing programs were passed in Congress through the Housing Act of 1968, setting goals for six hundred thousand new affordable housing units annually for ten years. The goals were never reached. However, when senator Robert Kennedy introduced tax benefits to private investors for investing in low- and moderate-income housing, production took off.

In the summer of 1969 Roger secured a new client, a up-and-coming organization called Settlement Housing Fund. He was eager to have me to work on their projects and especially their advocacy activities. Although I was still on Roger's payroll, I started there in October working for Clara Fox, the organization's dynamic founder and executive director.

The organization got its start through an affiliation with United Neighborhood Houses, at that time a federation of thirty-five settlement houses, many dating back to the late 1800s. Settlement houses, which were located mostly in poor neighborhoods, including Manhattan's Lower East Side, provided recreational and educational services for immigrants and low-income families. They represented noblesse oblige in the best sense of the term.

Clara, who died in 2007 at the age of ninety, was working for United Neighborhood Houses in 1968. Her first career had been early childhood education. Appalled by the housing conditions endured by her pupils and their families, she began to advocate for better housing programs. In the late 1950s and early 1960s her career shifted between housing and early childhood education. She worked for the state, encouraging ethnic integration in housing and originating the concept of preoccupancy education for residents of middle-income cooperatives. In later years when visiting various neighborhoods, she would often be stopped by people on the street thanking her for her work.

In 1967 mayor John Lindsay asked Clara to prepare New York City for its first Head Start program. She had six weeks to do it, and after she got the program launched she called Helen Harris, executive director of United Neighborhood Houses, and begged, "You have to get me out of here."

Helen hired Clara for a new position as head of the group's housing department. In that role, Clara wrote a grant proposal to create a new housing corporation called Settlement Housing Fund. The goal was to form cooperatives and provide technical assistance and seed money to settlement houses so they could develop low- and middle-income housing in their neighborhoods. To her surprise, the proposal was accepted and funded for two years.

Her next step was to contact Roger Schafer, whom she knew through his involvement in Rose Associates' developments in the Bronx. The two mavericks admired each other's brains and originality. Clara hired Roger as technical consultant for Settlement Housing Fund, and I was assigned to work there as Clara's assistant for policy matters. My tasks included writing a newsletter on housing programs, lobbying for federal programs that would work in New York, helping Roger obtain community approvals for projects, and writing submissions seeking government funds for housing projects.

On my first day at Settlement Housing Fund I arrived at my new office at ten in the morning. I'd told Clara I planned to stop at Roger's office first and pick up the necessary files. Clara forgot and was furious. She said I should remember that I worked for her, not Roger. Later that day I called Roger and told him I probably wouldn't last long in this job. That was in 1969. I stayed for forty-five years.

I quickly came to admire and respect Clara, who was a formidable force in the world of affordable housing and pioneered new approaches in the field. In those years, social workers were often the enemies of housing providers. Nonprofit owners hired social workers, who in turn organized rent strikes, which in turn led to the failure of a number of inadequately financed developments. In pursuit of a different approach, Clara created joint committees that included housing advocates, civic leaders, and social service leaders. She educated everyone on the importance of collecting rent to run a building, and worked hard to form important coalitions.

As executive director of Settlement Housing Fund, Clara called for a feasibility study of creating tenant-sponsored cooperatives in low-income areas. Working with Robert Kolodny, a professor of planning at Columbia University, the two developed an agenda for success. In the 1970s, the organization converted low-income buildings to cooperatives and worked to educate the residents about management, bookkeeping, meetings, best practices, and complying with regulations. Settlement Housing Fund sponsored and obtained the financing for several of these cooperatives. At least three of them, completed in the 1970s and early 1980s, are thriving today with a mix of low- and middle-income owners, including some tenants who had received public assistance.

Clara also liked to lunch with policy leaders and private developers. She was tough in manner but hilariously funny, and people hugely enjoyed her company. I in turn enjoyed seeing their startled expressions as she downed one or more vodka martinis, which she ordered straight up. Clara retained her panache until her death, along with what I used to call her "creative anger." Until the week before she died, she was writing letters to Congress.

Upon her retirement in 1983, she handed the reins over to me. In my thirty years as executive director of a greatly expanded organization, I grappled with the problem of survival every year. I often thought back to the organization's early struggles. In 1970 Clara had just enough money to keep it going for two years. Her annual salary was $14,000. Her staff consisted of a social worker who specialized in community organization and a secretary.

In 1969, thanks to the earlier leadership of senator Robert Kennedy, Congress enacted laws that gave significant tax benefits to private developers who would build or renovate affordable housing. The main benefit was rapid depreciation of the capital cost of construction and "soft" costs such as developers' reasonable profits, architects' fees, interest on construction loans, insurance, and funds for consultants. This translated into generous tax breaks, putting money into developers' pockets, and profits to boot.

These benefits were available to partnerships, and Roger convinced Clara that Settlement Housing Fund should get a piece of the action. Since, as a nonprofit organization, the organization did not pay taxes, tax breaks were not obviously attractive. The only way to take advantage of the new laws was to team up with the private sector.

Settlement Housing Fund and various community partners controlled five urban renewal sites owned by New York City. Through my work in Washington, I became familiar with the National Housing Partnership, an investor organization, and with Roger's help persuaded them to invest in low-income neighborhoods in New York. At first it was hard to lure investors, but it became easier as the demand for housing increased and the tax breaks became more attractive. We had sites on the East River on the Lower East Side, in East Harlem, on East 29th Street in Manhattan, and in Coney Island in Brooklyn.

After selecting the architect, we interviewed the private developers who would be our partners and asked them for proposals for sharing fees and profits. Then we visited their sites and reviewed their financial statements and references.

This approach usually worked well. Settlement Housing Fund controlled the sites, knew the technical aspects of the housing programs, and had support in the communities. The developers had the money to pay the initial costs for the architects, the banks, and Roger. We worked for two years to get commitments from local agencies and a feasible development plan for several sites.

Clara also worked on converting co-ops and seeking tenant support for upgrading numerous buildings. The owners wanted out because few reputable owners were eager to own buildings in poor neighborhoods, especially if their tax benefits had expired. Settlement Housing Fund renovated all these buildings, although some did not become cooperatives and were sold cheaply to private developers.

In 1974 Clara hired Susan Cole to work as a consultant to integrate a large project in the Bronx. The same year I became assistant director and eventually associate director.

Over the years I became increasingly well-known in New York and Washington in the small world of affordable housing development. I helped get amendments passed in Albany and in D.C., mostly to help federal programs deal with the realities of high costs in New York City. I was especially proud of a three-word amendment that allowed federal support for mixed-income housing. The amendment included the words "or part thereof," meaning that federal funds for low-income families could be used for a portion of a building instead of all the apartments.

The amendment was controversial because federal officials thought mixed-income buildings would fail. Discussing the closed debate on the issue, a congressional staff member later told me there had been no debate at all and that he and I were the only ones who even knew that the three words had been included in the act.

Also extremely helpful was Charles S. (Chuck) Warren, chief legislative assistant to New York senator Jacob Javits. Chuck, whom I met in 1970, is now a prominent environmental lawyer. He played a critical role in helping to make federal housing programs work in New York City. He served as president of the board of Settlement Housing Fund for more than twenty-five years and remains as the board's chairman today. The late Ed Koch was a great housing congressman and eventually an excellent housing mayor.

When I replaced Clara Fox in 1983, Susan Cole became the associate director. We hired excellent fiscal staff, and our annual budget grew from about $700,000 to nearly $5 million. In 2014, at the age of seventy-four, I retired as executive director, and Alexa Sewell became the new chief executive.

It wasn't easy to leave the organization after such a long run. But when I think back to all that the board and staff of Settlement Housing Fund accomplished during my years there, despite the bumps and the challenges and the setbacks, I feel lucky. It would be hard for me to imagine a better job.

PART II
A West Bronx Story

3

Walton and Townsend

This is the story of the transformation of a devastated neighborhood in the West Bronx into New Settlement Apartments, now a complex of eighteen buildings in the Mount Eden area that today forms the heart of a solid, working-class residential community. The neighborhood, located west of the Grand Concourse and north of Yankee Stadium, is still predominantly poor, with a median income of $27,000 for the local community board area.[1] Many local schools are still deeply troubled. Crime, although vastly improved, is still an issue. But compared to the picture three decades ago, the neighborhood turnaround is unfathomable.

Crime. Abandoned buildings. Drugs. Fires. This is still many people's image of the Bronx. Countless books and articles have been written about the borough's devastation. In 1977 the sportscaster Howard Cosell famously announced on national television during a World Series game, "Ladies and gentlemen, the Bronx is burning."[2] Nearly 33,500 fires were reported in the Bronx in 1974, three times the number in 1960.[3]

Rioting in cities around the country created an indifference to housing abandonment and destruction, especially in the decayed urban areas.

1. Community Board 4 document for 2016.

2. Jonathan Mahler's book *Ladies and Gentlemen, the Bronx is Burning: 1977, Baseball, Politics, and the Battle for the Soul of a City* (New York: Picador, 2005), which uses this comment as its title, describes the struggles to save New York City in the seventies and eighties.

3. Jill Jonnes, *South Bronx Rising: The Rise, Fall, and Resurrection of an American City* (New York: Fordham University Press, 2002), 261.

Based on census estimates, 321,000 apartments that had been part of New York's housing inventory were abandoned, demolished, burned, or boarded up by 1981.[4]

The area around the Grand Concourse north of Yankee Stadium had once been a showplace. The apartment houses, erected in the 1920s and 1930s and often named for the builders' wives or daughters, had decent bones and were well worth saving. Many of the buildings, featuring land-scaped courtyards and crenulated rooftops, were rich in art deco detail. When I mention the neighborhood to longtime New Yorkers, invariably someone can name an aunt or grandparent who grew up there.

But by the 1980s the area had been severely battered. Walton and Townsend Avenues, between which New Settlement Apartments stands today, were dangerous streets. Fourteen large, empty buildings within an eight-block area made the movie depictions of the neighborhood seem like understatements. All the clichés about the place seemed accurate. No one would go out at night. Criminals hung out in the vacant buildings, selling drugs and committing violent acts. When I first saw conditions there, I blanched.

Many people who still live in the neighborhood remember what things were like back then, among them Cynthia Cummings, an African American who participates in programs at New Settlement Apartments and lived through those years. Ms. Cummings moved to Walton Avenue and West 172nd Street in 1975 with her mother and three children.

"It was Jewish and quiet," she recalled of the area, "but then the build-ings became abandoned. They went down one by one. People were tear-ing the buildings apart. It was scary, really scary. I wouldn't go out—never north of 172nd. They were robbing people. "

"I wouldn't venture to Townsend then," Ms. Cummings added. "It was the drugs. Selling them and using them. I was fearful. There were packs of wild dogs—rampant—dog haven. Not safe."[5] I still find it difficult to imagine living under such conditions.

The late mayor Ed Koch, whose first of three terms in the office began in 1978, recalled of the area, "When I first came to office, people were leaving the Bronx like a flood. Every third house on the Concourse was city-owned."[6] The Concourse, of course, was the Grand Concourse, an

4. Nathan Glazer, "The South-Bronx Story: An Extreme Case of Neighborhood Decline," *Policy Studies Journal* 16, no. 2 (Winter 1987): 176–77.

5. Author interview with Cynthia Cummings, 2012.

6. Author interview with the Ed Koch, 2011.

Figure 3.1. Interior before renovation. (Courtesy of the New York City Department of Housing Preservation and Development.)

elegant boulevard often dubbed the Champs-Élysées of the Bronx located just one block from Walton Avenue and two from Townsend.

There are many theories about why the Bronx declined so badly during this period, but the consensus is that a combination of economic and social change, paired with government policies on all levels and those of private institutions such as banks, ignited the problems. When the first wave of crime began, residents, mostly white, started moving from the area. Some headed to the suburbs and others to Co-op City, a new complex of fifteen thousand affordable apartments in the North Bronx. Fires in the neighborhood were real and frequent—garbage, cars, and buildings burned. Building owners found that it was more profitable to collect insurance than to collect rents. When they stopped paying taxes, the city took ownership of their buildings. Local teenagers, called finishers, completed the wreckage by stripping away copper pipes and anything else they could take from the interiors.

Sweeping racial changes in many parts of the Bronx, combined with drug epidemics and municipal indifference, compounded the problems. The city became the owner of thousands of buildings and was widely considered a terrible landlord. At first developers and nonprofit groups bought vacant buildings from the city and fixed them up using federal housing subsidies. Then interest rates soared to 18 percent and the cost of fuel skyrocketed. Construction costs also kept rising. Several well-publicized housing scandals occurred. Starting with the Carter administration federal subsidies began to decline, and Jimmy Carter's successor, Ronald Reagan, eliminated the most viable programs.

President Carter had made Charlotte Street famous during a 1977 trip to New York when he visited this Bronx street, then a hodgepodge of garbage-strewn empty lots and half-standing fire-damaged buildings that had become an emblem of urban decay in the borough. Although he promised to rebuild the area, he never delivered. When Carter reneged on his billion-dollar commitment to Charlotte Street, Mayor Koch began thinking about a city plan to help the area.

Federal programs had ebbed and flowed over the years. Still, there was widespread agreement that substantial government assistance was essential to build and operate affordable housing in New York City and other high-cost areas. It was a nameless federal bureaucrat, working in the Office of Management and Budget, who would pave the way to mortally wound a fifty-year federal commitment to low-income housing in the Budget Act of 1983. He thought the programs were a giveaway. He preferred public housing, an argument that may have had some merit. Through a previous budget act in 1974, this gentleman established a new way of counting Section 8 housing subsidies, inflating the housing budget exponentially. This involved adding up all the funds contracted over twenty to thirty years and using the total as if it would be spent in the first year. It was like counting the thirty-year costs of your mortgage, utility payments, and repairs all in the first year you moved to a new house. The secretary of Housing and Urban Development said that because of this legislative trick, his budget went from one of the smallest in the federal government to one of the largest in just one year. The nameless bureaucrat hated the idea of trusting private developers with buildings for the poor. However, because public housing was politically unpopular, there was no other way to way to create new affordable housing.

Because of the new method of calculating costs, ending assistance for new housing became a great way to cut the budget. The Reagan administration did just that, determining that it was too expensive to support new low-income housing, and public housing advocates were not politically powerful enough to do anything about it.

As the federal government was cutting housing programs, New York State and New York City were recovering from the fiscal crises of the mid-seventies. New York State did not increase rent allowances for families on public assistance. A family of four was allowed $312 a month for housing at a time when a modest two-bedroom apartment rented for twice that amount. These families kept signing leases even though they could not afford the rent, and of course they were evicted. Often they became homeless.

To compound the problems in the late 1970s and 1980s, New York State "deinstitutionalized" vast numbers of the mentally ill, permanently moving them out of large and often troubled psychiatric hospitals where many had lived for decades, without taking any steps to accommodate them. Another blow to poor single people was the conversion of more than one hundred thousand cheap hotel rooms in single-room-occupancy hotels on Manhattan's Upper West Side into luxury housing.

Flophouses along the Bowery closed because they were no longer profitable. Crack cocaine and soaring crime rates helped spark a large prison-building program. But the people coming out of the prisons' revolving doors had nowhere to go. Single people, including many Vietnam veterans, were living on the streets of New York City, and families on public assistance were holed up in filthy and unsafe welfare hotels.

Cynthia Cummings of Walton Avenue was right in thinking that her neighborhood was scary. Public policies that had neglected urban neighborhoods encouraged disinvestment in places like the Bronx. Mayor Koch realized that local resources were needed.

By 1985 most New York politicians knew that housing in the city was in a sorry state and that something had to be done. The Coalition for the Homeless advocacy group successfully sued the city, claiming that the New York State Constitution in the health and welfare clause required shelter for the homeless. By then the city had become a major landlord, owning more than one hundred thousand apartments in tens of thousands of properties acquired through tax foreclosure. Included in that figure were fifty thousand apartments in vacant buildings, practically all of them in poor neighborhoods.

The Tax Reform Act of 1986 eliminated many tax benefits for depreciating real estate, ending the one remaining incentive that would have encouraged the private sector to stay in the game. Although some owners blamed state legislation that controlled rent increases, in many neighborhoods residents were so poor that they could not possibly afford the rent needed to cover a building's expenses. On Walton and Townsend Avenues, rent-control laws were irrelevant.

Thanks to all these forces, the Bronx became a national symbol of poverty and housing abandonment. Thousands of vacant buildings containing tens of thousands of apartments stood boarded up and empty. The buildings on Walton and Townsend Avenues became the setting for drug sales and drive-by shootings. Residents like Cynthia Cummings who stayed in the area were terrified every day.

City officials tried to appease the public by covering the windows of abandoned buildings with decals showing images of flower boxes, especially in neighborhoods that were visible from commuter trains and highways heading to the suburbs. In a 1976 speech, city housing commissioner Roger Starr suggested that letting buildings in the Bronx remain abandoned was preferable to rebuilding the area.

Although politically conservative, Starr believed passionately in good public housing and in other federal housing programs. Under his leadership, the rebirth of Times Square had begun with the development of Manhattan Plaza, two towers on West 42nd Street between Ninth and Tenth Avenues that contained 1,688 apartments, mostly for low- and moderate-income performing artists. Settlement Housing Fund created the marketing plan for this development and drafted the legislation and regulations needed to execute it.

Yet despite Starr's many accomplishments, he sincerely believed that a comeback in the Bronx was impossible. He thought that troubled neighborhoods in the Bronx should be demolished and become parks, an approach he described as "planned shrinkage."

In 1977 Starr left city government to join the editorial board of the *New York Times*. Two commissioners later, Mayor Koch appointed Paul Crotty, and his deputy was Felice Michetti, a lawyer and urban planner who knew the city's neighborhoods from her years in the Bronx office of the City Planning Department and in the Department of Housing Preservation and Development.

Mayor Koch, now in his third term, had been attacked for his neglect of low-income New Yorkers and his lack of concern for the homeless. Governor Mario Cuomo, though he had gained early fame for fighting on behalf of a group of middle-income homeowners in Corona, Queens, also had a mediocre record when it came to supporting housing for low- and moderate-income families.

In 1986, however, things began to change. By this point the city's homeless were in plain view, panhandling and sleeping in the parks, on the subway, or on the street. They were not attractive, especially to tourists. New York was compared to Calcutta. At the same time the city owned more than fifty thousand vacant apartments. Why, people asked, couldn't the city use the vacant buildings to house the homeless?

There were many reasons for inaction. Many city bureaucrats opposed local housing subsidies, which represented a potential budget buster. In response, housing advocates argued that subsidized housing creates jobs and thus brings new taxpayers to the city. Residents also buy furniture and appliances.

Some members of the Koch administration thought the city should continue its policy of auctioning city-owned buildings to the highest bidder and thus producing revenue. But this approach had been a failure. Buyers would operate their buildings briefly, take the depreciation for tax purposes, and then sell to someone who would abandon the building all over again. (As mentioned above, the Tax Reform Act of 1986 ended the automatic tax benefits to be accrued from such transactions.)

Some experts argued that if the city launched a large housing program, federal officials would feel justified in their large cutbacks for housing. They insisted that even the most generous local programs could not match the resources available at the federal level. This remains true today.

Even with the dramatic federal cutbacks, New York City always receives most of its support for housing from the federal government, despite the fact that the programs are complicated and hard to use. The city always had its own small housing program, but after the fiscal crisis of the 1970s few city resources were allocated to housing. City officials remembered when there was talk of giving them chits instead of salaries in order to balance the budget. Housing was a hard sell. Some officials with long institutional memories alluded to widely publicized scandals in the early seventies concerning a rehabilitation program known as the Municipal Loan Program. Again, it was easy to find reasons to do nothing.

In the 1980s the city used federal block grants almost exclusively to cover the costs of operating the poorly maintained properties it owned, known as "in rem buildings." The homeless had priority for vacancies in these buildings. But some of the working families who lived there did not welcome the homeless, and no one was satisfied with the way the city supported its buildings. Bill Spiller, a deputy commissioner in charge of occupied city-owned housing, once noted that it took fifteen approvals to get a single emergency repair approved.

Although managers of some of the buildings were heroic, assuring heat and hot water in decrepit, long-neglected apartment houses, the city had many problems as a landlord. Few if any records were kept for individual buildings. Tenants often neglected to pay rent, and city officials rarely tried to evict them. Legal Aid lawyers advised tenants that they did not have to pay rent if a building was in poor condition, or if it was a holiday. Some tenants were destructive. The city made patch-up repairs. By the time one thing got fixed, another was broken. Using $200 million a year to sustain these buildings this way was hardly a good use of federal money.

Then, seemingly out of the blue, there appeared a solution to the city's housing problems. In 1984 Meyer (Sandy) Frucher, a veteran of the Cuomo administration, was named president of the Battery Park City Authority. This was the agency that ran Battery Park City, which would eventually become an enclave of luxury residential and commercial buildings in downtown Manhattan. One evening in 1985 Frucher presented to Governor Cuomo his housing plan, under which excess revenues from Battery Park City would be used to pay for renovating vacant buildings in the Bronx.

Although Cuomo liked the idea, the immediate reaction among housing experts was that the plan would never work. In the 1970s all of Battery Park City languished. There was one large middle-income apartment house, owned by the LeFrak Organization and built just before inflation hit in construction costs, interest rates, and fuel prices. The rest of the landfill—now home of the Winter Garden Atrium, luxury office and residential buildings, hotels, museums, and gardens—was an empty stretch of sand.

The development, conceived by governor Nelson Rockefeller, was considered a failure. No one predicted that the World Financial Center would be built at Battery Park City in the early 1980s. But the landfill proved something of a cash cow. The office buildings in the first completed phase of Battery Park City would generate $3 billion in lease payments over thirty years, while bond debt service payments in that period amounted to only $800 million.

Mayor Koch, who as a congressman had been a member of the House Subcommittee on Housing, understood that affordable housing could not be built simply with creative financing. He knew that government money was essential. Governor Cuomo, a liberal Democrat, had previously committed the state to a small housing program, part for home ownership and part for rental housing. As mentioned above, Cuomo's initiation in politics had occurred when he successfully arbitrated a political battle involving public housing in Forest Hills, Queens, during the Lindsay administration. Nonetheless, as governor housing had not been his priority.

Local nonprofit groups became energetic advocates for the program Frucher had proposed. The New York Housing Conference played an active role. The aforementioned Tax Reform Act of 1986 launched a new tax credit program to encourage investment in low-income housing, which would prove effective (although compliance requirements could be daunting).

Since the days of Governor Rockefeller and Mayor Lindsay, the governor of New York State and the mayor of New York City were often at odds. The situation now was no different. Mayor Koch and Governor Cuomo, both Democrats, had each defeated the other in primaries over the years. The strains around Battery Park City increased. The city wanted to take over, and the state resisted successfully.

Happily, the mayor and the governor assigned some of their smartest advisers to work on a housing program. The result was a memorandum of understanding, signed by Koch and Cuomo in 1986, that committed $4.2 billion of mostly new money for housing over a ten-year period (a Port Authority official came up with sources of needed funds). At the time office buildings were attracting wealthy tenants, and it seemed unwise for the state agencies to remain as tenants in the World Trade Center. It was agreed that as the state agencies moved out and new tenants moved in, the increased rents would be paid into a fund to support housing. The fund, it was estimated, would produce up to $200 million. Another plan involved taking money that the Port Authority had allocated for redundant environmental programs and instead using it to create a housing development bank, adding an additional $250 million. Another Port Authority fund was supposed to produce $100 million. The state would add $250 million to existing housing programs, and the city would provide $2 billion from its capital budget. The city added another $1 billion the following year, and the Battery Park City Authority pledged an additional $600 million. Mayor Koch committed his administration to a ten-year plan to provide $5.2 billion for housing, which included everything from housing for the homeless to single-family homes for middle-income families. The initiative was called Housing New York.

The next step was state legislation to allow Battery Park City to issue bonds to support-low income housing. A committee of developers, bankers, and civic leaders formed to support the plan, but it had vociferous opponents. A group known as the Housing Justice Campaign sued the city on the grounds that too many apartments would be provided for moderate-income families, when the greatest need was for housing for the poorest families. Luckily, the city prevailed, and despite initial opposition in the Republican-controlled State Senate the legislation eventually passed, with the provision that the city handle the technicalities of issuing bonds and developing plans to use the money effectively.

Despite the new law, many of the creative ideas never materialized. In 1987 Battery Park Authority issued a bond for $400 million that provided only $148 million for housing. The rest of the money went to lawyers, reserves, Battery Park amenities, and financing fees. About $60 million came from World Trade Center lease increases. But the major source of money, the city's capital budget, remained intact.

Housing Commissioner Crotty and his deputy, Felice Michetti, identified sites throughout the city to be used for the program. Both nonprofit and for-profit groups geared up to become eligible participants.

Settlement Housing Fund received foundation grants to study the financing plan and make suggestions for implementation. I along with Anne Lindgren, a developer, board member, and former HUD official, wrote the resulting report.[7]

Despite initial skepticism, we were impressed with the creativity of the financing. Nonetheless we doubted that the city's goal of 225,000 apartments was realistic, and it turned out we were right. However, were reasonably upbeat that the new federal low-income tax credit program would help stretch local funds to create more units.

Our recommendation was mixed-income housing with up to 30 percent of the units reserved for homeless families. We also recommended using money from rents for social programs. We counseled the city to identify large assemblages of vacant city-owned buildings suitable for rehabilitation. Although many of these recommendations were familiar, our study became the subject of a legislative conference, and housing advocates were supportive of our work.

In 1986 New York City officially made affordable housing a municipal priority. The city committed record sums from its capital budget for housing, created new programs, and sought out qualified nonprofit and for-profit developers to carry them out.

The largest assemblages of buildings were in the Bronx and Harlem. A new program known as construction management was created for two large projects, toward which the initial bond backed by Battery Park City revenues was to be devoted. The Harlem site was financed through a different

---

7. Carol Lamberg and Anne Lindgren, *Evaluation of Housing New York* (New York: Settlement Housing Fund, 1986). A follow-up study in 1990 indicated that the programs were succeeding.

Figure 3.2. A new look. (Courtesy of the New York City Department of Housing Preservation and Development.)

program. The first and largest site, bounded by Walton Avenue, Townsend Avenue, Mount Eden Avenue and 171st Street, would become New Settlement Apartments.

Of all the developments I've been involved with over a fifty-year career, this is the one that transformed a neighborhood most dramatically. Countless good ideas emerged from the battles with contractors and bureaucrats, from the victories and mistakes. Although New Settlement Apartments received some publicity over the years, its success, spanning a period of nearly three decades, remains a well-kept secret. Still, the development could be replicated if government were willing to make a sufficiently large investment. The approach could have been modified and used to accelerate redevelopment of New Orleans after Hurricane Katrina and, after adjusting to local conditions, could provide a model for rescuing troubled cities like Detroit.

4
Deciding to Own and Competing to Win

Why would a nonprofit organization want to be a landlord? It's not a formula for popularity in the community. The evictions, the responsibilities, and the liabilities are daunting. The Settlement Housing Fund board was concerned about slip and fall lawsuits, as was I. Moreover, most housing programs were not set up to accomplish Settlement Housing Fund's ideas of best practices. It seemed much easier to develop affordable housing and turn it over to nonprofits (like settlement houses) or to for-profit companies.

There were other issues. We had advocated for mixed-income housing rather than concentrating very poor people all in one location. The city's response in the late eighties was to require 60 percent of a new building to be allocated to homeless families. We thought that was too much.

We had also claimed that government housing initiatives, other than the federal Section 8 program, did not allow operating budgets generous enough to keep buildings clean and in good repair. Although we believed in affordable housing, we let other groups become the owners. We hoped that some nonprofit groups could supplement their housing budget through philanthropic funds and that responsible for-profit groups would keep the buildings up because the tax benefits were great (and because there might be other incentives in the future). We were good at developing the properties and selecting the tenants. Once management was in place with a responsible owner, we would bow out.

But a part of me always wanted to retain the buildings we worked so hard to create, and our chance came in 1987. As discussed in the prior

30

chapter, Paul Crotty, a politically connected lawyer, had been named New York City housing commissioner. I'd come to know him when Settlement Housing Fund supported the legislation that implemented the new housing program Koch and Cuomo had initiated.

After surveying the huge numbers of vacant city-owned buildings, Commissioner Crotty and his able staff decided to find developers who would fix the buildings up to house the homeless and other New York families who needed affordable apartments. The city would use its own funds and be free from onerous federal regulations.

Several months after the legislation came into effect, Commissioner Crotty's secretary called me to set up an appointment at his office. I thought he might want Settlement Housing Fund to become involved with developments in Harlem. We had good relations with the Harlem community because we had successfully renovated an entire block front on West 111th Street. It turned out I was wrong.

When I showed up with Susan Cole, our associate director, Commissioner Crotty began by asking whether Settlement Housing Fund would consider competing to become the future owner of fourteen buildings in the Bronx, the largest assemblage in the entire program. Two other groups had been invited to compete as well. First deputy commissioner Felice Michetti was also at the meeting.

I was intrigued but had questions: Where exactly were the buildings located? What condition were they in? How would the rehabilitation be financed?

The financing, we were told, would be as good as it gets. The entire rehabilitation would cost us nothing. Excess income from the financially lucrative Battery Park City would be used for debt service on bonds, and the net proceeds of the bonds would pay the renovation costs. This was a terrific deal, one that would allow us to set aside money from rents for community programs rather than debt service.

Crotty went on to explain that the city would be the developer and would select a construction manager. Only large companies with strong track records would be considered. That sounded like a good idea. Construction managers can keep costs down by choosing subcontractors as they go along, rather than trying to guess at costs and pin them down in advance.

As for who would live in the buildings, although the city would require a 30 percent set-aside for homeless families, the choice of the other residents was up to us.

Deputy Commissioner Michetti asked who would be the managers after we became owners. She was savvy and knew that we did not have our own management company. I immediately said we would want Ashton Management, a small Bronx-based company headed by a brilliant woman named Linda Field and an electrical contractor named Bobby Garcia. Linda always spoke as if she were defending her Ph.D. thesis, in complete, elegant sentences. Linda and I had learned about management budgets together in the late 1970s. She eventually became a developer and then a building manager; I chose the nonprofit route. Bobby had different skills. He understood the physical plants of buildings and had a great eye. I had visited a few of their buildings and was amazed at how clean everything was and how high the standards were for repair and maintenance.

Deputy Commissioner Michetti asked if Ashton was big enough. At the time the company had only managed a few hundred units. She had a point, but I was more interested in quality and thought our organizations shared the same values. Susan, who had helped Ashton in tenant selection, agreed with me wholeheartedly. There were few managing agents we trusted at the time—in fact, there were only three. The first did not fare well on a difficult building we had sponsored on West 87th Street. The second had never worked in this area of the Bronx. The third was Ashton. I thought that even though they were small, they'd do a great job.

Commissioner Crotty handed me a map of the site, showing fourteen large buildings on Walton and Townsend Avenues, one block west of the Grand Concourse and fifteen blocks north of Yankee Stadium. I knew the city had spent a lot of federal money to rehabilitate the majestic old buildings on the Grand Concourse. The buildings on the map, however, had been empty and boarded up for about fifteen years.

I told the commissioner that we were pleased to be considered; we would look at the site and write a letter to explain our considerations. I was more than excited, thinking that this was a great chance to test our theories and make a significant impact. Susan was excited, too, but extremely nervous.

As soon as I got back to the office I called a few board members and then called Linda and Bobby at Ashton Management. They were enthralled with the idea of a co-venture.

Bobby drove me up to the site the next day. It was a beautiful, sunny morning. It is always dangerous to look at a site when the weather is perfect. All buildings look good in sunny weather, and it is easy to fall in love with them. I got out of Bobby's car on Townsend Avenue and West 172nd Street, eyes agape. Yes, these were burned-out shells, with debris everywhere, graffiti galore, and even wild dogs roaming the ground. But I focused on the crenulated roofs, decorative friezes, and courtyards, imagining how the buildings would look after rehabilitation. Bobby yelled at me, "Carol, get back in the car." I did not notice that there was a drug dealer in front of every building.

It certainly was a scary neighborhood. David Muchnick, a housing research expert, had done a study for the district attorney to track the sites where the majority of crack cocaine sales took place, and these buildings ranked near the top of the list. Reclaiming this neighborhood would be a serious challenge. How would I convince my board of directors to support this venture?

At least I knew that Susan Cole, who could be quite negative, would back me. She realized that this would be a worthy showcase for our organization. We discussed the project at our next staff meeting. Ann Loeb, our assistant director, who had a graduate degree in planning, looked forward to doing some actual planning. Ann also loved old buildings. She realized that there was great transportation to Manhattan because both the D and 4 trains stopped a block from the site. In addition, plenty of stores were located on nearby 170th Street.

The site also presented major problems. Sanitation, safety, and the quality of local schools left much to be desired. Sarah Kolodny, our director of social programs, was enthusiastic about the possibility of using rental income for community programs. She contacted her colleague Carolyn McLaughlin, who ran the Citizens Advice Bureau, a walk-in office where low-income families could get help with matters like entitlements, utilities, and just understanding the complexities of family life in the city. I was impressed with Carolyn's programs, and she became one of our first collaborators. Cindy Dial, an urban planner who had worked for the city, also wanted to play a role in the project; in due time she would help me in writing the proposal.

The project was the main agenda item for our next board meeting. Questions abounded. Jane Stanicki, a banker, was dubious. The fact that the city would oversee construction scared her. David Todd, a former landmarks commissioner, insisted that we would need our own supervising engineer, even though the city planned to have five full-time inspectors on site. Chuck Warren, an environmental lawyer who soon became our board president, thought a board committee should visit the site as well as the buildings owned and managed by Ashton Management. We arranged a site tour the following week.

The board understood how exciting the potential redevelopment could be. They were rightly concerned about the cost of the project. Would the city devote enough resources to do the job properly? In addition, it would

Figure 4.1. Board visits the Bronx site. (Courtesy of Settlement Housing Fund.)

clearly be important to hire our own engineer and to attend site meetings with the contractor and the city's engineers. Jane Stanicki had an unexpected worry about Ashton's management style—namely, that the floors and halls in their buildings were so immaculate. "Too clean," she said, worrying that too much money was being spent on operations. There Susan and I disagreed—"the cleaner, the better" was our mantra.

Three weeks later the full board met and decided that we should compete for the project, arguing that it would represent a great opportunity to make an important contribution to the city in keeping with our mission. The board noted, however, the we would need to create an entire neighborhood and new amenities. At the time there was no neighborhood. There was nothing there.

The board decided that we should begin by outlining our conditions in a letter to Commissioner Crotty. We wanted to be involved in design. We wanted to hire a supervising engineer of our choice. We wanted to attend job meetings during construction. The city and/or the contractor would be responsible for correcting latent defects after construction was completed. We reiterated that no more than 30 percent of the apartments would be reserved for the homeless, and a broad mix of income groups would make up the other 70 percent. There would be no taxes and no debt service. Community programs would be part of the operating budget. Most apartments would have two bedrooms.

Looking back at the letter today, I'm amazed at our chutzpah. The city had invited us to compete to own fourteen buildings, and we replied by saying we'd do so only if our demands were met.

Although we never received a written reply to our letter, Deputy Commissioner Michetti called and said, "Okay." Then we waited for the Request for Proposals to be announced, which took several months (it seemed like years). But we were not idle.

First there was a request open only to large-scale contractors for the Bronx site and for another one in Harlem, which would be owned by the New York City Housing Authority. One of our board members, an architect named David Castro Blanco, approached Lehrer McGovern Bovis, a huge international firm that had acted as construction managers for the Euro Disney Resort, the Central Park Zoo, and major hotels and office buildings. Their names were on signs all over New York. Apparently they decided to bid low. David had told me that his motto was "Get, the job, get the job, get the job"—and worry later. (I tended to worry before submitting a proposal.)

I attended the pre-bid conference for construction managers, joined by Cindy Dial from my staff. There were about a dozen of the largest contractors in New York in the room, including Lehrer McGovern Bovis and David Castro Blanco. This was during the time of high energy costs and uncertain construction outlays. Using a construction manager to play the role of general contractor was supposed to save money but seemed risky. We usually preferred the guarantees provided by a general contractor, and eventually we would see how right we were.

Nevertheless, we learned a lot by attending the meeting, including the fact that the construction standards would be high. Basically, the standards would be similar to those in public housing, which were much higher than the city's other programs. The goal was that any improvements would last for thirty years. That was important to us because we usually had to wage war to get the city to raise standards. In this case our work was already done.

We also learned that the city's Building Department would play a large role, with five inspectors on the site monitoring day-to-day construction. Minority and local hiring would be important.

Working closely with Linda Field and Bobby Garcia from Ashton Management, we began to make a list of items that would be essential for long-term maintenance. We did not like bifold or sliding doors on closets. Bifolds break, and sliding doors fall off the track. Both could become a management headache. We decided we would insist on swinging doors on all closets

We would argue for oak strip wooden floors but were not sure we would be successful because of the cost. Tile all over the bathroom, decent bedroom sizes, a reasonable roof guarantee—we had a long list, but not too long. We wanted to be reasonable. We thought that the list would show how much serious thought we would give to the proposal. It also mattered to the long-term viability of the development, especially since we would be owners for decades to come.

The next step was to seek out the neighborhood leaders who would support our undertaking, starting with members of the local community board. It turned out that the immediate area was home to few viable community organizations—no surprise, given its devastated state. We would have to create a community practically from scratch.

Two of our staff members, Sarah Kolodny and Ann Loeb, set to work on this. Both had been hired to work on special projects. Sarah was a certified social worker who attended community board meetings and reached out to local groups. One by one, she persuaded people to endorse us.

Eventually we would have letters of support from the director of the neighborhood day care center, an executive with the nearby hospital, local merchants, and many others. Thirteen organizations supported the plan and promised to provide services to the residents. Ann worked on the planning aspects of the proposal, describing actions needed to improve the community.

Transportation was excellent, and the major shopping strip along 170th Street would be easily accessible to families moving into renovated buildings. Because of the mixed-income nature of the new tenancy, local businesses would be likely to welcome the additional income and support. However, garbage collection and safety were major issues. Many nearby schools had closed because the area had lost so many residents, and we wondered whether the remaining local schools could accommodate the influx of new students.

Drafting the proposal became increasingly a labor of love. My cover letter and the letter from Linda Field of Ashton Management revealed how passionate we were about the opportunity to rebuild this broken community. The proposal had fourteen chapters detailing such issues as our approach to management, tenant selection, social services, tenant relations, use of nonresidential space, and the operating budget.

Tenant selection would be crucial to assure rent collection and safety. Obviously, attracting law-abiding families would be hard if we allowed dangerous applicants to live in the building. Similarly, we couldn't operate the building without prompt payment of rents, and we couldn't accept applicants with poor track records in this area. Grounds for rejection would include "falsification of information on the application, history of violent behavior of any family member, drug addiction or alcoholism unless enrolled in a treatment program, poor housekeeping observed at the home visit, bad credit, refusal to occupy the apartment without pets." We included our criteria as part of our proposal to the city.

We set goals to attract a diverse group of tenants. We knew the pool of applicants would be black and Latino but that there would be immigrants from Africa, South America, Puerto Rico, the Caribbean, and the Dominican Republic. We insisted on a wide range of incomes, extending from the public assistance level for the homeless to $53,000, higher than the annual median income at the time. We asked for good design and safety to attract higher-income residents.

At the time our approach was revolutionary. No one thought that higher-income groups would occupy the same buildings as formerly homeless families, especially in a neighborhood notorious for crime. We were uncertain, but we believed that the reasonable rents and nice layouts would attract working families. Maybe even some of the families who had moved away could be lured back.

We set three other income tiers in addition to the 30 percent required for formerly homeless: 40 percent of the apartments would go to low-income families, 20 percent to moderate-income families, and up to 10 percent to upper-moderate-income families. This was the range of the population in the neighborhood who needed housing. Families would pay between of 20 to 30 percent of their income for rent. The rents charged would provide enough income to cover the management budget, which was explained in detail as part of our proposal.

We submitted our proposal on August 12, 1987. As it turned out, only one other group applied. That was Phipps Houses, a much larger and older organization with its own management company and a reserve of money at least ten times greater than ours.

On a trip to Spain in March 1988 to speak at a conference, I ran into Steve Norman, New York City's assistant housing commissioner. When we met at the Ritz bar for a drink, he told me that Settlement Housing Fund had won the project, adding that the official notification would be coming soon.

The real work was about to start. Almost all the ideas in the proposal and the predictions about success were eventually realized. We succeeded beyond our wildest dreams. But many of the reservations and fears expressed by the cautious members of our board would come back to haunt us.

5
Collaborations and Battles

New Settlement Apartments was an ambitious undertaking. We kept planning and replanning the design, met with the members and staff of the community board, and obtained pre-construction grants from foundations to cover the cost of our efforts. However, we still had nothing in writing from the city officially designating us as owners.

It took months to get the official notice, long after the commissioner and deputy commissioner had called to congratulate us. I still wonder why it took so long. The official award letter consisted of one sentence: "You have been selected to enter into negotiations with the New York City Department of Housing Preservation and Development to become future owner of the Construction Management I rehabilitation site." It was signed by another assistant commissioner, who supposedly would oversee the design phase.

We had already completed negotiations regarding rents and financing. In retrospect it was a terrific deal, unique at the time. Setting the rents at levels that people could truly afford was gratifying to everyone at Settlement Housing Fund. Assuring that there was enough operating money to provide excellent services for the tenants was equally important. We wanted to get it right, and we struggled until we convinced city officials that we were right on this issue. Our income mix reflected the whole range of neighborhood families who needed housing assistance—from the homeless to middle-income families who could not find good housing at a fair price. After a long fight with city officials, we persuaded them to allow us to charge between 20 and 30 percent of a family's income for rent at initial occupancy. Today the target is 30 percent, sometimes even higher. There is a narrow band of families eligible for a particular development. A broader income range enables a housing owner to meet the needs of a specific community.

As explained in the prior chapter, there were four resident tiers: formerly homeless, low-income families, moderate-income families, and upper-moderate-income families. The rents were set for each tier. We had to keep reviewing the incomes of the formerly homeless families annually because of requirements that govern federal rent subsidies. There were 268 such families. Rents were set to be less than federally established fair market rents, which were adjusted every year to reflect changes in operating costs. Staff members knew that recertification meant getting families to come to the office and provide tax returns and third-party verification. This was costly and time-consuming. It also meant keeping great files. For the 625 working families, we did not have to go through this rigmarole each year. We reviewed the non-homeless families' income only once, when they first moved in. We could increase the rent each year according to the city's rent regulations. The fact that we did not review incomes each year for 70 percent of the residents meant that we saved both money and work for the management staff. I wish we could replicate this in our other buildings, but so far we haven't been able to do so. For New Settlement the arrangement was set in stone through the city's regulatory agreement, which would be in effect for thirty years. This was a revolutionary achievement at the time, although who knows what will happen in the future.

The initial rents and income levels are shown in Table 1.1. Rents are higher now (and will soon be higher yet because of the need for capital improvements).

Financially, the plan seemed to be in excellent shape. Our management budget was adequate. In addition, we had no mortgage, only a requirement to repay a pre-construction loan from the city's housing finance agency, the group that issued the bonds to pay for construction. We also had zero real estate taxes—my favorite number. Because we were not burdened with debt or taxes, we were able to set aside $578,000 a year for community programs, and we did so until 2013, when additional funds were available to launch new programs at our nearby community center.

And, at least at first, the design process went quite smoothly. The team created by our board member David Castro Blanco had been selected as architects and construction managers. Apparently their professional fees were lower than those of the other contestants. (David always recused

Table 1.1. New Settlement Apartments

Rents in 1990–1991

Apartment type	Rent	Utility allowance	Housing payment
Category 1: Very low income			
Studio	$260	$27	$287
One bedroom	$300	$29	$329
Two bedrooms	$350	$35	$385
Three bedrooms	$420	$39	$459
Category 2: Moderate income			
Studio	$365	$27	$392
One bedroom	$425	$29	$454
Two bedrooms	$485	$35	$520
Three bedrooms	$575	$39	$614
Category 3: Upper moderate income			
Studio	$440	$27	$467
One bedroom	$500	$29	$529
Two bedrooms	$565	$35	$600
Three bedrooms	$650	$39	$689

himself from voting on the project, thereby avoiding a conflict of interest.) David's partner, Bob Piscioneri, was the architect in charge of our development. The construction manager was Lehrer McGovern Bovis, who had a design representative. Professionals from the Housing Authority represented the city. I went to all the meetings, along with Cindy Dial, who was on our staff. Linda Field and Bobby Garcia from Ashton Management, and our engineer, Peter Franzese, also attended.

There were many areas of agreement. In general, the layouts were good. New wood floors would be provided in all apartments. Swing doors for the closets, moderately good room sizes, a lot of tile in the bathrooms, nice gray quarry tile in the lobbies, compactors, state-of the-art rubber roofs with fifteen-year guarantees—what more could anyone want? It seemed that all the players knew that a significant investment of public funds was involved, and it behooved us all to use the money carefully so that the buildings would last. This would also be Mayor Koch's showcase project, giving him terrific publicity right before the next mayoral election.

Typically there is tension between the staff of Settlement Housing Fund and city officials, who consider our management budgets excessive. City officials want to spread scarce government resources over as many apartments as possible, whereas we want to provide excellent service in a smaller number of buildings. The conflict is natural, and compromise is inevitable.

Our engineers said that modular boilers were preferable to the large, clunky ones the city had specified. The architects and Lehrer McGovern Bovis sided with the city. We had at least five meetings, everyone armed with statistics. I brought in a host of mechanical engineers to back me up, to no avail. The compromise we finally reached was that seven buildings would get modular boilers and seven would get the large ones. My favorite assistant commissioner, Steve Norman, whispered to me, "This is more than I ever wanted to know about boilers," and I secretly agreed. The debate still goes on about what is best. Over the years we have put in many improvements, like heat timers and, most recently, solar panels. Still, the tenants in some buildings are able to convince the porters to turn up the heat more often than do tenants in other buildings. After more than twenty-six years, the jury is still out. There are few, if any, perfect heating systems, and battles still rage. Various engineers feel passionate one way or another. Especially today when it is important to be "green," boilers without doubt are the issue du jour. I still have never met a heating system that pleases a building super and/or the majority of a building's residents.

Equally contentious was the confrontation about how to waterproof the building, otherwise known as the stucco wars. Our engineers and the management company swore that the brick walls should be pointed carefully and then patched with a state-of-the-art sealant. Sounded good to me. The city insisted on using stucco for the back walls. I was told by a slew of advisers that stucco was inappropriate for our climate. I was living in a building on the Upper West Side of Manhattan in which leaks were causing an uprising among the residents, largely because of stucco, which eventually had to be removed, a process that involved a lot of noise and money. The city officials and their advisers would not relent, and we got stuck with stucco. They promised, however, that they would supervise carefully to assure an excellent application.

We fought also about the tree pit covers. We did not like the design of the concrete covers, preferring wrought iron for both aesthetic and horticultural reasons. We lost that one, too.

The design meetings continued for a year. Building permits were obtained with difficulty, even though the city had agreed to expedite them.

In the meantime, construction costs kept climbing with every delay. The borough president and local community board members insisted on extensive hiring from the community and using minority subcontractors. We were called on to help negotiate compromises in some cases, and excluded from the process at other times. We were okay with that. It was comforting that at least we were not held responsible for high construction costs. Typically, in our other developments, we would be blamed if our estimates were high, but seldom praised when we came in under budget.

Approvals at all levels of city government were required. The local community board had to sign off, as did the City Planning Commission and the Board of Estimate, the legislative board with authority at the time. The City Council currently gives the final approval. There were many opportunities for contention, but no one wanted the buildings to remain vacant and dangerous.

In October 1989 construction began on the building on Townsend Avenue between 172 Street and Mount Eden Avenue. This is two blocks west of the Grand Concourse and about fifteen blocks up from Yankee Stadium. Mayor Ed Koch, borough president Fernando Ferrer, comptroller Harrison "Jay" Goldin, housing commissioner Abe Biderman, and I participated in a groundbreaking ceremony, shovels in hand. It was the chance to thank all who had helped and, of course, a great photo opportunity.

Even though we had the ceremony, we had not finalized our Land Disposition Agreement, the final legal document that designated us as future owners. We were represented by an excellent law firm, Stroock & Stroock & Lavan, at a 20 percent discount. An able young real estate lawyer, Peter Miller, was at our side. The city's lawyer, Dan Weisz, was competent and cooperative.

The Settlement Housing Fund board was worried about getting stuck with poorly reconstructed buildings. The construction management contract was between the city and Lehrer McGovern Bovis. We were not a party to it and had little recourse after the one-year guarantee period expired. But we did negotiate an arrangement that allowed us to determine when a building was finished and ready for occupancy, although we agreed to be "reasonable," an agreement that would cause problems in the future. The important achievement was that we had the right to sue the city for ten years to redress latent construction defects. The city, we thought, would in turn have the right to sue Lehrer McGovern Bovis.

The city would also provide 100 percent real estate tax exemption before title for any building would be transferred to us. Even though this kind of tax exemption is automatic for "gut" rehabilitation, the process

Figure 5.1. Groundbreaking. (Courtesy of New York City Department of Housing and Urban Development.)

can be excruciating. The Land Disposition Agreement put the onus on the city. We were pleased.

At the last minute, the city required that we fund reserves from the rents. We agreed, as long as we were able to manage the reserves ourselves. In new projects, the government usually must approve using the reserves, and we were pleased to have control. The city also added a clause in the contract giving them the right to ask for reports. The deal had been that we were not to be overregulated. Therefore we were hesitant to agree to provide reports, which we thought would be of little use. It sounds like a lot of chutzpah again, but we were wary. We agreed to give the city our audited report, if and when we were asked for it. We knew the city was within its rights, but we wanted as few diversions as possible from our work of providing excellent housing and community programs.

Many items were negotiated late in the process. The Board of Estimate required us to sign the agreement by the end of 1989, which we did—close to midnight, December 29, after ten hours of negotiation. A special assistant at the city's housing agency, Ilene Popkin, stayed late to type in the new clauses so that the secretary could go home. Ilene was a good sport about it. This was before the age of word processors or user friendly computers. There were side letters attached to the land disposition agreement. We were all exhausted but happy to have met the deadline. Peter Miller, representing us, and Dan Weisz, representing the city, did an excellent job. Many of the clauses negotiated at the time turned out to be important years later.

Construction began in earnest about two months after the groundbreaking ceremony. It always takes time to tool up, outfit the trailers for inspectors, negotiate with insurance companies, name everyone as "additional insured," complete the minority hiring outreach, finalize permits, and the like. There were special people from City Hall who were supposed to rush all the permits. The system was far from perfect, but it is certainly better than the bureaucracy we have today. Dealing with computer systems has always been and remains problematic at New York City agencies, even in the age of high tech. It takes eons to remove resolved violations or old tax debt of former owners from the computer system. At the same time, title insurance companies will not provide coverage until the violations are addressed, and as a result loans stop flowing. The lawyers get people to post bonds, but it takes many steps and causes aggravation, maybe even ulcers.

As often happens, construction started like gangbusters. Demolition was easy because the buildings essentially had been gutted by fire damage and the work of neighborhood gang members. Weekly meetings took place in a trailer in a vacant lot on Walton Avenue. City officials, their construction managers, and their architects met first, allowing my team to enter only after the discussion of such "privileged" issues as insurance. This seemed a bit patronizing, but I decided not to complain. Unfortunately, the pre-meetings often ran long, and our engineer and managers were often left cooling their heels for nearly an hour. Since I tend to arrive at places on time, I still remember the cold days, waiting outside the trailer. This was the era before cell phones, and the pay phones on Walton Avenue had long since been vandalized. Hanging out outside the trailer during the winter months was not much fun.

There were more serious problems. The quality of construction was disappointing, and costs kept going up. The required outreach to minorities and women subcontractors and workers required time, energy, and endless paperwork. Critics kept attacking the costs. It was all over the press. City officials and the contractors discussed ways to save money, and

we were not privy to their conversations. At first I didn't mind, because
we were not to blame for high costs. As it turned out, cost cutting involved lower quality and many mistakes.

At one time construction was halted because the comptroller discovered that a convicted criminal owned the drywall company, running the
operation from his jail cell. He was on the state's list of approved minority
subcontractors. I testified on behalf of the city that the work should continue, minus the individual who was in jail. No one bought my argument,
which was unfortunate, because drywall work stopped for six months, and
the contractor, who had done good work, was replaced by a less competent organization.

Even worse, another subcontractor took his first payment, went to Las
Vegas, lost everything, and never came back. (I couldn't make this stuff up.)

Our engineer kept voluminous records about the poor quality of construction. Sometimes the construction manager and city officials listened
to us. Often they did not. We were a bit of a pain. A major issue, as predicted, turned out to be stucco. There should have been pointing, followed by wire lath so the stucco would stick to the walls. Our engineer
said the workers just slapped the stuff on, and that there would be leaks.
My interpretation was that the city was trying to cut costs. The city inspectors said all would be fine. I hoped they were right.

We agreed to become owners of each of the fourteen buildings as they
were finished. However, our team's definition of "finished" was quite different from that of the construction manager and city officials.

We were upset about the paint job, for example. In response, the city
official in charge of architecture said, "Just turn the lights down." One of
the construction managers asked us, "What do you care about the finishes? You know who is going to live there." That infuriated me.

I caved more often than I should have. The city officials and contractors wore me down. I was afraid that the buildings would be vandalized
if left vacant. So as soon as each building was "complete," we took over
ownership, and our staff cleaned up the mess. This proved costly.

The closings were agonizing. We had twenty-five pages of "punch list
items" for each building. The contactors would have to return and fix
such things as windows that did not open, compactors that were installed
incorrectly, and nonworking gates and intercoms.

At one building the retaining wall had not been sealed; as a result, rats
were rampant. When no one from the construction team responded to
my calls, I went to the company's president, who referred me to a vice
president. I invited him and the city officials to come uptown to see the

"wildlife preserve" and other construction problems. Again, we got only half of our demands met.

Our biggest battle involved the playground for the complex, which was to be built on an adjacent vacant lot. We didn't love the design but had been pleased that a playground, or tot lot as we called it, was part of the project. The construction was less pleasing. Our engineers said that the foundation was too shallow and that organic rubble was part of the fill. As a result, they predicted the tot lot would sink. Lehrer McGovern Bovis's engineers provided assurance in writing that the foundation was fine. Crossing our fingers, we took possession of the tot lot in August 1991. This was the last parcel to be completed.

Our final annoyance involved obtaining the real estate tax exemption that had been promised. The city was supposed to give us the buildings with all the information for tax exemption in place. Zero real estate taxes had been part of our deal, and city officials had promised to make it easy for us. Take the buildings anyway, we were told. Tax exemption would be granted retroactively, and city officials would handle everything. That was the good news. The bad news was that the law did not allow retroactive tax exemption for projects like ours. The statute is called J-51, referring to a section of an act few people had ever read. I had read most of it. It's what I like to do. However, neither I nor the city attorneys had noticed that our particular type of nonprofit corporation was not eligible for retroactive tax exemption. We took the buildings anyway, because we thought they would have been destroyed if left vacant for too long. Our board president, Chuck Warren, and I were able to get the State Legislature to amend the real estate tax law, providing retroactive tax exemption for projects that fit the exact description of New Settlement Apartments.

But even after the governor signed the new law, we weren't out of the woods. Next we needed the City Council to enact enabling legislation, a process that took about eight months. Then we had to submit individual tax exemption applications for each of fourteen buildings. All of this took two years. In the meantime tax bills were accumulating, and our buildings ended up on the list for tax foreclosure, which meant automatic ownership by the city. This in turn meant that every month I had to contact various government agencies to make sure that this did not happen. Finally our tax exemption certificates arrived. But then it still took eight additional months for the city's computer system to stop spewing out tax bills.

In retrospect, we made the right decisions, but the process was arduous. The city was no help regarding the poor quality of construction. Nor did

the city comply with its contractual obligation to provide all the information for tax exemption. We could have refused to take possession of the
buildings, and we would have been within our rights to do so.

Apparently the New York City Housing Authority experienced a
similar situation with its contractor, involving a large rehabilitation project
in Harlem, and the official in charge of signing off was more difficult than
we were. The agency refused to take possession of what it described as
"incomplete" buildings, which stayed vacant for months while various
city agencies fought with another. Many of the buildings were vandalized,
needing a new rehabilitation before they could be occupied. We took our
buildings not just because we were smart—we took possession because
we were worn down.

6
Here Come the Families

People often ask how we choose our tenants. So many people in New York need housing, and there are usually hundreds of applications for a single apartment. At New Settlement over fifteen thousand families applied for a total of 893 apartments.

Selecting tenants was never my strong suit. If left alone, I would tend to accept everybody. My first summer job in housing, while still in college, involved interviewing tenants for a building on Bruckner Boulevard in the Bronx. The developer was an idealist who wanted a racially integrated building. The year was 1959, and it was acceptable to have quotas. Not enough white people applied, and the search for diversity (meaning whites) was on. But when I interviewed black or Latino families who seemed nice, and medium in skin color, I would check the "white" box on the application form. I hated turning anyone down. I messed up the files and soon realized I was better suited for other tasks.

Today the law requires lotteries. Developers must reach out to achieve integration, mainly through advertising to those least likely to apply. Goals are fine, but quotas are forbidden by law and regulation. To me this is a silly distinction, but the Supreme Court disagreed in the late 1980s when refusing to hear the appeal regarding Starrett City's tenant integration plan, which had been deemed unconstitutional by the appellate court. The new laws are extremely complex, so complying with them is difficult and costly.

After decades of work in this field, I came to realize that careful tenant selection is crucial for the long-term success of a development. Tenants need to have good credit scores and should not have recent criminal records or a history of destroying property.

Susan Cole, who was associate director of Settlement Housing Fund through 2010, knows everything there is to know about tenant selection. She established this niche early in her career, long before New Settlement Apartments existed. She is both a licensed real estate broker and a certified social worker. Over the decades of her professional career, Susan has trained many others. Large developers who get tax breaks for reserving 20 percent of their apartments for low-income tenants hired Susan and her staff to select the families in their buildings. This was a good line of business for Settlement Housing Fund, and it has continued under new leadership. The work is hard. Many rejected applicants file an appeal. Some get hysterical, sue, threaten, lie, and harass. We had to call the police on several occasions. Susan, using the services of her favorite attorney, always won the lawsuits. We comply meticulously with all laws and regulations. But even when we win the lawsuits, there is an emotional cost and a significant cost in dollars.

Nowhere was the process more arduous than at New Settlement Apartments. Initially we worried that few people would want to live in such a troubled neighborhood. Luckily we were wrong. As stated in our original proposal, we had four income tiers. Of the 893 apartments, 268 were reserved for homeless families, 357 for low-income families earning less than 50 per cent of the area's median income; up to 268 for moderate-income families earning less than 80 percent of median; and up to 10 percent for upper-moderate-income families essentially paying market rents. This last category depended on demand.

Apartment sizes ranged from one to three bedrooms, along with a few studios. The majority were two-bedroom units. The various apartment sizes were proportionately distributed among the four income tiers. Every floor of each of the fourteen buildings was to be economically integrated. The goal was that families not know the income levels of their neighbors. We also hoped that the working families would not know who had been homeless.

Our proposal to the city outlined a comprehensive system for selecting tenants, which has since become the model for a citywide protocol (although changes are on the horizon). The process of selecting tenants began with an extensive outreach program, which involved visits to schools, community organizations, churches, and local employers, as well as a presentation to the local community board. We distributed a fact sheet and maintained a list of the people who inquired about it. We advertised in local and citywide newspapers. Potential tenants were required to request an application in writing. The deadline for returning the application was four weeks after the ads were placed.

The application forms called for information needed to determine eligibility: income, family size, and family composition. Applications were on paper that could not be copied, although unfortunately a few applicants would copy applications and even sell them. The applications had to be mailed back to a post office box. We did not list our phone number because our lines would have been jammed with inquiries.

Huge bags with over fifteen thousand applications were picked up and brought to the management office. We used a logbook and entered all the names, date- and time-stamped. This was all done manually, and the process was tedious and nerve-racking. Today the government sends a representative to watch us, which can be okay. It's often much better to have them there than to hear them complain later.

The next step was the credit check, followed by an office interview and then a home interview. Susan did the final sign-off on every tenant who was accepted.

Reasons for rejection included incomes that were too high or too low, poor credit history, failure to pay rent, falsification of information on the application, history of violent behavior by anyone in the family, poor housekeeping observed during the home interview, and drug addiction (unless in an active rehabilitation program). Pets were not allowed. This sounds harsh, but we knew that maintaining the buildings would be harder if dogs were wandering around.

We set up two selection processes, one for families considered homeless and one for all others. For the homeless, we reached out to the directors of over twenty family homeless shelters, asking for names of qualified families. We wanted families without a history of violent behavior or recent substance abuse. Susan along with Sarah Kolodny, our director of community programs, did all the "home" interviews at the various shelters around the city. I would have liked to have been there, but Susan and Sarah were horrified at the very thought. They thought I was clueless and would get in the way. Sarah is one of the most politically correct people I have ever met. She was also astutely aware that if the homeless families in our Bronx building acted out badly, our experiment in economic integration would fail. Susan, an intuitive social worker, is blunt and unafraid to "tell it like it is." They had great mutual respect and were an excellent team. They performed more than six hundred home interviews to select the 268 families. Most of the shelter directors were helpful and supportive of our goals. Others were advocates for their clients above all, making it difficult at first for Susan and Sarah. They managed to navigate the maze, but it wasn't easy—and it's even more difficult now.

Another problem involved timing. Mayor Koch wanted to dedicate the first building before the November 1989 election. He was justifiably proud of his housing program and thought that having these buildings complete and occupied would make him a shoo-in for a fourth term. He was wrong about the election but right about the legacy of his housing program.

The first "completed" building was not really ready for actual occupancy when we had the dedication, but we allowed a few tenants to move in anyway, before repairs were done. One was a single parent, the head of a homeless family that included a son and three daughters. We thought she had leadership potential: she was quite articulate and had stubbornly stayed in a shelter for four years waiting for the perfect apartment.

The mayor was stunned when he heard her story. "Four years in a temporary shelter? Unheard of," he said with a scowl. In fact, she was somewhat problematic as a tenant, but relatively harmless. She has since passed away, but two of her children have separate apartments at New Settlement. They are doing quite well.

Susan and Sarah went to all the home interviews together, because two sets of eyes and ears are needed to make this kind of decision. Sometimes one of the children would distract the mother or jump up and down a lot, or otherwise be disruptive. The interaction between the parents and children provided useful information about how the family functioned (or failed to function). Some screamed at or pounded their children. Others were great.

Many of the shelter rooms or apartments were immaculate, and the children were well behaved. In other cases there were clear signs that children had been neglected or even abused, physically or emotionally. Dirty, torn clothes, unpleasant odors, stuff strewn on the floor, screaming, or loud fighting at an interview were all indications of problems. And there was everything else in between. One woman had three children, all busy with toys or puzzles during the home interview. She had been evicted and at one time struggled with serious drug problems. But nonetheless she had a certain charm. At the end of the interview, she turned around and asked with a smile, "Well, what do you think of my kids?" The pride in her voice endeared her to Susan and Sarah. She did well for a while but eventually got back into bad habits. She had two more children; of the four, one died at a young age, one went to jail, and two did well.

We conducted a number or workshops in our office or at the shelters to describe our goals, and most of the staff members at the shelters approved of our program and wanted it to succeed. In recent years the staff at the shelters have been under great pressure to move families out—the faster, the better. Sometimes they will vouch for families who are not ready to live independently. These families end up failing to pay rent and causing problems for their neighbors. Many homeless families leave the shelters, only to become homeless again. Good supportive housing is needed to help such families.

Selecting tenants presented other problems. Politicians, community board members, and others with connections sometimes tried to use their influence to circumvent the system and get friends or constituents into New Settlement Apartments. Happily it never worked. Susan would not tolerate such shenanigans.

Selecting the working families who would live in New Settlement Apartments was less of a problem, but still time-consuming. Often families did not show up and did not even call. If this happened twice, they became disqualified.

We encountered extra complexity because of the three income bands in addition to the homeless. Since each floor of each building was economically integrated, each apartment had to be designated for a specific income range. We had to establish initial rents and register with the state agency that supervised rent regulations. In addition, the city's regulatory agreement was specific and correct about eligibility and equal opportunity. We had no problem living with the regulatory agreement for all this time, although after fifteen years we did negotiate an amendment to allow more flexibility.

Many families turned out to have bad credit, or they lied on their applications—grounds for automatic rejection. We required applicants to provide tax forms and letters from the landlord verifying that the families paid their rent promptly. (Some landlords were happy to provide the letters, hoping to vacate the units and raise the rents or just hoping that difficult tenants would leave.) We also required letters from a school administrator that the children attended school on a regular basis. We had to go through about ten thousand applications in order to choose 893 eligible families with acceptable credit and housekeeping ability. Much of the problem involved income eligibility—most incomes were either too high or too low.

To me, this all seemed a bit much—although I never admitted it. I know I would be annoyed if I had to find my own records and amass letters from landlords, school administrators, and others order to qualify for an apartment. The policy of not doing favors for politicians was sound, and I admired Susan for her guts. I'm not sure I would have had the courage to say no to powerful people.

Mayor Koch was responsible the lottery system. There had been bad publicity about a project in Harlem. People had lined up around the block simply to apply, and the crowds got out of control. Newspaper articles claimed that few apartments were available because tenants who were friends of the developers had been preselected for most of the units. Furthermore, the mayor, who was great at being outraged, declared that from that moment on, tenants would be chosen through lotteries. Susan figured out the mechanics of how the lotteries would work at New Settlement and at other buildings where Settlement Housing Fund was a consultant.

New Settlement Apartments was the first complex with a specified broad mix of incomes, ranging from the homeless to tenants with incomes in excess of $65,000. Our Land Disposition Agreement with the city stipulated that we would take over ownership of each of the fourteen buildings as the renovation work was completed. We were told to be ready with approved tenants ahead of time.

We held the initial lottery for over fifteen thousand families in August 1989. However, the first building was not ready for occupancy until the following January, the next in February, the next in April, and so on until the project was complete in August 1991. We would get schedules from the contractor, but they were never accurate. The process was difficult.

At the time tenants were moving in, a new mayor was taking office. In 1989 Ed Koch was defeated in the Democratic Party primary by David Dinkins, who went on to win the general election. Felice Michetti became the housing commissioner, and she wanted the buildings filled immediately.

After half the tenants were selected, the city officials announced a new definition of homelessness. A study by an advocacy group had shown that many families lived doubled-up in public housing. These were deemed the "hidden homeless." Not only were the apartments overcrowded, but the wear and tear and the extra use of utilities became expensive for the New York City Housing Authority. We were instructed to stop recruiting families at shelters and to reach out to public housing officials to find these "hidden homeless." Luckily we had good relationships with the Housing Authority. Susan and Sarah visited the apartments in projects in which two or more families inhabited one apartment. Unfortunately, because of a complicated part of our contract, our fee was reduced because of this change in policy. Even though we had philanthropic support, we needed fees to cover the costs of our staff, all the credit checks, and more. The fee (known as the EARP, or Emergency Assistance Rehousing Program) was only available to owners who took families from shelters. We were happy to get any fee at all, but we lost over $400,000 because of the new policy. Interestingly, we thought that the families in the shelters at that time adjusted more easily to living in permanent housing than did those who had been doubled up in public housing. The tenants in public housing were mostly children and grandchildren of tenants, and they had never lived independently nor paid rent before. They had few responsibilities. The shelters at that time provided some training in such areas as parenting skills and budgeting,

The construction delays continued to cause serious problems for the leasing process. We should have expected delays, but we could not count on them, and we wanted to have the families ready just in case. We did not want finished buildings to remain empty—a clear invitation to vandalism. By the time we notified the families that their apartments were ready for occupancy, some of them were no longer interested. Applications can get stale. In some cases income levels change and the families are no longer eligible. Or they have moved somewhere else, or they have changed their minds.

Sad to say, the contractors' definition of readiness remained dramatically different from ours. Windows were covered with cement. Towel racks were missing. Ceilings weren't painted. Garbage compactor chutes were in the wrong places. Doors didn't close properly. We suffered for many years because of these defects. When we made repairs on the facades in 2013, we found places where the brick under the window sills was missing, with the sills attached to interior sheetrock

It took a long time to achieve full occupancy because of all the legal and regulatory complexities. We had serious operating deficits at the start, because it took months to get the rent subsidies that were owed to us, and we never made up that loss. City officials were angry at us, especially blaming Susan. "I will cut your heart out," Commissioner Michetti screamed at Susan at one of our meetings to which we brought our board president. "What's the matter?" asked the commissioner. "Does Susan Cole have to look in someone's refrigerator before they can move in?" The city's staff members suggested bringing vans of homeless families so they could see the site and move right in. We thought that the families needed to demonstrate independence and get to the interview themselves.

The commissioner, who is now in the private sector, later became one of Susan's close friends and deserves every kind of accolade for her original vision. Felice's company manages New Settlement and most of Settlement Housing Fund's buildings. But no one would ever have predicted the friendly relationship. The tension was brutal.

It did not look good to have vacancies while so many people were looking for apartments, and the city and the contractor wanted "out" of the whole thing. The city had experienced cost overruns and started to receive bad press, which is the worst state of affairs for bureaucrats—even the good ones.

Eventually we decided to place a new advertisement for apartments. City officials allowed us to take families as they applied, without going through another lottery. This is now called a rolling lottery, frequently used when the first lottery does not produce enough eligible applicants. It takes a lot of work to get officials to agree to this.

Decades later, I realize that Susan's careful process of tenant selection had been prudent. We learned the lesson the hard way in another neighborhood by taking over thirteen distressed occupied buildings for which we did not select the tenants. Tenants paid rent sporadically or sometimes not at all. About half the families kept their apartments in complete disarray, making the staff afraid to enter. Mice, dirt, piles of dirty dishes, diapers in the hall, and odors of marijuana and cigarettes were pervasive. We improved the buildings and eventually sold them.

The situation at New Settlement Apartments was and remains different. Now over 98 percent of our Bronx tenants pay their rent on time and keep their apartments in good condition. Units are inspected at least once a year. Susan, Sarah, and the managers did a great job of tenant selection. But it was not easy.

Suddenly it was time for them to start moving in. To welcome them to their beautiful new homes we planned orientation sessions and took measures to assure safety. We reminded them that our community programs would take a while to develop.

We were bringing 893 families to new homes in a neighborhood that had been the scene of crime, abandonment, fires, and economic failure. We had to send a message that the past was over and a new community was about to be born. We congratulated the families for "winning the lottery."

But the fights with the construction management team continued to escalate. As we were preparing apartments for move in, there were no toilet paper holders, windows were stuck, gate hinges fell off, tree pits were already cracking, paint was peeling everywhere, glop was all over the floors, child guards were missing from the windows, and on and on. The contractor gave us a schedule of when each building would be ready. It was wrong. The whole thing was a nightmare

We ended up doing a lot of cleaning ourselves. In fact, many of the new tenants commented that they liked the smell of the strong cleaning fluid we used on the floor.

The first thirty-two families moved into 1532 Townsend Avenue in January 1990. We had a loan from the New York City Housing Development Corporation and foundation grants to cover costs of staff, supplies, and equipment. We hired a director, who had been a public housing manager and was on the managing agent's staff. We also hired a director of maintenance, a sort of super-superintendent. Our third employee was a director of programs, who started to plan for the future.

Families attended orientation classes and seemed happy to do so. We stressed the importance of prompt rent payments. They paid attention. I went to a session about using the equipment, including the garbage compactor. Only environmentally correct items could be thrown in the compactor. We required recycling way in advance of city regulations. The instructor demonstrated the best way to tie a garbage bag. I think about that class every time I throw something out at my apartment building.

Originally we planned to help organize a tenants' organization. Settlement Housing Fund's founder, Clara Fox, believed that a system with floor captains and real tenant involvement would help to create a sense of ownership among the renters, assuring that peer pressure would prevent destruction of the property. Clara had taught classes for owners of cooperatives that had been financed by New York State. With her help, we included an elaborate tenant lesson plan in our proposal to the city. Tenants were expected to learn the history of the development, the cost of running a building, and the importance of acting as a watchdog for the development and the community.

On paper this sounded like a great idea. But none of the working families participated. They were too busy and had no gripes about the buildings. The participants argued among themselves. They wanted a dedicated room, a telephone, and money. We let the program die quietly.

We decided that concept involved a fuzzy kind of paternalism. It was not a good idea for the landlord to create a tenants' association. Over the years we learned that when problems arise, tenants are quick to organize on their own. We had a brief problem with mice, and the tenants of that building did not hesitate to band together. We met with them and fixed things, of course.

Instead we concentrated on helping the tenants settle into the neighborhood. We gave every new tenant a welcome basket with cleaning supplies, fruit, vegetables, and, for some reason, salt. I think that was supposed to be good luck. We handed out a brochure that described the neighborhood, the schools, transportation, shopping, and where to get help in opening up accounts for electricity and telephone service. (Cooking and heating gas were included in the rent.)

One of the first tenants to move in was Maria Santana, a teacher who had taken time off to care for her children—or so she thought. Our new director of Bronx programs, Tom Gonzalez, convinced her to launch an after-school program, which started after we took title to our second building, a structure that included two large spaces for classes as well as a management office, a kitchen, and a small conference room. Sarah Kolodny, who oversaw community programs at all Settlement Housing developments, believed in creating programs "organically." That meant starting small with high standards of quality. Ideally a buzz would form in the community and people would want to participate.

That's exactly what happened with our after-school program. Parents wanted to become involved, and we kept expanding. Maria ran the after-school program for over twenty years. In 2014 she retired and went back to her home in Ecuador.

We also launched co-ventures with neighborhood organizations and tended to avoid wheel reinvention. We made an early connection with the Citizens Advice Bureau, later renamed BronxWorks. The group had offices in various Bronx neighborhoods. I visited one with the executive director Carolyn McLaughlin, and you could tell immediately that something good was going on. Neighborhood residents obtained help in filling out forms, qualifying for public aid, opening accounts with utility companies, and accessing health care and other benefits.

We provided rent-free space and a small grant. There was an outside entrance so that residents of the entire community could take advantage of the services. In fact, all our programs are open to the entire community, not just to our tenants. This has been a successful policy. We became a vital part of the neighborhood instead of creating an "us versus them" ambiance. A few years later we obtained a grant from Citibank and opened a larger office for BronxWorks, which has since been renovated again and still operates today, providing services for our tenants and their neighbors.

We also contacted the Board of Education (now the Department of Education) to alert the agency that 893 families, most with school-age children, would soon arrive. Iris White from the board was assigned to assure that the children registered for school, and she was effective. Several interns worked for us, and quite a few ended up there permanently or participated in other co-ventures. Among the latter was Bob Hughes, a lawyer who became CEO of New Visions for Public Schools, the group that invited us to create a school complex twenty years later. That's another story for another chapter.

The one collaboration that should have been a natural was a disaster. Settlement Housing Fund emanated from United Neighborhood Houses, the federation of settlement houses. We had thought that one of the settlement houses would run programs at New Settlement, in collaboration with our director. Even though we had two licensed social workers on staff, we were the housing experts and they were the social service experts. Or at least that was our theory. We obtained a generous grant from a foundation to cover the initial planning costs for New Settlement. We suggested a meeting with United Neighborhood Houses, which resulted in an even more generous grant for them. However, for a series of complicated reasons, the idea fell apart and it took months to repair the damage.

However, this story has a happy ending. We all get along famously now. At our suggestion, BronxWorks officially became a settlement house and a member of United Neighborhood Houses. Then, in 2010, New Settlement Apartments also became a settlement house and joined United Neighborhood Houses.

The arriving families adjusted fairly well to their new surroundings. Management did a good job. We stuck to our guns about tenant selection. We asked tenants to report the need for repairs early, before problems became serious. We hired great housing coordinators to handle work orders, relaying information to the handymen and porters.

We made repairs promptly. The coordinators got to know the tenants well. The porters, hired to keep the buildings clean and in good repair, were also trained to be alert for social problems—loud noises in the apartments, signs of domestic problems, bad smells, and the like. They would report such conditions to the tenant coordinators, who would make referrals to the appropriate agencies.

We had one frightening incident early on. One of the tenants stabbed her live-in girlfriend. The assailant went to jail, and luckily the victim survived.

We were concerned with security from the get-go. In interviews, potential tenants asked about safety again and again. We provided photo ID cards for the residents, who were happy to have them. After much internal debate, we decided not to hire our own guards, but to use a security firm. We had three guards during the day and four from 3:00 p.m. to 11:00 p.m. for the fourteen buildings. They walked up and down the stairwells and around the outsides of the buildings. They kept in contact with one another with walkie-talkies. We had gates and vestibule doors that were locked at night. Tenants had fobs, but they had to go downstairs to let guests in. They paid fines if they lost their fobs or keys. If the fobs were stolen, we could disable them through a computerized system. This was new in 1990, and we fought hard to include the system in the project budget.

Most important, we decided to hire a director of security, who would supervise the guards provided by the security firm. Our choice was Chester Paul, a former detective with the local 44th Precinct. Chester made sure that the guards did their jobs. We had relatively few incidents and dealt with them appropriately. There was one case in which a guard became too friendly with a female tenant, and they ended up on one of the roofs, having disabled the alarm. That guard was promptly fired. Chester established good working relations with the precinct. This was during the Dinkins administration, which had emphasized community policing. Workshops were held in which the police captain would advise residents about safety. The precinct also hosted retreats, so everyone would get to know one another. Our system was a good one. Chester retired in 2011, and another retired officer from the 44th has been hired to replace him.

It took a year to reach full occupancy. We struggled to pay our bills and spent a lot of time cleaning up the mess left by the contractors. We had problems, but looking back, I realize that things could have been much worse.

7

The Stucco Falls Off
and the Playground Collapses

I hoped I was wrong about our disputes with Lehrer McGovern Bovis and the city inspectors. I hoped that the stucco would adhere to the buildings, that the tot lot would be stable, and that no other potential defects would materialize. Sadly we were right about almost everything.

In 1993, in response to our advocacy, a new public school for very young children, P.S. 170, opened on Townsend and Mount Eden Avenues, next to one of our buildings. Lehrer McGovern Bovis conducted a tour. Although the school was great, as I looked out the windows I could see cracks on the rear facades of some of our buildings. I asked our managers and our engineer whether the buildings were supposed to look like that. The answer was a resounding no.

The next day I visited the buildings with our manager and the engineer, who was carrying a small hammer. As he tapped gently on the facades we heard a hollow sound. Using that low-tech method, he could assure us that the stucco would fall down in the future, resulting in serious leakage, thereby damaging the entire renovation. Great . . .

We immediately notified the city officials in a letter that also mentioned problems with the tot lot, a bad paint job in the hallways, and sewage repeatedly backing up in several ground-floor apartments. Our contract required the city officials to repair latent defects for ten years after obtaining a certificate of occupancy for each building. Settlement Housing Fund board members had insisted on that clause, and unfortunately it turned out they were wise to do so.

We were in year 2. We checked with the attorneys who represented us in 1989, and they approved our notice to the city.

The construction contract had called for a 2 percent holdback, providing potential funding. If the city did not respond to our request, we would have the option of doing the work ourselves and billing the city. If we did not have the funds in our reserve, we were empowered to sue the city. We thought that the city would be able to get reimbursed either by using the holdback or by suing Lehrer McGovern Bovis. The city officials agreed to the logic when we negotiated the contract. But that was then.

To our dismay, the city responded by claiming that the cracked stucco and all the other problems were caused by poor maintenance, and therefore that everything was our fault. That was a ridiculous claim, since our buildings and grounds were spotless and in great repair. There were articles in the press celebrating our work, especially compared to the abandoned and burned-out buildings that had occupied the site previously.

We then learned that the city had already released the holdback to Lehrer McGovern Bovis. The city sued the firm but lost. Apparently the construction contract gave the city no remedy after a brief period.

New inspectors arrived. One admitted that the stucco contractor should have used wire lathe before applying stucco to attain long-lasting adherence to the walls. He later tried to wiggle out of that opinion. The city officials dismissed the problems with both the stucco and the tot lot. Our laundry list of complaints included many other items, ranging from leaking bulkheads to the wrong screws having been used for the closet shelves. Some complaints were addressed, often after long disputes. Most were ignored.

However, the Housing Authority's project in Harlem was experiencing disastrous problems, delays, and disputes that made ours seem insignificant to the officials who were handling both developments. Nevertheless, we would not be ignored.

It took months to arrange the necessary meetings, and no one took us seriously. When I complained to a friend, he remarked, "You mean the city 'gave' you buildings and a playground for a dollar, and now you want to sue them?"

But we felt we had no choice.

Luckily, one of the city's top law firms, Davis Polk & Wardwell, had taken us on as a pro bono client. Our legal team included John Fouhey, our corporate partner. the one who agreed to take us on originally. John is someone that you want on your side. He is quite brilliant. He brought in the top litigation partner, the late Denny Lewis, to assist us, as well as a smart, conscientious young associate, Joe Warganz.

Then at a reception I ran into Bob Rubin, a great construction lawyer. He was with another firm that specialized in real estate and construction law. I had seen him in action representing a good contractor. I described our situation, and he said, "I would like to join the team."

Denny, Joe, and Bob were the best of the best. They meticulously combed through our thousands of pages of files. They spent hour after hour working on our behalf and did not charge a cent. Especially after visiting the site, they were passionate about the righteousness of our cause.

We tried for over a year to settle our dispute without litigation but got nowhere. Then we asked our lawyers if we could sue Lehrer McGovern Bovis instead of the city. After considerable research, our attorneys said we did not have that right because we were not a party in the construction contract.

We then had to hire engineers. We chose the firm of Feld, Kaminetzky & Cohen, who were considered experts. Dov Kaminetzky, one of the partners, had written an interesting book about construction failures, titled *Design and Construction Failures: Lessons from Forensic Investigations.* We also consulted experts on soil and foundations.

With the arrival of Mayor Dinkins in 1990, a new team of city officials had taken over, and they seemed even more determined to ignore us. Meanwhile our problems were escalating. Not only was the stucco cracking, but sidewalks around the perimeter of the tot lot were cracking, too. This was caused by settlement from the rubble used as fill in the foundation. Cracking occurred all over the place. Bleeding paint spoiled the appearance of the complex's ground floors and community rooms.

In February 1995 we filed an official complaint against the city. Not surprisingly, the city filed a counterclaim a few months later. There were endless interrogatories. Back and forth. Back and forth.

We were worried that if jurors ever visited our buildings they would be impressed with how great everything looked. There were as yet no actual leaks as from the damaged stucco. Some of the jurors might even think, "I wish my apartment building looked that good."

Meanwhile, we had to close the tot lot. We were sad to deprive the children and their parents of this amenity, but we worried about safety. Our engineers and attorneys advised us to hire experts to perform test borings to see if the foundation was in fact unstable and therefore dangerous. When a small truck was driven onto the playground for that purpose, a large area of the playground collapsed. No one was hurt, but city officials could not deny that something was seriously wrong with the foundation.

We were successful in obtaining private philanthropic grants to pay for the engineers and to start planning a new tot lot. By this point, we could sense from the attitude of the city's lawyers that a partial settlement might be possible. By 1995 Jack Doyle, our excellent new executive director, had just come on board to oversee New Settlement Apartments (more about Jack in the following chapter). He and his community program staff met over a few months with parents, program participants, and community stakeholders to solicit their ideas on how the new playground should be designed. As owners of the project, we wanted to assure that the design included all the latest safety features. We also wanted the playground to look good and to be appropriate and fun for young children. To this end we hired an experienced playground designer, Donna Walcavage.

But when we discussed our plans with the city's attorneys and staff in the comptroller's office, they were horrified that we were planning to improve the playground. "No betterments" was their reaction. We knew that we could build our beautiful new playground for less money than had been spent on the unsafe one. The biggest expense would be the new foundation. Our engineers and the New York City Building Department determined that we needed to dig down fourteen feet and replace the rubble with solid fill.

The meetings went on and on. Various lawyers for the city accused us of everything from maliciousness to stupidity. It was an emotionally draining experience.

Still, no one really wanted to go to court. Although we thought that a judge and jury would be more sympathetic to us than to city bureaucrats, we did not want to take the risk. The fact that we were not paying anything for legal costs was a huge advantage, and the city attorneys were well aware that our legal team and our engineers were highly regarded professionals. The battle continued for years, and the acrimony grew worse and worse. The good news was that we did arrive at a settlement on the major issues. We held a celebratory party for the attorneys and everyone involved, at which we gave out coffee mugs with the inscription "Stucco, Never Again."

Our initial plan had been to remove the stucco from the buildings, do a good pointing job, and apply state-of-the art sealants to the walls. The tenants would hate the noise, but we wanted to secure the buildings from leakage. We asked several well-regarded waterproofing firms to bid. The lowest bid was more than twice the price awarded in the settlement. The engineers then proposed a new plan that involved coats of stucco and

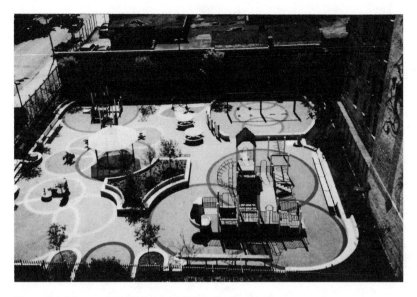

Figure 7.1. New tot lot. (Courtesy of New Settlement Apartments.)

staples to secure proper adhesion. It worked well and lasted over twenty years, but we are just now repairing some of the rear facades.

We built the tot lot within budget. We raised funds in advance of receiving the actual settlement award. Members of the community and local teenagers participated in a Community Build Day, October 22, 1998, for the final installation of play equipment. I was there to be a part of a joyous occasion. The tot lot is still beautiful, immaculate, and safe. It is locked when not in use, and when open there is a staff member is on duty to supervise activities.

In 2012 Mathew Wambua, then the commissioner of the city's Department of Housing Preservation and Development, visited New Settlement Apartments. He gasped when he saw the tot lot and said, "This looks like a playground in a rich, white neighborhood."

Although the tot lot and the stucco were the big-ticket items, we had a huge list of latent defects that plagued us. Naturally, the city's estimate was much less than the cost of repairs. Eventually we agreed to a grant plus a 1 percent loan that costs us $32,000 a year, part of an annual budget of more than $6 million. (It is now about $12 million.) The loan replaced a purchase-money mortgage with $41,000 a year in debt service, part of our original agreement. Thus we actually saved a little money when all was said and done. For nonprofit owners, however, all is never said and done.

Our deal about latent defects would expire ten years after taking title to the last lot—August 2001. Settling the lawsuit took just about that long. We were not compensated for every defect, but we managed to get enough funds to keep the buildings in great shape all these years. There are still lawyers on the staff of the city housing agency who have not forgiven us for initiating a lawsuit and subsequently have made life difficult for some of our projects. No fun . . .

All in all, our board was wise to worry about construction defects. Our original attorneys, Stroock & Stroock & Lavan, negotiated a good deal for us with the city. The original lawyers for the city understood and supported us. It got messy later on. Thank goodness we had Davis Polk & Wardwell on a pro bono basis. It was a good thing to sue the city.

8
Finding Jack

Managing a building involves a million things: hiring, firing, tenant relations, paying the bills, oversight, maintenance, preventive maintenance, security, green consciousness, and much more. In housing and community development, management should be everything. While it requires a herculean effort and a few miracles to get anything built, even more challenging are the day-to-day chores involved in sustaining affordable housing. Great building managers are heroic.

When I first started to learn about housing in the sixties, many developers never gave a thought to management. In fact, they created their management budgets by working backwards. They'd start by estimating rental income. Then they would subtract the amount needed to cover interest and amortization of the mortgage. Whatever was left would be the management budget.

That was a recipe for default, disaster, and worse. A good management plan requires detailed estimates of operating costs, including utilities, the salaries and benefits of those who take care of the buildings, repairs, routine maintenance, supplies, insurance, security, reserves, and the unexpected. As people have learned more about the importance of upkeep, the situation has improved. But even today, underestimating management and maintenance costs is all too common.

Linda Field, president of the company we had hired to manage New Settlement Apartments, started her career working for the city and then became a housing finance consultant for private developers. The two of us learned how to estimate management costs together. We went to see a management guru, Morris Stutman, who taught us how to write a management plan and gave us a sample to follow, the details of which were quite impressive. It spelled out how often the porters would mop the hallways. It described work order procedures, inventories, equal opportunity policies, and much more. The plan consisted of about twenty pages, plus documents outlining the costs of about thirty categories of expense.

Linda and I used this plan for proposals for many projects. Years later Linda teamed up with a contractor, Bobby Garcia, to form Ashton Management. They were a great combination. Bobby was an expert electrician and knew all about the physical aspects of housing. He was especially knowledgeable about heating plants. Linda was a good writer and adept with numbers. They were both smart and aligned with us in terms of mission.

When we prepare management plans, we look at the latest operating statement we can find and try to predict the costs for each item several years into the future. At that time we would usually project a cost increase of about 3 percent a year.

The staff members of various city agencies often quibbled with our operating budgets over the years, and they still do. We always try to avoid underestimating the cost of keeping a building spotless, safe, and in great repair.

When we compiled our management budget for New Settlement Apartments in 1990, we had to figure out the staffing pattern for fourteen buildings comprising 893 apartments. We decided to employ a managing director, who would be supervised by Linda and Bobby. All staff members would be paid from the project budget. Instead of a live-in superintendent, we'd hire a director of maintenance. Four handymen would be hired. They would have boiler licenses and possess various maintenance skills, and they would live on the site.

Then we would hire fourteen porters, one for each building. They had to assure that the buildings were spotless. Over the years we kept adding porters, and at one point we employed twenty-nine. When we had cash flow problems in later years, we reduced the number to eighteen. Today there are twenty-two, but they take care of more program space and several additional buildings. We even planned to have painters on staff so we didn't have to hire outside contractors—and believe it or not, the first painter we hired was named Picasso. Settlement Housing Fund would always be an active asset manager, inspecting the properties, keeping the books, and supervising community programs.

We had many original ideas. We included three "housing coordinators" as part of the operating budget, who would get to know as many of the 893 families as possible. They would also keep on top of rental subsi-

dies for the formerly homeless and refer families to city services and programs. They would also oversee apartment inspections and report on the
results. This system worked well, and several of the original coordinators
are still on staff twenty-seven years later.

Settlement Housing Fund is a hands-on owner. In the first twenty
years, associate director Susan Cole would "walk" the buildings of New
Settlement at least twice a month. She would go up and down the stairwells, examining basements, facades, courtyards, and more. Susan had an
amazing eye. Once I saw her point to a spot behind a light fixture in the
ceiling. Practically screaming, she announced, "There is a piece of chew-
ing gum stuck behind that light!" The entire staff at New Settlement and
all our other developments respected and admired Susan.

I'd examine the monthly financial statements: city officials had feared
the project would be a cash cow, throwing off huge profits, but they were
wrong. We barely managed to cover costs and reserves.

One of the most important functions of management is collecting rents.
An owner cannot pay for heat and services without sufficient rental income. We wanted the rent checks to be sent on the first day of every
month. After ten days we would send a warning letter, and after thirty
days we would start eviction procedures. It is expensive to evict a tenant,
and the New York City Housing Court process is far from user-friendly
for either tenants or landlords. Still, we needed the word to spread that
we were serious about collecting rent. Many nonprofit owners have been
hesitant about evictions, and their buildings ultimately failed. We were
rigorous about rent collection, and the residents respected our policy. In
fact, those who paid their rent promptly resented tenants who were late
or who did not pay. We did not like evictions but knew they were necessary. That was one of the reasons we used professional, for-profit managing agents, who acted as a buffer between us and the eviction process.

Collecting rent from the residents became relatively easy. However, obtaining Section 8 federal rent subsidies for the formerly homeless families
from the city agencies was excruciating. As required by law, every apartment had to be inspected. However, the inspectors often failed to show up
for appointments or fill out reports. As a result, the city staff either delayed
payments or skipped them entirely. Because of this, we lost $85,000 to
$100,000 a year, which we desperately needed. Housing homeless fami-
lies without these subsidies was impossible. The importance of Section 8
cannot be overstated.

Unfortunately, it seemed that our first project director was not up to
the job. Things did not move quickly enough, and we were concerned

about inefficiencies. The second, third, and fourth managers also presented problems.

Because of these difficulties, Susan and I decided to revisit the structure of our management hierarchy. We did not think there was sufficient understanding in the management entity of the value of community programs. We did not think that we had enough control of overall operations. We called Rosemary Bova, our executive leadership consultant, a woman who had advised me when I became executive director of Settlement Housing Fund. We met among ourselves and with Linda and Bob, the two principals of our managing agent.

We finally decided that the next project director would be on Settlement Housing Fund's staff. That person would be entitled to our benefit package, attend our staff meetings, and become loyal to us, not just to the managing agent. In fact, this director would supervise the on-site management staff. At first Linda and Bobby were skeptical. The consultant acted like a therapist, and we came to terms with our problems. We had a plan.

Now we had to find the right person, someone who would understand the importance of integrating community programs with taking care of the buildings. Magically, the perfect person for the job appeared on our doorstep. Jack Doyle grew up in the Bronx. His father was a member of the New York Police Department. One of his brothers was a public attorney who had defended those accused of capital crimes. Most recently, Jack oversaw all homeless services for the Red Cross but left because he felt that the agency was losing interest in such programs in favor of other undertakings. We had both served on Mayor Dinkins's Task Force on Homelessness. Jack had helped me when I was figuring out a social service budget for our transitional housing project for homeless families in Crown Heights, Brooklyn. I learned a lot from him.

Susan Cole knew him because many of the homeless families at New Settlement came from the Red Cross shelter that Jack had supervised. We both admired his skills and his ideals. Jack, in turn, was intrigued by our model at New Settlement, and he came to work for us in 1995.

On his first day of work, as he walked around the neighborhood, a local teenager hit Jack with a BB gun. Thank goodness he was not seriously hurt. Also thank goodness he did not tell his wife, who might have influenced him to have second thoughts about this new position.

Jack never hesitates to walk around the neighborhood, and it has always been fun to accompany him. He is six feet three, handsome, and still youthful though in his sixties. Everyone greets him, "Hi, Jack. Hi, Jack."

Figure 8.1. Jack Doyle. (Photo by Damon Winter. Courtesy of New York Times / Redux.)

People are enthusiastic when they run into him on the street. Soon he became the unofficial mayor of the neighborhood. He is interested in everyone and their life stories. He has a quiet dignity that is infectious, radiating respect for others.

Jack thoroughly understands the value of community programs. He had studied public education all his life and knew that learning was key to upward mobility. He knew that people needed to celebrate and have a good time, and therefore he always organized festivities. He knew the importance of security. He has a command of the physical aspects of maintaining a building, and like Susan he has a great eye. When he walked around the buildings, he carried a notebook, jotted down problems that needed attention, and followed through immediately.

Jack is truly the Platonic ideal of a housing and community development guy. I still get up every morning and think about how lucky we were that he appeared at the right moment. One of the great strokes of good fortune for New Settlement Apartments was that Jack was hired as its impresario.

Jack and I did not have the same style at all. He took his time making a decision, reviewing all the ramifications involved. I tend to be impatient. I have told other staff members that "wait" is a four-letter word. Jack's approach was often the correct one, but not always. Sometimes if you do not respond quickly enough, the problems keep getting bigger. We managed to work well together despite—maybe even because of—these differences. Our goals were the same, and we trusted one another. Susan's involvement was a key factor in our success. She insisted on consistency as the key to fairness.

Jack was a great asset at the meetings in which we settled our lawsuit with the city. He could speak about the details of the construction defects without losing his cool, something the lawyers appreciated. He also worked well with the management team, at least in the early days.

Linda and Bobby's company kept growing. They managed a project nearby for the Catholic archdiocese and started to invest in new developments. Then they took over the management of Parkchester, a twelve-thousand-unit complex that was about to undergo renovation with the residents in occupancy. This was an enormous and highly publicized endeavor. Linda and Bobby stopped paying such close attention to New Settlement Apartments, although they assigned a good member of their staff to do so in their stead. Nonetheless, the buildings started to lose their luster. Susan and Jack were appalled.

One day Jack and I went to look at one of the basements to see if it was suitable for a community program. There we found one of the porters fast asleep, using two chairs as a bed. That did it for me. I knew we had to make a change.

Doing so was difficult. Linda and Bobby had helped with our original proposal. Their input was key to our success, both in planning and early implementation. They were also close friends of ours. We worked well as a team for a long time. But their company was no longer doing its job adequately. We were losing money, and therefore eating into our reserves. The place started to look different. It was time to move on.

The solution to our problem was found downtown. Settlement Housing Fund had worked for decades in the Two Bridges urban renewal area

on the Lower East Side with a local partner, the Two Bridges Neighborhood Council. Four of the six residential sites were managed by Grenadier
Realty Corporation, which managed twenty-five thousand apartments
citywide. We had a great deal of respect for many of the firm's principals.
The new president of Grenadier was none other than Felice Michetti, the
very person who had identified the site for New Settlement, the brains of
Mayor Koch's ten-year plan and commissioner during the Dinkins administration. Even though we often struggled with her as a city official,
we always admired her intelligence and vision.

Grenadier was a champion of racial equality, and its major development, Starrett City, was famous for values that were close to ours. Included on the staff were engineers, labor experts, accountants, and more.
Susan Cole knew all the Grenadierians well, especially Natalie Weinthal,
who, albeit somewhat grumpy, is an expert who keeps on top of every
detail about all the buildings in the Grenadier portfolio. The company
has real depth.

After lengthy negotiations, Grenadier became the managing agent at
New Settlement. Susan Cole continued to walk the buildings, sometimes
with Jack and sometimes with a member of the Grenadier staff. Gradually everything got better. We raised some rents, but not all. We reduced
the number of porters to eighteen. Grenadier assigned top-notch staff to
oversee management at New Settlement, most recently Eliner Tuitt, as
head of the on-site team. She and the management team have reduced
the number of vacancies, always low, to practically zero. Natalie Weinthal
keeps a watchful eye over the properties and meets with Jack regularly.

Grenadier was a great choice. One of the key staff members, Barbara
Tillman, is an expert on utilities. She keeps track of the cost of fuel and
electricity like no one else. Each year she would call, and we would discuss the pros and cons of locking in the rates for heating gas. Usually we
chose to do so, preferring predictability over gambling that prices might
come down. We were always happy with the decision, and usually we
saved a lot of money. She also advised us about various grants that resulted in significant energy savings. The best thing we did was replacing
the windows on seven buildings in 2012, reducing the utilization, and
therefore the cost of gas, dramatically.

This isn't to say there haven't been problems. Over the last quarter
century, I remember about four fires, several of them serious. Luckily, we
had good property insurance. Even though Grenadier had its own insurance experts, in 2003 Settlement Housing Fund joined with seventeen
other large nonprofit organizations across the country to form our own

insurance company, covering both property and liability insurance. Under that system, we saved 20 percent in premiums the first year and even received dividends. Over the years, I learned the importance of having a good insurance company, a good broker, and a good claims officer. Some companies dispute claims or delay payments. That never happened at New Settlement. After our own insurance company began operations, we tried harder than ever to keep our buildings in excellent repair to avoid claims or accidents. Our dividends went up and our premiums dropped in years when we had the fewest claims. Still, the idea of a fire is terrifying. Every time I hear about a fire near any of Settlement Housing Fund's buildings I shudder. Luckily we've had very few.

Good housing owners must be concerned about the security of the residents and building staff. Prospective tenants always ask about security. At New Settlement we have three or four guards walking the site, depending on the time of day, supervised by a director. Our first director, Chester Paul, was there for twenty years until 2011, when he retired. Jack gave him a good party. Both Chester and the current director, Daniel Scanlon, had been police officers in the local 44th Precinct. It was only natural that we would maintain excellent working relations with the police. Whenever there is an incident, officers respond right away.

New Settlement Apartments is a safe place to live, but there have been incidents. The stabbing in the first year of occupancy was worrisome. Even worse, there was a brutal incident in which a husband shot himself and his estranged wife in front of their eleven-year-old child. The woman had obtained an order of protective custody that prohibited the husband from entering the complex. However, he parked his car next to one of the buildings and waited for his ex-wife to appear. Every year for a long time there was a candlelight vigil in the victim's honor, commemorating her death and the broader struggle against domestic violence.

One night when Jack stayed late to write a report, he noticed several police cars in front of one of the buildings. Hurrying over to investigate, he learned that a cache of guns had been found in one of the apartments. Jack knew the young man involved and told him that regardless of whether he was convicted, he could not return to the building. The man, who had been in prison before, was not a legal tenant. He was in the building to care for his mother, who had cancer. Jack was sorry to have had to ban the man from the apartment, but safety in the neighborhood had to be a priority.

Guards are expensive. We paid four guards salary plus fringe benefits to work between 4:00 p.m. and midnight and three during the day; we spent over $450,000 annually for guards, plus $60,000 a year plus benefits for the supervisor. Recently, installing security cameras and using off-site monitoring seems to be a more cost effective approach. It is important to establish good relations with the local police precinct, which is not always easy to do. However it gets accomplished, people need to feel safe in their homes and neighborhoods.

When it came to running New Settlement Apartments, the development benefited from the active participation of a special committee of Settlement Housing Fund board members. Settlement Housing Fund's developments were each owned by separate corporations, all with their own boards. This protects each development from liability for the others and is required by government funders. There are advantages and disadvantages. It would be good to create reserve funds across a portfolio and using them where they are needed most, not just for the specific building.

Susan and I kept the boards informed about every problem, not just the victories. We were accountable, and the board members had great ideas and connections. Our policy has been that the individual project boards should comprise members of the Settlement Housing Fund Board and/or staff. That practice precludes disputes among factions. Most important, we are accountable to these boards, report all problems, and often get great advice.

The staff members at New Settlement Apartments and Settlement Housing Fund cherish the seventeen buildings that now make up the complex, and they are passionate about the Mount Eden neighborhood. An eighteenth building is being built on the parking lot, probably to be completed late in 2017. Others are in the planning stages.

We think that the city was smart to have chosen us as owners in 1987, even though we had never owned any buildings before. We had 100 percent financing and no interest or amortization to pay. It proved a good investment, as one sees by walking around the neighborhood. But without a thoughtful plan, an adequate budget, good management, and constant attention by Settlement Housing Fund, the story could have been much different.

And yes, another secret to our success was finding Jack.

9
Community Programs, Philosophy, and Achievements

So, tell me, what's a social program?" asked Felice Michetti, who at the time was the city's tough-minded housing commissioner and author of Mayor Koch's housing plan. Felice, a nuts-and-bolts professional, admired Clara Fox, the founder of Settlement Housing Fund and longtime advocate of including "social programs" as part of a housing plan. Felice was only half joking.

Looking back at how things evolved at New Settlement, Felice's question wasn't so surprising. Some of the programs outlined in our original proposal were implemented, but the high-quality programs offered today exceed our wildest dreams.

Although I worked with community groups for a good part of my career, I am not and have never been a social worker. I've visited many settlement houses and programs run by other groups. Sometimes you walk into a place and know immediately that something's wrong. Things seem disorganized, and nothing appears to be happening. In other places you can sense the active involvement of people and realize that something good is underway. When I take people on tours of New Settlement Apartments, I invariably feel great about the programs there.

When New Settlement opened, we started off with an allocation of 10 percent of gross rental income that could be used for community programs—$578,000. This was permitted in our regulatory agreement, as was the ability to raise the allocation by 10 percent a year. This policy has not continued for most other affordable housing developments, but it should.

We did not use all the funds in the first two years, when the apartments were not fully occupied and therefore not producing enough revenue. After Jack Doyle came on as executive director of New Settlement in 1995, we attracted new money for additional programs. Jack raised $3 million annually (and sometimes as much as $12 million) from foundations and government contracts. We did not increase the amount of the allocation from the rental budget until 2012, when launching a new community center. Still, that initial source of funding allowed us to remake a devastated neighborhood into a great community. We could also use the funds flexibly, even to pay for reports and essential administration, a hard sell to government or philanthropic organizations.

Our plan to organize a tenants' association fizzled. Only the homeless families seemed to want to participate. There were factions. One night a brother-in-law of one of the tenants somehow got ahold of a gun, which fortunately was not used. However, there was an unpleasant squabble that evening. Soon thereafter we quietly allowed the tenants' association to fade away and turned our attention to other kinds of programs.

Sarah Kolodny was Settlement Housing Fund's director of community programs. She always talked about "organic" community programs. That meant creating a small, high-quality program—getting it just right. Then people would tell their neighbors that something good was happening, and participation would keep growing, leading to new and expanded programs. Although I silently laughed at the social work jargon, this organic theory not only made sense but actually worked.

As described in our proposal, we hired a community program specialist, Tom Gonzalez, to get things going. He was both a social worker and a nice guy. Tom recruited Maria Santana to run an after-school program in our first-floor community room. She did a great job. In fact, decades later her program is still running strong. Known as the Multicultural After-School Program at New Settlement Apartments, it offers tutoring and group activities with an emphasis on the development of academic skills, specifically in the areas of science and literacy. The program currently serves one hundred children, and there's always a waiting list.

When Maria moved back to Ecuador after twenty-four years of running the program, about seventy people attended her going-away party, among them one of the original funders. The event was a festive tribute to Maria's many years of service, with all the guests dressed in the Ecuadorean national colors of red, blue, and yellow. Maria got the accolades she deserved.

Sarah's theory became reality, and the parents were pleased with the after-school program. As Tom and Maria got to know the parents, they learned about their interests and soon expanded our roster of programs to include adult education opportunities.

Next we added teen programs to the list. Megan Nolan, a social work student and intern at New Settlement, was supervised and mentored by Sarah Kolodny. She and Jack Doyle worked closely together. After graduation, Megan came to work full-time (and then some) at the organization as program associate, a job she kept for ten years. Tom moved on to another job.

One of our better ideas was to offer programs to the whole community, rather than just our tenants. As a result, we became quite popular in the neighborhood (and remain so today). When we were first deciding whether to compete for the project, Linda Field at Ashton Management reminded us that we would have an opportunity to make a real impact on a deeply troubled neighborhood. For example, we could organize the parents to form a voting block that would press for better schools, an effort that would not only help better educate neighborhood kids but could also help increase the value of our property.

One of our major activities was to organize the parents. In 1996 a group of parents from the After-School Program started the Parents' Action Committee. When Jack Doyle came to New Settlement, he made a connection with the Annenberg Institute for School Reform, which had been at NYU and is now at Brown University. The staff there provides professional expertise to the New Settlement parents.

A formalized group of parents from our buildings and the community began to meet every Monday night, hoping to secure a good education for their children. For starters, the group petitioned the city's schools chancellor to fire the principal of P.S. 64, the local elementary school. They regarded him as incompetent, citing problems ranging from poor academic achievement to a lack of toilet paper in the bathrooms. The parents arrived at the chancellor's office carrying bouquets of balloons, and asked to meet with him. He listened attentively to their concerns, and a change was made.

Unfortunately, the next principal was also ineffective, and not surprisingly, the relationship between the Parents' Action Committee and the school's leadership became strained. Nonetheless, a private-public partnership later chose New Settlement to run a large after-school program at the school, based on Maria's favorable record of accomplishment. The program proved popular, serving two hundred children.

After that, relations with the school leadership improved dramatically. New Settlement obtained funds from the Trust for Public Land in 2007 to create a "Community PlayPark" in the school yard, which had been a hodgepodge of parking spaces and trailers. New Settlement staffs the PlayPark after school hours and on weekends. The New Settlement staff also raised funds from City Arts and NASA to enable young people from the community to paint a seven-thousand-square-foot mural on a school building wall with fantasies of life on Mars. However, the school did not improve academically and was closed in the final year of the Bloomberg administration. Two new schools have replaced it. Hopefully the situation will improve.

The Parents' Action Committee also joined with neighboring groups to form a district collaborative. One of their accomplishments was to launch the Lead Teachers Program. Master teachers would spend part of their time in the classroom and the rest coaching less experienced teachers. The master teacher would receive an extra $10,000 in salary. The collaborative had the support of the teachers' union, the principals, and other community leaders. The successful initiative was incorporated citywide, but without sufficient funds to sustain activities at the necessary level.

Along with after-school programs, New Settlement runs two active summer day camps for three hundred children, ages six through ten, with activities that include trips to upstate New York and sailing excursions on the Hudson River. Another one of my favorites at New Settlement is the Bronx Helpers Program, which has won various awards over the years. A group of teenagers meet to decide on a community service venture and then implement their idea. One year they helped to clean up a building damaged by lead paint. Another time they visited with children living with cancer. They marched down the Grand Concourse to meet with the borough president and raised over $20,000 to help hurricane victims in Haiti. Recently the group has been involved in a number of projects that promote nutrition. The Bronx Helpers group has a long waiting list of young people who want to participate. The program makes one feel upbeat when thinking about positive ways to channel the energy of teenagers. In 2013 the program moved from a basement community room to expanded space on the first floor of our newest building. The staff is delighted.

Today at New Settlement there are adult education initiatives to teach English to newly arrived adults, drama programs for young women, and an initiative that offers education and job readiness for young people who are neither in school nor working. In 2016 New Settlement won a grant from the Department of Labor for its YouthBuild Program. Young people who are out of work and out of school first receive their General Equivalency Degrees. Then they either go to college or receive certification as construction workers (sometimes both). Settlement Housing Fund has a similar program at its Brooklyn development with a long track record of success.

The programs, though not a cure-all, have been quite successful. Megan Nolan was always concerned about young people who were hardly model citizens. Jack, in a rare moment when he let his guard down, said that "she never gives up on the knuckleheads." She recalls a group of teenagers that hung out on a street corner and would wave to her as she came to work in the mornings. She befriended one of the young men and told him a few months later, "I will no longer greet you if you keep getting high." The story ended with Megan driving the young man to his first day of college. Social workers are not supposed to get too close to "clients," but there are welcome exceptions to most rules.

Another success story involves the College Access Center, located on the first floor of the building we added in 2001, 1563 Walton Avenue, across the street from the tot lot and adjacent to the parking lot where our eighteenth building will soon be completed. This was the last city-owned building in the neighborhood. There were only six families remaining in this twenty-six-unit building, which was a wreck. The families were relocated, and four of them returned after renovation.

The College Access Center was the brainchild of our associate director Susan Cole, who came up with the idea of replicating the Options Program run by Goddard Riverside Neighborhood Center on the Upper West Side. Jack thought this was a great idea. The staff at Goddard obtained funds to help us get started. Now our program receives funds from several foundations, including the Robin Hood Foundation, which is rigorous in requiring successful outcomes.

Anyone can walk into the College Access Center and learn about opportunities to go to college or other post–high school educational options. The center offers free SAT preparation classes, one-on-one counseling, and college visits. Staff members help with college and financial aid applications. There is information about scholarships and stipends to help with expenses ranging from textbooks to eyeglasses to transportation home during school holidays. By 2011, 1,400 young people used various programs offered, and 275 young people went to college and received financial aid through the program. The first-year annual college retention rate was 85 percent. And all this is in a neighborhood in which only 6 percent of the residents are college graduates.

The College Access Center has recently expanded to sites at two nearby high schools. According to the program's director, Allison Palmer, about

1,500 young people participate each year: about 450 students receive intensive, one-on-one college advising each year; another 575 college students receive support to stay on track through graduation; still 475 additional students participate in early awareness workshops, financial aid seminars, SAT prep classes, and college visits.

We started the first anti–domestic violence program in the Bronx. We also have a Girls' Program Initiative with about two hundred participants, ages nine through eighteen. One of the activities focuses on theater, in which young women write, produce, and direct original plays. Some of the topics include resisting negative peer pressure, being true to self, problems with violence in relationships, and the power of story—all serious issues.

In our original proposal we promised to reach out to owners of adjacent buildings to help them improve living conditions for their tenants. They could use our power hoses to remove graffiti. We would provide information about loans or tax abatement. In cases of negligence, we would contact the appropriate enforcement agencies.

Initially this arrangement was informal. In 2005 New Settlement obtained funding to establish the Community Action for Safe Apartments (or CASA) organization, which has been effective, staffed by enthusiastic and able tenant advocates. In fact, one of the more notorious landlords contacted members of the Settlement Housing Fund board in an attempt to end this work. Needless to say, the board was totally supportive of our efforts, which have won awards. Although our own buildings are still affordable and well maintained, over 50 percent of the families in the surrounding area live in buildings that are in poor repair and/or unaffordable. Much work remains to be done.

As our programs expanded, we outgrew our space. In 2012 we opened up New Settlement Community Campus, a twenty-four-thousand-square-foot community center with a competition-sized swimming pool, adjacent to three public schools that we would develop and manage (more on this in the following chapter). We were up and running almost immediately. We offer swim programs at all levels of ability, Alvin Ailey American Dance Theater–led programs, a green roof learning garden, cooking classes, and much more. We can use the connecting high school's magnificent gym, auditorium, and other spaces on weekends and evenings. There is a staff member who coordinates activities at the schools with our community programs. We offer so many other opportunities as well. How often do you hear about a place that provides not only Zumba and kickboxing but also free prenatal yoga and belly dancing? We do charge fees, but they are modest compared to local health clubs and YMCAs. Some of the classes are free, supported by grants. There are six thousand family participants. Middle and high school students use the pool, as do second graders from neighboring schools.

One hears of young people who have drowning accidents because they did not learn to swim, and we needed to address that issue.

One happy story involves a sixteen-year-old boy from the neighborhood who had never learned to swim. After less than a year of lessons he decided to take lifeguard classes. He excelled in these classes and now is one of the lifeguards at our facility.

I have taken many people on tours of our housing and community programs, which always generate a feeling of excitement. Something valuable is always going on. Sarah was right to start small and watch the programs grow organically. But I doubt that even she could have imagined how things would end up—beyond our wildest dreams and worth all the trouble.

10

New Settlement Community Campus
The Schools, Center, and Pool

By 2003 we had been operating New Settlement Apartments for fifteen years. Our programs won awards and had waiting lists, but there was no place to expand. From the beginning it was clear we needed a community center. Jack Doyle occasionally reminded me of this. He thought he was being subtle, but I took him more seriously than he knew. Although the basements and first floors of our buildings were great spaces for our programs, we needed more room and visibility. My friend, a lawyer, public servant, and developer named Susan Fine, approached me about building a small New Visions high school. Half joking, I said we'd do it if we could build an adjoining community center on the site. New Visions for Public Schools is an organization that worked closely with the city to build and operate small, high-quality public high schools and stressed the need to alleviate overcrowding, especially in the Bronx.

One rainy night that spring after a community meeting, I walked over to Jerome Avenue and 172nd Street to check out a site that was available for $3.2 million. It covered most of a block front, certainly large enough. But that was the best thing I could say about it. The property was a burned-out former parking lot, surrounded by dilapidated automotive use and a live chicken establishment (yes, a place where they kept live chickens and sold them to restaurant owners and others, known locally as a "liveria"). Even worse, the site was next to the elevated subway track and therefore very noisy. The rain did not make the site look any better. I could not imagine how Jack Doyle, our brilliant leader, could have suggested this as a good location. When I visited Jerome Avenue on a sunny day with

Jack later that week, I did see some nice churches and a beautiful Catholic school north of the site, all next to the subway. El or no el, I thought, let's try it.

I invited Susan Fine and Adam Rubin, an idealistic young man from New Visions, to see the site on a sweltering day in July. Jack and I met them at the site, and I was expecting a negative reaction. To my amazement, everyone, sweat dripping from their bodies, liked the site, especially because of its proximity to public transportation. The real estate experts at the New York City School Construction Authority were also pleased with the site and encouraged us to buy it. This venture would change everything about our reputation for being risk averse.

New Visions for Public Schools was headed by Robert Hughes, the litigator who had obtained equitable funding from New York State for schools within the five boroughs of New York City. The group had also received funds from the Bill & Melinda Gates Foundation to help non-profit community development organizations work with the city to plan, build, and operate small schools. By coincidence, Bob had been an intern at New Settlement in his law school days, helping families to enroll their children in local schools.

In the fall and winter of 2003 I attended a number of large meetings, along with executives of other nonprofit groups eager to build New Visions schools. They either owned sites or were looking for them. Joel Klein, then chancellor of the Department of Education, was a fan of innovation, and the New York City School Construction Authority (SCA) was to become the reluctant partner agency of a dozen or so groups. The SCA was known as a huge, bureaucratic, rigid agency that spent too much money on construction and took too long to get anything done. Years ago it had been involved in a series of scandals, and therefore the staff went out of its way to avoid anything remotely corrupt. Prequalifying and vetting all partners and professionals was the order of the day. Anyone with a demerit could not even go near a potential site.

The Settlement Housing Fund board did not object to this new venture, although there were a few raised eyebrows at the meetings. We began to negotiate in earnest with the School Construction Authority; in 2004 we received a letter encouraging us to pursue a joint venture that eventually would result in a long-term lease with the city. The next step was to obtain an option or enter into a contract to buy the property.

Jerry Deutsch, an active member of the Settlement Housing Fund board and a brilliant negotiator, was pleased to assume the task of negotiating a deal. The owner was Sander Wallick, a six-foot-two, eighty-two-year-old gentleman with long white hair and a penchant for white shoes. He told us all about his life, his gin rummy game in Florida, and that he was a widower and had a new girlfriend. Jerry found out through his Florida connections that Mr. Wallick was a notorious gambler, paying his beloved gin rummy for high stakes. He was also a nonstop talker and did not seem to make much sense. "Crazy like a fox" was the conclusion of our general counsel, Lee Warshavsky, who helped Jerry with the deal. Setting Mr. Wallick's eccentricities aside, where would we get $3 million?

Somehow we were able to convince HSBC Bank to give us a 3 percent loan, and we signed a contract in the summer of 2004. Jerry negotiated the price down from $3 million to $2 million. He held his nose and wined and dined Mr. Wallick in New York and Florida. Goodness knows what Jerry promised, but the reduced price was a stellar accomplishment. My admiration for Jerry still knows no bounds.

We borrowed $400,000 from HSBC for two interim payments and signed a contract for the rest. In addition, Wallick would have to pay for environmental remediation over $500,000. We had to close in twelve months.

We then began serious discussions of the details with the SCA. The Department of Education's staff had determined that our local elementary schools were even more overcrowded than were the high schools. Therefore we decided to build two schools: one comprising kindergarten through grade 5, the other grades 6 through 12. The two schools would be in one building with two entrances. I was concerned that the high school kids would taunt or beat up the little ones, but Jack said that the presence of small children often made the teenagers surprisingly gentle. Susan Cole, our associate director, wouldn't let up until we added preschool classes to the elementary school. The plan later expanded to include eight classrooms for children on the autism spectrum.

Then Megan Nolan, who became the Settlement Housing Fund director of community programs, started complaining that there was nowhere in the neighborhood for people to swim, and that many young people never learned how and subsequently drowned. Okay, okay . . . We ended up deciding to build prekindergarten–grade 12 public schools with a community center and a swimming pool.

We decided that we should also acquire two adjoining plots as well as the chicken establishment, if the School Construction Authority staff agreed. Not only did they approve these additions, they also decided to acquire additional parcels so that we would have the entire block front. We never expected that reaction; needless to say, we were pleased. Sandy Wallick knew the "chicken guy" and badgered him for months until he would sell. Sandy chased him in person and by phone, finding him in the Dominican Republic or wherever he happened to be. It turned out that his brother was co-owner and had to agree to sell. It got done, mainly because of Sandy Wallick, but there was a lot of drama. The other sites were acquired from recalcitrant sellers by the SCA through eminent domain, the right that allows a government agency to acquire property for public use. We agreed to pay Sandy $170,000 for his work in obtaining the $2.4 million site. He did not have a broker's license, and therefore the payment was recognized as a consultant fee. The lawyers for the SCA despised Sandy and would reimburse us only for $25,000. We are still out $145,000.

I was putting Settlement Housing Fund at serious risk. I signed a contract and borrowed money to buy the property without a written agreement from the SCA. All I had was a nebulous letter signed by the SCA's chief executive. Even before the financial crisis of 2008, it would not have been easy to sell the property if city officials backed out of the deal. But they didn't. Eventually I would sign a seventy-five-year renewable lease for a community center and pool attached to a magnificent complex of public schools. We would be in charge of maintenance.

Jack had a great relationship with the local community board. One night when he was busy I made a presentation to the board's education committee. The reception was overwhelmingly collaborative and positive. Even the people in the audience were enthusiastic and after the meeting they greeted and encouraged me.

We started to negotiate our lease with Ross Holden, general counsel and executive vice president of the SCA. Susan Fine and Adam Rubin were at my side, along with Lee Warshavsky, our general counsel. Ira Sanders, a veteran and talkative attorney, was assigned to represent the SCA on the details of the lease. From the start, Ross said we would be responsible for paying for the community center. I thought that the school structure would set aside 25,000 square feet out of maybe 150,000 for our use. For housing developments, the mortgage covers building the core and shell of space for a nonresidential tenant. We call this a vanilla box. The tenant would then have to put up partitions and provide all finishes. I thought we would need to do the same, and I had figured a cost of $2 million, which I thought was conservative. I knew that Bronx borough president Adolfo Carrion, Jr., would help us and that New Visions would find additional funds from the Gates Foundation and all their other contacts. I agreed that Settlement Housing Fund would pay for building the community center.

We were to be the developer of both the schools and the community center and pool. The SCA and Settlement Housing Fund would be jointly responsible for design and bidding. A new nonprofit subsidiary would have the sole responsibility for construction. The SCA would reimburse us for expenditures. That meant we would need a loan to pay initial costs, but I did not think that would be a problem. TD Bank was interested in playing that role, although it seemed silly to all of us. It seemed like a better idea to have us approve requisitions and let the SCA pay vendors directly, but I did not think it worth fighting about this point.

I was adamant about choosing the architect. I wanted a firm that would be loyal to Settlement Housing Fund. At the same time, I wanted a firm that knew a lot about schools and the SCA process during design. Our choice was Edelman Sultan Knox Wood, a firm that had designed most of our buildings over three decades. Susan Fine and the New Visions team questioned my choice, but I insisted. The firm's principals, especially Judy Edelman and Andrew Knox, had an eye for design and were practical about costs. However, they had never designed a public school and needed to go through a lengthy process to be preapproved by the SCA. They did so, much to my relief. I looked at a list of architects who had a solid track record with the SCA and asked the Edelman team to interview two or three of them to form a co-venture. We jointly agreed that Dattner Associates would be the best. The chemistry seemed excellent.

Part of New Visions' agenda was to show the world that nonprofit groups could build a school more quickly and less expensively than could the SCA, all without sacrificing quality. But I knew we could not even pretend to be able to do that. We were required to conform with SCA design standards and to use competitive bidding to select the contractor, who had to be preapproved by the agency. We'd also need to pay union wages.

Unlike the process mandated by the School Construction Authority, I prefer to have the contractor and the architects work together during the design phase. Contractors often know idiosyncratic ways to save on construction costs, and it's great when the design reflects these methods of saving money. Also, when architects and their engineers complete full construction drawings without input from contractors, the contractor does not take ownership of the design, which inevitably results in higher prices.

I wanted this to be a showcase of cooperation between a public agency and a nonprofit entity. Everyone's eyes would roll when I said that, but we eventually achieved a good approach to teamwork and mutual respect.

However, I soon learned that not only would we have to follow SCA rules, but we would also need to pay for the entire construction of the pool and community center, not just the interior. Well, I thought, I would not need to bid competitively for our part, and our standards would be lower. Still, according to my mental arithmetic, the cost went for $2 million to $8 million. This was in 2004. The economy was starting to heat up, and construction costs were escalating.

With the help of our pro bono law firm, Davis Polk & Wardwell, we negotiated a draft lease. In fact, the word negotiation was a something of a euphemism. We caved on pretty much everything, but at least we were getting the land for a community center free of charge. In my head, I thought we could amend the lease to save money later, as we improved our relationship with the School Construction Authority.

Next came the design kickoff meeting, late in December 2004. There were over twenty people from the SCA present, including architects, cost experts, construction experts, real estate and budget staff, and lawyer Ira Sanders. Staff from New Visions attended, as did a few people from the Department of Education. I was supposed to be in charge of the meeting, but I had no problem letting the SCA architect take the lead. I spoke out as often as I pleased, but I had a totally different way of developing a building and wanted to hear the typical SCA practices. The New Visions staff members later admonished me; they thought that I should have asserted that I was in charge. That was not an issue for me.

Meetings would continue every two weeks for the next two years, we were told. Our architects had to present three sets of schematic drawings. We debated all of them. When the site expanded, everything had to be changed. We added prekindergarten classes and urged that adequate administrative space be included (it was). The SCA staff members fought rather viciously with one another and scorned our architects, but it became clear to me that they cared about the children. They wanted the building to work for the students and faculty.

After a few months of this, the SCA attorneys realized that we were supposed to have a competitive bidding process when we selected the architects, something they'd neglected to mention earlier. But they came up with a solution. Dattner had a so-called open contract with the SCA, allowing them to work on all projects without competitive bidding. "All" we had to do was to reverse the roles of the two firms. Dattner would be the lead contractor, and the Edelman firm would be subcontractor. I was worried about losing control, and the Edelman architects were extremely nervous about the arrangement. But we had no choice and just hoped for the best.

Before signing the lease for the site, I had to demonstrate that I could raise the money for the community center. My plan was to obtain about $1 million from the Bronx borough president. I thought that New Visions would help me raise the money, and that Susan Fine could get me funds from Fisher Brothers, a large real estate firm where she worked. I also hoped that the New York Yankees and the Goldman Sachs Foundation would pay the rest. I met with Sam Freas, head of the Swimming Hall of Fame, and I was sure he could come up with money for the pool. I had a million ideas, but few of them materialized.

We closed on the site in May 2005. We were repaid for our down payment, the cost of environmental remediation, and other preliminary expenses. The draft lease had a total budget of $65 million for the entire project. I still thought that our share would be no more than $8 million. I hired a consultant to help with a capital campaign plan. After he and I went met with individual Settlement Housing Fund board members, the board, to my amazement, pledged to contribute $900,000. I got letters of support from others, such as one from a group that had allocations of federal New Markets Tax Credits, which would produce 20 to 30 percent of the cost. I also obtained a letter of intent from Citibank for a low-interest mortgage. However, the SCA would not allow a mortgage. I then approached a wonderful philanthropist, famous for his anonymity, and obtained a loan commitment from him. I thought it would not be needed, but it was great to have just in case. The anonymous philanthropist even committed to an interest rate subsidy when I complained that his rates were too high.

We signed the lease with the SCA, a document which eventually would be assigned to the city's Department of Education. Eventually both agencies would need to approve. We would codevelop and oversee construction. We would receive a fee of $2 million for our work, with a down payment of $200,000. I fought hard to obtain the fee because it was essential, considering the amount of time we were investing. We would need to pay a construction supervisor and had already found a great firm, the URS Corporation.

Our first fund-raising victory came in January 2005 through the Borough President Carrion. As a planning student in the1980s Carrion had interned for us, gaining practical experience that he never forgot. He was a fan of New Settlement Apartments, as had been his predecessor, Fernando Ferrer. We obtained a commitment of $1.4 million from his office's share of the city's capital budget, which, with pledges from the board, brought me to $2.5 million. I then had to show that we could raise the rest of the funds, estimated to be $8 million at the time.

I met with Diana Taylor, mayor Michael Bloomberg's "significant other." She could not ask for money, she said nervously, but she called both Randy Levine, president of the Yankees, and an officer at the Rockefeller Foundation. I had a meeting with Levine but no commitment for money, and the foundation officer was not available and then quit.

Two bus rides to visit New Settlement Apartments proved critically important. First, in the fall of 2006 I invited "luminaries" on a bus tour, including Sandy Frucher, who at the time was president of the Philadelphia Stock Exchange. He had been president of the Battery Park City Authority and convinced governor Mario Cuomo that Battery Park City revenue could support a bond to renovate vacant city-owned buildings. That resulted in the financing for New Settlement Apartments. I also invited bankers, intermediary executives, foundation staff, Carol Tweedy (CEO of Asphalt Green, the city's leading swimming organization), and others. They were all enthusiastic, but few volunteered to raise money. The exception was Denise Scott, the New York head of the Local Initiatives Support Corporation (LISC). She knew about a potential federal grant and hired a consultant to help us obtain it. It was a difficult application, but we were told we were ranked number one in the country. That resulted in $650,000, approved in 2007, bringing us to $3.15 million. Denise also said that LISC could also help us to obtain New Markets Tax Credits, a complicated program that could provide about 25 percent of the total. We were getting there. However, I knew I would need an interim loan. FJC, a philanthropic lender, came through with the financing and saved the day.

The next bus ride came later. Our relationship with the staff of the School Construction Authority had been rocky. I thought they were overbearing, treating us as if we were incompetent. I suggested to the executive vice president and general counsel, Ross Holden, that we meet for breakfast. To my surprise, he said yes. He had cereal, befitting his lean physique, that of a serious runner. We actually had a good time. I suggested taking the SCA staff for a tour of New Settlement Apartments, so they would understand why we needed a community center. He thought it was a good idea and suggested we schedule it for a time that SCA CEO Sharon Greenberger could make it. I had met the former CEO, but not Sharon. We were on.

The bus picked up the SCA staff at 8:30 outside their office in Queens. About twenty of them joined the tour, including the CEO, Ross Holden, Ira Sanders, the heads of architecture and construction, and others. I baked ginger scones for the occasion. On the way to the Bronx I handed out photographs of the neighborhood as it looked back in 1987, and asked everyone to remember the photos when they saw the buildings as they looked today.

The first stop was a public school playground that was renovated and improved with funds we had raised. We ran programs at the playground that were quite impressive. When we visited our buildings, everyone was impressed with the level of cleanliness and repair. One of the SCA staff members who had grown up in the area was in tears.

After that trip, our relationship with the agency improved dramatically. Although we did not agree about everything, we developed a mutual respect. We continued with design meetings every two weeks, and I was struck by the fact that the SCA staff seemed to care deeply about how the students would use their new space. They had great ideas.

The design ended up with the schools on the north corner; the auditorium and gyms in the middle, along Jerome Avenue; and the pool and community center on the south end of the site, with a door connecting the community center and school spaces. It was essentially one building. Since we had 13.8 percent of the square footage, we would pay 13.8 percent of the cost. We would have a beautiful seventy-five-foot pool, dance studios, an art space, a green learning roof terrace, meeting rooms, and more.

The only issue on which I lost involved the lack of natural light in the cafeteria. The SCA cost experts insisted that we use the large basement area for the cafeteria. The savings were so dramatic that we could not take issue. The architects designed a system of translucent paving that allowed natural light from above the cafeteria, but the SCA staff rejected it. Although we were supposed to have joint control of design, we did not win on this issue. Whenever I see translucent paving I am often furious, although other times I shrug and think about the chipped glass that could have been a maintenance headache.

The cafeteria itself is great, featuring different kinds of seating. There is a full kitchen and a chef who prepares meals on site, offering many healthy options.

Costs kept going up. We finally had an approved design in the spring of 2008, and we began the bidding process. I checked references of dozens of preapproved contractors and found five that we liked. Office meetings and site visits were arranged. Bidding packages were mailed out. Included was an introductory letter from me, explaining our role. The bids, due six weeks later, were to be delivered in person in sealed envelopes. I went to the bidding room with the SCA official in charge. Nobody arrived for some time. Finally the representative of one contractor showed up.

The cost had been estimated at $89 million, or $517 per square foot, which had seemed unconscionably high. When we started working on the project, our estimate was $375 a foot. Housing at the time cost about $200 a foot.

The bid came in at $106 million. I thought the whole project would be scrapped. Instead, the cost experts at the SCA negotiated the price down do $103 million. We were about to go ahead when a scandal hit the headlines. Our one bidder was being investigated by another agency. Several months went by, and the investigation dragged on. After a decent interval, we all decided that we should go through the bidding again. There were a few design changes, causing further delays.

But before the process could move forward, in November Ross Holden and his boss, Sharon Greenberger, asked if I could come to a meeting at the SCA. Our general counsel, Lee Warshavsky would accompany me. I had no idea what to expect and was nervous.

At that meeting Ross asked if we could renegotiate the deal to let the SCA be in charge of construction. Ross did not say why, but he thought that unusual arrangement with two entities controlling construction had discouraged the bidders. He assured us that we would still have a seat at the table and would still receive our fee.

I thought his suggestion made sense. Adding an additional layer of approvals to the construction process was pointless. We renegotiated the lease. Our attorney from Davis Polk & Wardwell, Susan Kennedy, did a great job. Ross had expected us to object, and I said this was not about ego. Our relationship got even better.

The bidding process started all over again. The woman in charge for the SCA was a consummate professional. However, the bidding process was open, and the company that inherited Lehrer McGovern Bovis was not excluded. This was the reconstituted firm that had caused so many problems for our apartment complex. I was nervous but told myself that it was a different company now. However, it was clear at one of the bidding meetings that the philosophy of the company was out of sync with ours.

There were two companies that I especially liked. One was a small outfit whose CEO had advised me about working with the SCA. The other, Turner Construction, was huge. Their representatives seemed to be doing the most homework, bringing representatives of subcontractors to the meeting and frequently visiting the site. I also liked the Turner website, especially the fact that it highlighted a training program the company sponsored for low-income students This time eight companies made bids, including Bovis. We were fortunate that Turner's bid was the lowest by far. This was mid–December 2008, and during the previous six months the U.S. economy had collapsed. Turner's bid was $83 million, more than $20 million less than the previous bid.

With contingency and soft costs, I thought our share of the costs would be $14 million at most. I tried to get the SCA to agree to a dollar cap for our share of the cost. The answer was a firm no. I kept trying to negotiate while we were raising money and getting ready for construction. It would have been so much easier to have a fixed budget.

The good news was that the SCA chose URS to supervise construction, the same team we'd selected when we thought that we would oversee construction. As it turned out, much work lay ahead of us.

Plans had to be changed and permits secured. There were countless details, mainly dealing with environmental remediation. The initial environmental study did not show some of the illegal automotive uses on the site and the resulting soil contamination. For starters, the project required extensive soil removal, costing over $2 million. Because the soil was under the school, not the community center, we thought we would not be required to pay for the work. We were wrong. "The site is the site," said Ross Holden. The second change order involved the foundation under the area where the soil would be removed, another $2 million. This time, thank goodness, after intensive negotiations, the SCA officials agreed that we would not be responsible for a share of the cost.

We broke ground on August 11, 2009. We did most of the planning for the ceremony, in cooperation with the city Department of Education. I was on NY1 cable TV news, interviewed by Dominic Carter. I had my fifteen minutes of fame. Unfortunately, two weeks later Mr. Carter was arrested for domestic violence. He had been at the groundbreaking with his wife and family, so the whole thing was hard to fathom. The deputy mayor was there, along with all the local elected officials and the newly appointed lieutenant governor, Richard Ravitch, a friend of mine. Everyone from the community, the SCA staff, and the world of politicians were ecstatic. The children from our day camp were also there wearing blue T-shirts, making the photo ops unbeatable. The enthusiasm was palpable and genuine.

I still tried to get a cap for our share of the construction cost. Assuming a budget of $14 million, I figured that we could raise about $9 million from known sources. This included about $4 million from government, $1 million from our board, and $2 million from foundations that had been friendly to Jack Doyle or to Settlement Housing Fund. I thought we could also use the federal New Markets Tax Credit Program to generate

Figure 10.1. Groundbreaking ceremony for the campus. (Courtesy of New Settlement Apartments.)

over $2 million. It would all be easier if we had a cap. It was strange that I had to beg for the privilege of raising $14 million, something that could have been the responsibility of government.

I went to the mat. I met with the deputy mayor, Dennis Walcott, who invited the SCA representatives. I had board members join me. The deputy mayor, as he had promised, called me the next day. I lost—there would be no cap. At least we stayed on good terms with the SCA, and we signed the new lease with them in January 2011, when construction was 40 percent complete. My (hopefully) final budget would be $15.8 million. Costs had certainly escalated during the years of planning, design, and bidding.

As if that weren't enough, Susan Cole retired at the end of 2010. I no longer had my collaborator there with me. She is four and a half years younger than I am, but no matter, she'd had enough of the stress and was ready to go. I knew I should start to think about retiring, but I could not do so until all the funds were raised for the campus.

Our next job was to secure the investment from the New Markets Tax Credits, the only federal program that helped generate investment in low-income neighborhoods. We had planned to obtain the funds through LISC, the group that had written a commitment letter in 2007, subject to feasibility. I had no idea what I was getting into. I made calls in January 2011 to get the process rolling. In the meantime, we had raised about $7 million, and prior to January it was uncertain whether Congress would extend the program. Thankfully there was a new allocation, and we had to secure a commitment. Our general counsel, Lee Warshavsky, reached

out to the Goldman Sachs Urban Investment Group to contribute. A dynamic young man named James Patchett was assigned to represent Goldman. He pushed the process along and never lost his cool. Who could
have predicted that Goldman Sachs would work so hard to achieve a
project for the community?

We gained respect from the LISC staff by bringing Goldman "to the
table." We hired Matt Wexler, an excellent consultant, at the suggestion
of LISC, and thank goodness we did. I had worked with every complex
housing finance instrument over a period of forty years, but I have never
encountered anything like the maze of contradictory requirements of
the New Markets program. It turned out that we needed an allocation
from another organization as well, and the Low Income Investment Fund
stepped up.

In order to generate about $3 million, I was ready to sign up for tor-
ture. There were weekly conference calls with both financial intermedi-
aries, the investor, three sets of lawyers, our accountant, and the consultants, who wrote the agenda and sent it out in advance in addition to
keeping everything running smoothly.

Somehow, with fees, contingencies, and interest, the total costs went up
to a little over $18 million for the purpose of calculating the credits. Over
$2 million of the total were fees that passed through to the various entities
without creating cost increases for us. I had to borrow almost $8.5 million
from my reluctant "standby" philanthropist bridge lender. The term of the
loan increased from four to seven years. All the money went into an investment fund; with the Goldman equity and fictionalized loans, I would
have all the money to finish construction. The lender reluctantly agreed,
but a few months later he changed his mind because of a reasonable concern about guarantees. He even required Settlement Housing Fund to
take out an insurance policy for $4 million on my life, making me worth
much more dead than alive. The lender had insisted on closing before the
end of June, which the Goldman people liked a lot. However, the lender
and investors (really, their lawyers) could not agree about the provisions
of the loan documents.

We went on with the calls, tense about the philanthropic bridge loan.
We raised other funds from government sources. Our comptroller pointed
out that the lender had already given us $4 million and that the loan would
be safer with the Goldman investor on board. Eventually the lender came
around, but my board had to approve pledging everything we owned as
collateral. We had never guaranteed anything before, so this was monu-
mental. I could no longer claim an aversion to risk.

The staff at the SCA also had to cooperate, and I was astounded as to how helpful they were. They were great.

A few weeks before the closing, the people at Goldman Sachs had a falling out with the people at LISC. I had just received an honorary award from LISC, and I wanted to keep Goldman as the investor because the loan officer was the best person on the deal. We made peace, but it took a lot of babysitting.

We closed in August 2011. There was a diagram made showing all the entities through which cash had to flow. Everyone who looks at it gets a headache. Living with it involved insomnia and dyspepsia. All sorts of charades were necessary to disguise what should have been a grant to make it look like a loan—true debt. I call it a "groan." It was difficult, but we netted $2.919 million. I was still short over $5 million, because Settlement Housing Fund was obligated to repay the bridge lender. However, at least all the money was there to finish construction.

Although we had commitments from the city and state, it was next to impossible to actually get the funds. The fiscal crisis and multiple unrelated scandals unleashed dozens of extra bureaucratic hurdles. Many groups lost their allocations of government funding. Luckily we did not. But Settlement Housing Fund had to pledge its assets over and over again. My board members held their breath and approved all the transactions.

Construction proceeded smoothly, on schedule, with relatively few change orders. The construction supervisor, Tim Fitzgerald of URS, ran great meetings, twice a month. Either Jack or I attended all of them. The School Construction Authority staff was thorough. Two sets of architects were there, as well as the team from Turner Construction, including a colorful female representative. The contrast between these meetings and the ones for New Settlement Apartments was dramatic in that they were characterized by teamwork, not dysfunction.

It was time to start planning the educational component at the school. Jack Doyle had been thinking about education forever, working with the parents to try to improve existing schools. To help us proceed, we needed a consultant. For that role we chose Xenia Cox, an education activist and innovator in architecture. We had numerous meetings with the staff at New Vision for Public Schools, which had changed its focus to charter schools, mainly because of the organization's funding needs. Our first meetings at the Department of Education were not promising. The tune changed after a few public meetings when it was overwhelmingly clear that we had the respect of the community and local elected officials. There seemed to be a new spirit of collaboration.

In the meantime, fund-raising continued. Our director of development, Kathy McAulay, became an expert in applying for Resolution A
funds from the city's capital budget. In 2008 all we had to do was write a
short letter to the borough president or City Council member. By 2010,
after a scandal or two, the application grew to a ninety-page online form.

That year we were awarded $1.5 million, but it took ten months to re-
ceive the funds, a nail-biting period during which we were paying $260 a
day in interest. To complicate matters, when the funds finally arrived, the
bank accidentally sent the money back to the SCA. We finally straight-
ened things out and made a large payment to reduce our loan, originally
$8.5 million, now less than $7 million.

We were also raising funds privately. I was sure someone would want
their name on the center wall, but the huge donors did not appear. We
did get private grants from individuals on our board and from the foundations that had supported us before. This due in large part to Jack Doyle,
who was well-known and respected in the neighborhood and in the
foundation world.

Around this time we also had productive meetings with officials at the
city Department of Education. A planning committee of education experts and representatives of the community met to write a proposal for
the schools. The design called for one prekindergarten–grade 5 school,
a school for grades 6–12, and one for students with special needs, which
turned out to be classes mainly for autistic children. After the buildings
were practically complete, one of the officials wanted to change the configuration, which would have been expensive in both time and money. It
did not happen.

For the "upper" school, we selected a successful middle-school principal who wanted to expand his school to include a high school. For
the lower school we chose the impressive assistant principal at the same
school. The city officials applauded. Jack and our newest consultant, John
Garvey, spent hours at the schools, seeing how well everything worked—
except for the custodian in charge of maintenance. We decided finally that
we would try our hand at doing the maintenance ourselves. We thought
it could be a headache but did not want to risk losing control.

There was a minor hiccup when someone at the Department of Education decided we could not use the name New Settlement Community
Campus. We won on this issue, but it sapped our energy.

We were about $5 million in the hole. I approached a lot of wealthy
people, including Mario Gabelli, a billionaire who was born in the Bronx,
and Mickey Drexler, CEO of J.Crew, another Bronx native. We had many

visits from people at Cablevision and made multiple requests to Goldman Sachs. No one said no, but neither did anyone say anything close to yes.

Our City Council member and the Borough president encouraged us to make a big request for Resolution A capital funds. This would be our last chance, because the building was just about complete. Our board used every connection to help personalize the request.

The Resolution A application added many more obscure requirements. Chuck Warren, our board president and a terrific lawyer, said that the contradictions meant that the agencies could do whatever they wanted. After a good deal of exertion, we got the application in at the end of January 2012. We applied for $5.4 million. In May we learned that allocations totaling $4.2 million had been approved. That plus the unspent funds in the New Markets disbursement account would be enough to re-pay the bridge lender. Whew . . .

It looked like the money was all there—until it wasn't. On June 23, 2012, we got word that the Mayor's Office of Management and Budget (OMB) had pulled the funds. We were not eligible because we had bor-rowed funds and the building was almost complete. That made us not eligible? I learned about this while I was coming back from a trip to Washington, D.C., and stuck on the tarmac for two hours. I reached Jack and the staff by phone and told them we *were* eligible because of an ex-ception for buildings that had received this kind of funding in prior years. Everyone on the plane overheard my conversation and added their two cents. We were reinstated for consideration. On June 27 at 10:30 p.m. Jack called me at home (he was still in his office) to let me know we would get our $4.2 million. It would still take all kinds of work to receive the funds, but—oh my God—we did it.

The building was complete in July, and it looked dazzlingly beautiful—better than I had even imagined. Awards started to pour in from various architectural and construction groups.

The school opened in September 2012. Mayor Bloomberg made ours the first stop on his tour of city schools on opening day. The community center opened the next week. Jack was unprepared for the ecstatic re-action from the neighborhood. On the first night there were lines around the block. Residents wanted tours of the center and the chance to apply for membership. I came the second night, spoke to people from the com-munity, and broke in goose bumps multiple times.

We dedicated the center in late October. Former borough president Adolfo Carrion, Jr., current borough president Ruben Diaz, Jr., City

Figure 10.2. The schools. (Photo by David Sundberg / Esto.)

Council member Helen Diane Foster, deputy borough president Aure-lia Greene, and Assembly member Vanessa Gibson all spoke eloquently, as did Jack. We had signs around the center naming various rooms for contributors, including the Harold and Pearl Lamberg sky lobby, named for my late parents, whose foundation had provided a grant. At the end of the ceremony our board president, Chuck Warren, presented a pair of swim goggles and a bathing cap to me, announcing that the swimming pool would be known as the Carol Lamberg pool. I was embarrassed. But later, when I saw the kids in the pool taking lessons, it felt pretty good.

But there was still no Resolution A money. After multiple agonizing phone calls, I was able to schedule a meeting with the city's OMB for January 9, 2013. Usually the staff refused to meet with anyone other than city officials.

Scott Ulrey, the OMB counsel, was there, along with two other OMB staff members, one of whom was loud and unpleasant. Also present were representatives of the local City Council member, Helen Diane Foster; representatives of Borough President Diaz; Rob Goldrich from the may-or's office; SCA officials; a representative from the City Council Speaker's office; our board president, Chuck Warren; Lee Warshavsky, our general counsel; Jack Doyle; and me. The office was strange. There were no signs on the outer office doors or on anyone's desk. Everything was gray. It was

Figure 10.3. The pool. (Photo by David Sundberg / Esto.)

hard to find anyone to guide us to the conference room. At most government offices there are metal detectors and security personnel. Not at OMB. But we had our meeting.

I prepared a two-minute opening statement and gave out beautiful photos of the campus. Then OMB staff began to brutalize our application. They asked why we waited to apply for the last round of funds instead of applying for more money in previous years. We were even accused of dishonesty. After going back and forth endlessly, Scott Ulrey gave us one glimmer of hope. If we could prove that we had relied on promises from the borough president and City Council member before construction started, OMB might be able to release the funds.

Chuck Warren asked me for more information about the earlier financing. Then he drafted a letter that was strange but truthful. We sent it to the Council member and borough president for their signatures. Neither of them understood, but luckily staff members were able to explain it. The letter went out. About a month later OMB actually accepted the letter and released the funds. It took a few more weeks for the SCA and OMB staff to agree on the reimbursement schedule. Finally we got the word that the check for $4.2 million was ready. Our bookkeeper, Kofi Appram, went to the SCA Queens office, picked up the check, and deposited it in

Figure 10.4. Art program. (Photo by David Sundberg / Esto.)

our account. It cleared the next day, and I delivered a Settlement Housing Fund payment to the bridge lender, thereby reducing the loan from the original $8.5 million to $597,000. I included a photo of the check in the package for our board meeting two days later, on April 6. Chuck Warren suggested champagne, and we did in fact celebrate.

The next problem was reconciling the New Markets investment so that we could access the remaining $600,000. It took weeks of calls assuring the lawyers that we were following proper procedures. We were successful and the entire bridge loan was repaid.

New Settlement Community Campus, as the complex is known, represents the culmination of twenty-five years of community rebuilding at New Settlement Apartments. In 2017 we began the fifth year of operations. We have the Alvin Ailey Company teaching dance, swimming lessons for everyone, over six thousand family memberships, cooking and nutrition classes, and an outdoor green garden terrace. Eighteen thousand people use the center annually. Over one thousand school children take swimming lessons each week during the school year. Nine summer camps use the pool as well. So far forty-four high school students have been certified as lifeguards, a summer job that often pays as much as $15 an hour. Athletic groups are beginning to hold swim meets at the pool. There are also special hours for people with disabilities.

Figure 10.5. Cooking class. (Photo by David Sundberg / Esto.)

As for the schools, the first senior class graduated in June 2016. Out of 109 students, 101 graduated. The other eight will be in remedial programming. Even better, eighty-nine students are heading to college.

The staff and participants are palpably energized and enthusiastic. After four years of heavy use, the place shines. Let's hope that upkeep continues and that the lease will be renewed after its seventy-five-year term expires.

11
A Few of the Families

New Settlement Apartments is now a complex of eighteen low-rise buildings renovated or constructed between 1989 and 2017, providing 1,082 apartments in the Mount Eden section of the Bronx. Its mission is to offer clean, safe, and affordable housing along with community programs and amenities for residents and the wider neighborhood.

There are many ways to measure success: the condition of the physical plant, financial health, safety, and the viability of the surrounding area. But one thing I had always wanted to do in my years at Settlement Housing Fund was to survey the tenants of our various developments to see what they thought about their buildings and communities. That did not happen. In writing this book, however, I wanted to hear at least a few of their voices.

As I was writing, I found a report from 1994 describing the situation of 252 New Settlement families who had been homeless. It had been written by a social worker whose job was to assure that the homeless families were settling into their new surroundings.

Most of the families had moved to New Settlement between 1990 and 1992. Forty-one of the families had serious problems, such as domestic violence, mental health issues, drug addiction, poor housekeeping, or children engaging in criminal activities.

Of the twelve New Settlement residents I interviewed, a few were among those formerly homeless tenants who had serious problems. By the time I met them, more than two decades later, they'd turned their lives around. Their apartments were immaculate and beautifully maintained. Their

Figure 11.1. Maria Martinez. (Courtesy of Maria Martinez.)

children had graduated from college and had good jobs. One of the original residents had earned a master's degree herself. Although good housing doesn't guarantee improvements in the lives of tenants, in these cases the effect was more than positive.

I found their stories, and in fact the stories of all the residents I interviewed, remarkable and even inspiring. I hope they reveal something about the courage and values of the people who live in these buildings.

These residents were kind enough to thank me for the work that I had done over the years, and they also thanked God. They seemed to enjoy talking about New Settlement. I certainly enjoyed talking with them.

Maria Martinez

Maria Martinez moved in 1990 to 1512 Townsend Avenue, the second of the complex's initial fourteen buildings. At the time she was a twenty-two-year-old single mother with a three-year-old son. She had been living with her mother and too many others in an overcrowded apartment.

In her mother's apartment, Maria said, things had become dysfunctional. Nevertheless, she managed to complete a few years at Long Island University and landed a job as a receptionist. At first, being pregnant, she had applied for food stamps and welfare. But when she started working, she called the welfare agency and said, in effect, "Thank you, but no thank you." She has not needed the assistance ever since.

When she first walked into the new apartment building, she could hardly believe that she had her own key. "This was actually mine," she thought, beaming. She immediately noticed how clean it was and that everything was in great repair. There was an emphasis on maintenance. Because she had a son, she qualified for a two-bedroom apartment. Today, in most government-assisted buildings, mothers and young sons are required to share a bedroom. She still has the same apartment, even though her son has left.

Maria worries about some of the neighbors, among them those who arrived at New Settlement in recent years. She wonders if the tenant screening is as rigorous it used to be. Some of her neighbors are noisy, she said, and not so clean. She gets annoyed by those who smoke pot in the hallways, by children playing in the hallways, and by trash left around, especially because she sees how often the floors are mopped, how well the hallways are painted, and how repairs are made at once.

Even in the beginning things were hardly perfect. When Maria first moved in, her apartment was burglarized and all her housewarming gifts were stolen. For a few months she slept with a knife next to her bed. However, she is quick to assert that New Settlement Apartments is a safe place to live. The security guards are alert and polite. The burglary was an unfortunate fluke.

Maria believes that in many ways New Settlement Apartments keeps getting better. She gives the credit to Jack Doyle, Megan Nolan, and other staff members. She can always go to them with her problems. She singled out Barbara Cooper, a longtime housing coordinator, as a "caring, understanding human being who will work with you." She considers herself fortunate to have an affordable apartment, compared to people she knows who spend almost all their money on rent.

She made $18,000 when she first moved to New Settlement. Now she makes "a lot more." But at New Settlement her rent does not go up just because she makes more money. Of course, the rent does go up a small amount every year because of increased operating costs.

After the receptionist job, Maria went to work for West End Intergenerational, a Manhattan residence for low-income seniors and the formerly homeless. She learned a lot from the professional staff members, who believed that people could improve their circumstances when offered adequate support.

She was able to obtain help from the staff to enroll her son, Kenneth Chabert, at a school that was near her new job. Maria had hated the idea of sending him to the local public school in the Bronx (which was closed many years later). When she went to enroll Kenneth in that school, she heard one of mothers cursing at her child in a loud, violent manner. That was enough for her. That would not be the school for Kenneth. Then, the school near her job and started a bilingual program, and the administrators tried to place Kenneth in the Spanish-speaking class, based on Maria's last name, ignoring the fact that Spanish was not Kenneth's first language and he was half African American. Maria became furious. She and Kenneth's father appealed to the school leaders successfully. The child transferred back into an English-speaking section. This incident led Maria to become interested in helping others. It became clear to her on that day that if she had not spoken English and had not known her rights as a parent, Kenneth would have been placed in a program solely because of his mother's last name.

Maria's son is a New Settlement success story. He attended the summer day camps and then the sleepaway camp run by New Settlement. At sleepaway camp he learned to be independent and overcame a tendency toward shyness. He was also actively involved in the Bronx Helpers Program. At one time he got into some trouble with the young people in the neighborhood. With the help of Jack Doyle and Megan Nolan, Kenneth got back on the right path. He graduated from St. Raymond's High School for Boys, and he won the Martin Luther King, Jr., scholarship to Providence College. He graduated with a bachelor's degree in management in 2010. He stayed in Providence, and now works in the computer programming at Alex and Ani University, where he is one of twenty-five "Prezxi masters," which has something to do with a unique Hungarian software program. When reeling off her son's accomplishments, his mother is visibly proud.

Maria is an example of a person who took advantage of opportunities for upward mobility and has not stopped. When she was pregnant and had to find a job, she failed to complete her degree at Long Island University. But she continued her education and has obtained numerous certifications and her bachelor's degree in business. She is currently enrolled in CUNY's School of Professional Studies.

While working at West End Intergenerational, she became interested in helping victims of domestic violence. She went on to work for the Violence Intervention Program, a program to aid victims of domestic violence and to prevent such incidents. She is currently the organization's program coordinator in the Bronx, a role in which she works closely with New Settlement.

In 1996, a man fatally shot his wife in front of one of the New Settlement buildings. Until recently there was an annual candle light vigil commemorating her death and highlighting the need to combat domestic violence. Maria hopes that the vigil will be reinstated.

Maria says that New Settlement keeps getting better and better, as do the community programs. She loves the new campus and hopes to get around to taking up yoga. However, she believes that problems in the neighborhood are worse than they used to be. There is more gun violence. She can hear the shots at night. She is all too aware of many instances of domestic violence, bullying, and related violence in the immediate area. She believes that the new community center offers a safe place for children and teens to benefit from positive mentors.

Although Maria earns much more money than when she first moved in, she would never leave, because finding this level of cleanliness, good repair, and positive environment would be difficult. She ended the interview with the following statement: "Can you imagine if there were developments like New Settlement Apartments all over New York? Everything would be so much better."

Emma Nunoz and Her Mother

Emma Nunoz and her mother, who asked to be identified simply as "the lady who lives in 1A," moved to New Settlement in 2002. Emma remembers that it was the year after 9/11. They had been living in a Red Cross shelter, and the family now receives Section 8 rent subsidies to help pay the rent.

The interview took place on a Saturday because Emma's mother works every weekday from 8:00 a.m. until 8:00 p.m. She is a home-health-care provider. She seemed pleased that she has the long hours and knows that her work is important. She said that at times life as a single mother had been stressful. However, she seemed proud of her daughter.

In Emma's opinion, the best aspects of New Settlement are the community programs. She always had "something to do, instead of just being outside." Her mother nodded in agreement. The worst times are when there are no activities and "nothing to do."

Emma and her brother participated in the programs at the College Access Center. Emma is in her second year at Bronx Community College, and her brother is in college in North Carolina. Emma has not decided on a career as of yet. She is keeping her options open. Her mother had plans all along for her children to attend college. Again, they both valued the many educational and recreational programs at New Settlement.

Emma's mother said that her building is in good repair and keeps getting better. Repairs are made promptly. During our Saturday interview, I could see that the electric outlets in her apartment were being repaired and that new kitchen counters were being installed to replace the original ones, which dated back to 1991. The radiators were being adjusted so that it would not be too hot during the heating season. (Some tenants complained of too much heat, while others felt too cold. It's hard to please everyone.)

To both Emma and her mother, the building seemed safer than it used to be. New surveillance cameras had been installed, which made a real difference. No one was smoking weed in the hallways any more. The surrounding community seemed much "calmer" than it had in previous years.

Ramon Cepeda

Ramon Cepeda met me in his apartment. Although the entrance doors and courtyard could use some sprucing up, the vestibule and hallways were spotless. Ramon's apartment was simply and tastefully furnished. It shined. "After all," he said, "this is my home."

Ramon moved to the building in 1992. He had previously been living in the Washington Heights neighborhood in Manhattan. In 1998 his family moved back to the Dominican Republic for a while and then to Pennsylvania, while his son attended Carnegie Mellon University for graduate studies. However, in 2002, it was the right time for him to move back to New York City. Ramon called New Settlement, only to discover that there was a three-year waiting list. Nevertheless, he sent in his application with his old photo ID for the building. Miraculously, he said, there was an opening, and he has remained as a tenant ever since. He gave God part of the credit.

He said that the best thing about New Settlement Apartments is the maintenance. He clearly respected the level of cleanliness and repair.

When I asked what was the worst thing about New Settlement, he thought for a while, and then said that the laundry room was inadequate. There were only two washing machines for thirty or so tenants. On weekends it was especially hard to get the laundry done.

To me he seemed amazingly aware of every detail—mostly positive, but sometimes quite negative. He is a passionate and enthusiastic sup-

Figure 11.2. Ramon Cepeda. (Courtesy of Ramon Cepeda.)

porter of the staff and of all that has been accomplished in the neighborhood over the twenty-three years he has been there. He thinks that the
housing coordinators he knows, Barbara Cooper and Beverly Williams,
do a great job and that the security staff is responsive and professional. He
thinks that Jack Doyle, "the very tall man," is totally devoted to the community and respects the residents. If Ramon calls anyone on the staff, his
call is returned within twenty-four hours.

Ramon thinks that the tenant selection process is less rigorous than it
was when he originally moved to New Settlement. Some people don't
take care of their apartments, he said, and they leave garbage in the hallways. At night he hears mice scurrying around inside the walls. Some
tenants have hidden dogs, even though leases stipulate that pets are not
allowed.

He thought that management should warn the tenant with one infrac-
tion, require fines for the second violation, and then evict people who

do not abide by the rules. Ramon said that one family can ruin an entire building.

Of course, Jack Doyle said that the tenant selection process had not changed. There was still a pre-application, an application, a credit check, an office interview, and a home interview. Furthermore, it is not at all easy to convince a judge to evict someone.

Ramon considered the building reasonably safe, though he thinks that cameras should be installed on every floor, not just at the entrance, and noted that the glass on the front door gets broken from time to time.

The exhilarating part of the interview concerned Ramon's two children. His son started New York University at fourteen and was the youngest graduate in the university's history. There was an article about him in the NYU newsletter. He majored in engineering and is now working on getting a master's degree in electrical engineering. His daughter started college when she was sixteen and graduated from Manhattan College in Riverdale with a degree as a civil engineer. Although she is working, Ramon said she was looking for a better-paying job. Both his son and daughter had benefited from the College Access Center. Ramon said that the staff was especially helpful in getting scholarships for his children.

I was a little skeptical about the graduation ages he reported, so I went to the College Access Center to check things out. The staff there confirmed everything Ramon had told me. The article about the NYU graduation was posted on the wall for a long time in order to encourage other students.

Ramon receives Section 8 housing subsidies, but he might soon lose his eligibility because his daughter's employment might result in too much family income to qualify for the program. This family of three might have to move to a one-bedroom unit because of the scarcity of funds for Section 8. Ramon certainly does not want to move from his apartment, and one could hardly blame him.

Pedro (Peter) Morales

Peter Morales moved to New Settlement in May 1991, having previously lived on the Lower East Side and then with his family in the Bronx. He lives on the first floor in a one-bedroom apartment and works in a program that serves women and children with HIV-related problems. At the time of our interview he was looking for less stressful work.

His housing coordinator at New Settlement said that "although he's not home a lot, Peter always makes us aware if he sees anything going on in the building." He praised the people who work at New Settlement. When I asked what was best about New Settlement, he said, "The maintenance."

He has the utmost respect for the work being done to "help the impoverished" and to prevent and address domestic violence. He liked the community Halloween parties, which are much better than having the children go from door to door. He also valued the tot lot, especially because it was secure and supervised. Peter had good things to say about the youth programs, the College Access Center, the pool, and the community center. He has not used the programs because of his heavy work schedule but is trying to find the time to swim.

He has seen dramatic changes for the better in the neighborhood. When I asked about problems, however, he gave me an earful. He believes that management is no longer selective when approving tenants, and that some residents engage in illegal activity. He mentioned one woman on the sixth floor who has people in and out of her apartment day and night. He also said there is definitely drug activity. Sometimes there is drug trafficking in the vestibule, although the cameras have helped with this. On one occasion thieves entered the building and took one of the front doors off its hinges. Peter was outraged. This kind of thing did not happen in earlier years. When he calls security, the guards do come, as did Chester Paul and now Daniel Scanlon, the security supervisors. There was a time when the police actively patrolled the neighborhood. Peter felt "calm and secure" at that time. He regretted that the gates are no longer "locked and private."

Although maintenance is great, some of the tenants are not. They throw garbage on the floor even if they live right next to the compactor. Peter advises them not to do this. He had a leak from upstairs during Hurricane Sandy and hopes that the repair will last. He is concerned that there had been some debris in the pipes.

Peter believes that the rules are the rules. Someone had circulated a petition to allow dogs in the building. Peter explained that he had given up his dog and left it at his mother's apartment. The lease had a clear "no pets" clause, and he felt that it was wrong to ignore it: dogs are too hard to clean up after, and some are dangerous.

He misses the friendliness that had been part of his building in the early years. People would decorate the vestibule at holiday time, schedule events, and get dressed up, but that no longer happens. Some of the best residents have moved out.

Overall, Peter "cannot complain." He is proud to live at New Settlement Apartments. The programs and the diversity are "awesome." Yet there are little glitches here and there. One time his money order was not in the right form and it was not counted as a rent payment. He got it cleared up but thinks that the process took too long. That was in 2004. He pays his rent promptly every month. That is his "Bible." He gives credit to the New Settlement staff and to God. New Settlement, he says, has "come a long way."

Nancy Vandross

Nancy Vandross has lived at New Settlement Apartments for twenty-one years. She had previously lived in another area of the Bronx, sharing an apartment with her daughter. When her daughter got married, it was time to move. Her apartment and her building are immaculate.

Nancy described the service at New Settlement as "fantastic." Her eyes lit up as she spoke. The place is so clean. If anything is scribbled on the walls, it is immediately removed. The porters are constantly keeping everything clean. The porter in her building is especially good and hard-working, but she was also pleased that there was someone else there to cover when he goes on vacation. Barbara Cooper, her housing coordinator, is in her words "a wonderful person."

Nancy retired several years ago. She worked at Woolworths for a long time, and then for a legal firm in Manhattan. Her daughter and son live nearby. She grew up in South Carolina and sometimes thinks of going back, but she considers herself a "citified person." She does not drive a car. The neighborhood is well served by the D and 4 trains. Occasionally she will take the bus. She likes to read and always brings a book or magazine for the bus. In good weather she likes to walk from her building, which is near 172nd Street, down to the shopping center at 161st Street. She also shops on 170th Street, and her bank, JPMorgan Chase, is there as well.

When I asked about the worst things at New Settlement, she hesitated before discussing a few of the newer tenants who litter or create other problems. She mentioned a woman who lives down the hall on the sixth floor as a real troublemaker, as she both deals and takes drugs. One of this woman's male visitors would kick the door when it was locked and once even tore the lobby door from its hinge. Another time, he broke the glass window on the door, "but they fixed it right away." She hoped that the woman would be evicted. (Eventually, an eviction did take place.) When I mentioned that her neighbor on the first floor had said the same thing, she said she knew Peter and thought he was a nice guy. She has many friends in the building. She liked the fact that some of her friends were

Figure 11.3. Nancy Vandross. (Courtesy of Nancy Vandross.)

Puerto Rican and that others came from Africa. She had nice things to say about a "cordial older couple." She has many good friends and enjoys going with them to church, the movies, and dinner. She just returned from a cruise to South Carolina and the Bahamas.

She likes the programs for the children, although she did not live at New Settlement when her children were growing up. Her son did go to the College Access Center and pursued higher education for two years.

She has not signed up for programs at the community center, although one of her friends who is trying to lose weight is taking Zumba lessons. I told her that the yoga programs looked excellent. She said she would consider it.

On the whole Nancy feels safe in her building and in the neighborhood. The only time she was robbed was getting off the escalator near her job on East 55th Street in Manhattan.

She said that the front gate of her building used to be locked and that she wishes it would be made secure. However, she also said that the managers were putting in a new system, which hopefully will help.

She believes the neighborhood is pretty safe and has been over the years. Few people loiter in front of the buildings, as they do a few blocks away. Occasionally there are car break-ins. Sometimes children vandalize the shrubbery, but not at her building. Nancy said, "I love it here. What else could you ask for?"

Emma

Emma did not want me to use her last name. She moved to New Settlement Apartments in 1991, after having lived with her brother in another area of the Bronx. Her apartment and her building look good. She is trying to throw out some of the things she had accumulated over the years, but it did not look cluttered to me.

To her, the best thing about the development was "security." She also said that most of the staff members responded to requests right away. Garbage does not accumulate. Most of the time everything is clean and in good repair.

The worst problem has to do with some of the residents in her building and the building next door. "It never used to be like that," Emma said. "So much loud noise, loud music. It used to be quiet, especially on this floor. It is still quiet, but sometimes someone is in the hall." However, all in all, she says that the neighbors are pretty good. In the summer the streets are noisy, she added. She complained that some of the tenants or others let their children destroy the flowers in the courtyard. She reported them to city services a few times and one time even called the police. She is glad that dogs are not allowed in the building, as they could be messy and even dangerous.

Emma has twin daughters now in their thirties. They participated in New Settlement's after-school programs and other programs when they were young. One of her daughters was awarded a prize. Both graduated

Figure 11.4. Emma. (Courtesy of Emma.)

from SUNY New Paltz. It was good for them to be together in college. Emma wants them to get their master's degrees. She said she pushes them a lot. One of her daughters works at Lehman College, so it would be "easy for her to get a graduate degree, since she's right there."

Emma has not been to the community center but says she might go for a meeting of CASA regarding community organizing. She also might try yoga. She currently does push-ups and other exercises. She also enjoys playing on both her piano and her keyboard.

She was confused about her rent. At one time she received Section 8 payments, but then she earned too much money to be eligible. She was confused about a notification that she got from the New York City Finance Department about the Senior Citizen Rent Increase Exemption (known by its initials, SCRIE). She was worried about possible rent increases in the future, to which she did not think a senior like her should be subjected. That was the only thing she would change about New Settlement Apartments—the "rent rules." She was gracious and watched to make sure I was safely in the elevator when I left.

Jane Terry

Jane Terry moved into New Settlement Apartments as a young single mother of two in 1990 after having lived in a shelter established by governor Mario Cuomo's son Andrew (before he himself entered the world of politics). She was escaping a broken marriage and had little money. Susan

Figure 11.5. Jane Terry. (Courtesy of Jane Terry.)

Cole and Sarah Kolodny remembered interviewing Jane at the shelter. They were impressed by the way she interacted with her sons. Jane still has fond memories of Susan. She says she "grew up" at New Settlement.

Jane gave New Settlement credit for what she described as her self-esteem. Sarah interviewed her in 1996 and remembers her will to succeed. The staff at New Settlement suggested a reading program at the local public library, and it was there that Jane learned she needed to acquire new skills. She overcame her problems, got her General Equivalency Degree, continued her studies, and became a registered nurse. She is now retired but works part-time as a home health-care provider.

Her two sons, Kevin and Max, took part in the after-school programs and other youth programs until they went to college. Kevin graduated from Morgan State College; Max went to John Jay College of Criminal Justice, part of CUNY, and then entered the military, which became his career. Jane proudly showed me his picture in uniform. Jane was determined that her children would not emulate their father or suffer because of the problems she had faced as a young mother. She would make sure her sons did not "drop out and there would be no drugs." There were rules in her home regarding school attendance, homework, and chores.

Jane's apartment is pristine, decorated with many photos of her sons along with their wives and children. Jane is happy with the maintenance and security. She said she feels safe, especially compared to back when some of the tenants used to sit at a front desk to watch the entrance. In her twenty-four years of residency, she was never cold or without hot water. She remembered what the neighborhood had been like in the eighties, calling it "a ghost town."

Jane praised the staff, especially Jack Doyle and Maria Santana, who oversaw the after-school programs. She had few complaints. In fact, to get her to share some I had to drag them out of her. She missed some of her friends who passed away. Her upstairs neighbor was noisy late at night, though Jane thought it was the children who lived there. She also wished that her rent did not increase whenever her income went up (as required by Section 8). However, she said that her non–Section 8 "peers paid thousands of dollars a month" for inferior apartments.

She has noticed changes in the neighborhood population—namely, more people from Africa and some who do not speak English. However, she is fine with the changes.

She took a tour of the new community center and thinks it is "fabulous—out of this world." However, she has not had time to enroll. She walks miles around the neighborhood and also runs around a track on 161st Street. Next year she will look into yoga for seniors.

Jane seemed genuinely pleased to be interviewed. She sent her love to Susan. She congratulated me for retiring, hugged me, and gave me a beautifully wrapped present. The gift was a small pillow and eyeshade so I could travel comfortably now that I am retired. She is a gentle, charming, and inspiring human being.

Dana Smalls

Dana Smalls moved to New Settlement in 1992. In 1997 she began having trouble with the stairs to the entranceway because of an injury and so relocated to another building in the New Settlement complex, one block away. Both apartments are great, she says.

She had lived with her grandmother in another area of the Bronx but moved when other family members moved in and the apartment became too crowded. When she applied initially, she failed to send back one of the forms with the application. She was rejected but followed the appeals process. She then sent in the appropriate form, and her appeal was successful. She was elated.

In Dana's opinion, the best thing about the development is its wealth of programs for young people. Her son participated in everything. He won a prize as a member of the Bronx Helpers. He was in the after-school program, and even the boat-building program that had operated in one of the basements. He went on overnight trips to Maine and to Pennsylvania. Through the College Access Center he found an appropriate college and graduated in 2010. "He turned out well," Dana said. "The programs kept him out of trouble. No drugs. No gangs."

Dana also used the College Access Center and graduated from Lehman College. She is currently working for a master's degree in health services. Unfortunately, after recently getting a job, the hospital where she worked laid off all the new hires after just five months. She was not eligible for unemployment insurance. She is looking everywhere for a new job. Her computer is her best friend.

She said the maintenance of the building is excellent. Recently there was a leak through her fire alarm. She called, and it was fixed the next day. Her apartment and the building were immaculate. She is a big fan of Woody, the head of maintenance. All her friends tell her how great her apartment is.

She thinks her building and her apartment are safe. Security is good. There are problems if someone gets in the building without proper permission. Dana calls security right away. She will never open the front door for someone she does not know. One of her neighbors reported that her son was in the basement and called security. She was surprised. It turns out that her son had gone with one of the security guards to check out smoke coming from the basement. Security is good indeed, and her son is a model New Settlement citizen.

She says that the neighborhood is safe. There was a shooting a few months ago, but she believes it involved people who were not from the area.

She appreciates everything about New Settlement Apartments. I asked her what the worst thing was about the development. She hesitated a long time and then said she wished there were parking facilities. When I asked her if there was anything at all that she wished she could change, she hesitated again. Then she said that the washing machines did not always work. The dryers are okay, but she wished that there were new washing machines in her building.

She raved about the new community center. She takes Zumba lessons and hopes to start swimming. She thought that the ballet classes and other programs for young people were great.

She praised Jamilah Colvert, her housing coordinator. Jamilah is there for her, always helpful and understanding. One time she was behind on her rent because her ex-husband was in a coma after an automobile accident. Her money order was on top of her armoire, but she couldn't get away to retrieve it. She was in a quandary. Jamilah helped Dana to resolve her case in court and quickly got her back in her apartment. Dana understands that rent has to be paid on time. She feels lucky to have Section 8 to get her by in hard times.

She would stay forever if she could. She is thinking of moving to Maryland for work but seemed reluctant. If that happened, her son would stay in the apartment. She appreciates all that Jack Doyle does, and I appreciated the opportunity to talk with her.

Juana Diaz

Juana Diaz came to New York from the Dominican Republic when she was twenty and later moved to New Settlement Apartments in 1992. She had arrived in this country with her mother and knew no English. Her mother worked in a garment factory next to Settlement Housing Fund's main office on West 37th Street, and Juana decided she would work there, too. She stayed for eleven years and was earning good money until the company went bankrupt. She learned English from listening to other people, and the bankruptcy proved a lucky event. It gave Juana the impetus to go to college and improve her English. After getting her associate's degree she went to work at a methadone clinic, where she has been ever since.

Juana's children went to Catholic schools and the local high school. Her oldest daughter, a registered nurse, is now getting a master's degree. Her son is a chef. Her youngest daughter, who is majoring in human development and psychology at SUNY Binghamton, hopes to become a social worker. She encouraged her children to speak both English and Spanish, which helps them when looking for a job.

Juana said it helped her, too, because so many clients at the clinic speak only Spanish. She thinks that methadone is addictive. Many of the clients have mental health and other problems ("A lot of crazy ones," she says). She works from 6:30 a.m. to 3:00 p.m.

Before moving to New Settlement, Juana lived nearby in a one-room apartment with her husband, son, and daughter. Her mother heard about New Settlement, and Juana was happy when her application was accepted. She had another daughter after moving to New Settlement. She lives in a spotless three-bedroom apartment. She was especially happy to have an extra bathroom. She painted one bathroom pink and the other blue—one for female family members and the other for males. (She and her husband are now divorced.)

In her view, the best thing about New Settlement is that people come to fix things right away and everything is clean. The building looked great when I visited. Juana said that the building is safe.

Her children took part in all the programs: after-school, the Bronx Helpers, and basketball. They also liked the tot lot, which they called "our park."

Juana enjoys the new community center. She took up swimming but had to stop because of leg cramps. She had great things to say about Barbara Cooper and the staff at New Settlement. Barbara greets all the other tenants, who are always polite to her.

Sheila Hines

Sheila Hines moved to New Settlement Apartments in 1991. She had lived in a house in Queens, but the owner sold the building and the new rents were way too high.

For a time she received public assistance, but then she got a job. At first her rent was $300 a month, but when she was successful in her application for Section 8 the rent went down to $63 a month, a fact that she described with obvious pleasure. She has worked most of her life but lost her job a year and a half ago. Her unemployment benefits expired after six months. She was a receptionist for a nonprofit organization and then promoted as an assistant to the executive director. The nonprofit lost funding and had to downsize. She has computer skills and is eager to get back to work.

Despite all this, she seemed cheerful. She likes life at New Settlement Apartments. She feels comforted having security guards on site. She is also pleased that repairs are made promptly and that the building is so clean. She had seen dramatic changes in the neighborhood, all for the better. She remembers the drugs and violence down the block from her on Mount Eden Avenue, before the police cleaned everything up. She believes that her building is safe now.

Sheila, who has four grown children and has legally adopted several grandchildren, lives in an apartment that is immaculate. One wall is devoted to photographs of her children and grandchildren. There are small chairs in the living room for a granddaughter, age seven, who lives with her, as does her daughter (the child's mother).

When Sheila's children were young they participated in the community programs. Her daughter was in the program for girls, and a grandson used the College Access Center. Sheila pulled out trophies and certificates for merit and perfect attendance that were awarded to her children and grandchildren.

One of Sheila's grandchildren, a second grader, is gifted in ballet, art, and drama. She is also a skilled baton twirler and takes swimming lessons twice a week at the New Settlement pool. Sheila thinks the new schools and the community center are beautiful.

Sheila wishes that that her rent could be lowered now that she is out of work. Although she had Section 8 at one time, when her daughter started working their family income exceeded the Section 8 limits. She is having trouble making ends meet.

Sheila understands that the rent is set to cover program and operating costs. She was interested in the original favorable financing of renovations and the fact that there are no mortgage payments included in rent. She pays $1,133 a month for three bedrooms and one and a half bathrooms. She all too aware that there is nothing comparable in New York City. She was extremely proud that she has never missed a rent payment in all the twenty-three years she lived at New Settlement. She also has never missed a payment on her utility bills. Her mother taught her how to be frugal, telling her "Keep some money under the mattress. You might need it."

Sheila does not spend much time with friends. She sees one neighbor two or three times a year. Between working and raising four children and grandchildren, she had no time for friends. Her daughter is her good friend, and she considers her daughter's friends to be her friends, too. They all call her "Mom." In fact, they all went on a trip to Niagara Falls together. They try to get her to go to the movies on Tuesdays, when the cost is only $7.50. She likes the movies, but she likes the popcorn even better.

Maggy Torres-Morales

Maggy Torres-Morales moved to New Settlement in 1990 and was one of the first three residents in her building. She was born in Puerto Rico but grew up in the Bronx. Her family lived on Macombs Avenue in a Section 8 development.

Maggy is a survivor of domestic violence. After she left her abusive husband, she and her three children lived for three months with her aunt in Roosevelt Gardens, a Section 8 complex in the neighborhood. She had to leave because of regulations about overcrowding and ended up at a shelter.

She was ecstatic when accepted at New Settlement. She knew the neighborhood and remembers the terrible conditions in the eighties. When she saw the renovation underway, she thought that it symbolized "a new dawn of hope."

For Maggy, having known domestic violence, New Settlement was and remains a "safe haven." The residents, the security guards, management, and the program staff all had the same focus: making New Settlement safe and a great place to live. All the buildings are secure and in great repair.

Maggy became an ardent community activist and joined the program for domestic violence survivors. She enjoyed meeting all the social work interns at New Settlement, including the former community center director, Megan Nolan, who had been an intern, and Amy Watkins. When Amy died tragically in a random act of violence near her home in Brooklyn, everyone despaired. Maggy helped with a mural in Amy's honor on one of the neighborhood buildings.

An important visit led to a great opportunity for Maggy. The wife of an assistant district attorney from Brooklyn was a guest speaker at the work-readiness program she attended. She spoke to Maggy, who then volunteered to translate from English to Spanish for women in court cases, many of whom had no idea what was going on in these English-language legal proceedings.

Through this work, she met Brooklyn district attorney Charles Hynes, who hired her as a receptionist in his office, even though she had not graduated high school, on the condition that she continue her education. Thrilled, she told him that her childhood goal was to become a judge.

While working for Hynes, Maggy got her General Equivalency Degree and then graduated from Empire State College, after getting help from the New Settlement College Access Center. Maggy worked in the Brooklyn DA's office for fourteen and a half years. She was promoted from community aide to the criminal court felony homicide and grand jury paralegal. Then she became a zone supervisor. The work made Maggy become, as she said, "a stronger woman." She never stopped her advocacy for victims of domestic violence and for community safety. Maggy retired in 2007 when she was overwhelmed by so many deaths in her family.

Maggy is indefatigable in reaching out to help those in need. On September 11, 2001, Maggy was in the subway train under the World Trade Center when the South Tower began to fall. Everyone had to vacate the train. Maggie's sister had worked in 1 World Trade Center but fortunately had stayed home that day. When Maggy saw what was going on, not only was she horrified and shaken, but she also noticed an eighteen-year-old woman who did not know what to do. The young woman had been in the area for her first job interview. Maggy took the young woman's hand, and they both walked the substantial distance from the Lower Manhattan to Maggy's apartment in the Bronx. Then Maggy managed to find a taxi to take the young woman to her home in Queens.

Maggy admires the cleanliness and maintenance of the buildings at New Settlement. She thinks the neighborhood has become more violent in recent years, probably because there is a for-profit shelter without any services across the street on Townsend Avenue. She believes the residents in the shelter are destructive and responsible for the upsurge of graffiti. There was a recent shooting at the building. Gun violence has increased, and domestic violence is on the rise as well. Maggy did say that the police are responsive. When the shooting occurred, the police were there "in seconds" after a call to 911.

Maggy's three sons went to P.S. 64 and attended the New Settlement after-school program. Two of her sons graduated from college. Maggy recently got married. She and her husband are raising her seven-year-old great nephew, Jonathan, who swims at the community center and attends the Mount Eden Children's Academy, which is part of the New Settlement Community Campus. "Jonathan is an awesome kid," she explained.

I asked Maggy what she would change at New Settlement. She thought an "elder outreach program" would be a good idea. People pass away unnoticed. They should be commemorated. Maybe more help should be offered. The elders should be more connected to New Settlement.

New Settlement Apartments, Maggy says, offered her "a second chance of life."

Adjoa Julie Abdul

I was eager to meet Ms. Abdul because when I spoke to her on the phone, she spoke vociferously about various problems at New Settlement. At times she sounded somewhat incoherent. Then, the second time I spoke to her, I heard more complaints, but they were interspersed with positive

Figure 11.6. Adjoa Julie Abdul. (Courtesy of Adjoa Julie Abdul).

comments. When I got there, she greeted me cordially. Her apartment was pristine. She immediately charmed me with a big smile.

Ms. Abdul has lived in New Settlement since 1994. Previously, she lived with her youngest son in a one-bedroom apartment on Crescent Avenue. During that time she traveled to Ghana to retrieve her other three sons who were there with her husband. Unfortunately her husband had died.

Ms. Abdul was able to get all her children to the United States. After two years she was accepted by New Settlement Apartments and assigned a three-bedroom apartment. Ms. Abdul's mother lived with her, which allowed her to work as a nurse's aide. She was injured on the job and now receives disability payments.

Her sons have been successful. Three of them went to college. One works for JetBlue Airways. Her youngest son, who had a learning disability and was in a remedial program, now has a high school degree and will attend Bronx Community College.

Ms. Abdul is a tough customer. She had a slew of complaints.

When she moved in, the apartment had not been properly repaired. The previous tenant had mice and roaches, and the paint job was terrible. Ms. Abdul painted everything herself and bought her own refrigerator. She said that Troy, the handyman at the time, was helpful enough to patch the areas where the mice had been gaining access, alleviating the problems with vermin.

Ms. Abdul said that her housing coordinator, Jamilah, is great. She is responsive and works hard to provide good service. Ms. Abdul also said that the maintenance is excellent. Woody, the head of maintenance, is the very best professional, and she praised Eno, the porter. She also thought highly of Troy, the former handyman.

Ashton was a good management company. Grenadier, on the other hand, "is terrible."

She went on to detail the most serious problems. The washing machines, she said, are dreadful. She cannot understand why we do not get new machines. The second problem involved the security cameras: "They are cheap. They do not catch everything. We need better ones." Furthermore, her kitchen cabinets and appliances need to be replaced. The floors also need to be repaired because they creak. Finally, the windows need to be cleaned, at least every three years.

Ms. Abdul thinks that the neighborhood is dangerous, too. There are drug sales going on, even in the building. She complains, but no one seems to hear. She misses Chester Paul, the former director of security. She tried to tell Daniel, the new head, about various problems, but he is not responsive. "Daniel can't talk to people." The security guards are afraid of the drug dealers, some of whom arrive on motorcycles and do not even live in the neighborhood. She tells Jamilah about the problems, so that Jamilah can talk to the security guards and the supervisor. Ms. Abdul also calls city services to report the problems.

Ms. Abdul said, "Jack does not know how to talk to tenants." They only spoke on the phone once. Jack complained that Ms. Abdul was yelling at him. She said she wasn't. Having spoken to Ms. Abdul quite a few times, I am well aware that she can sound angry and, as she admits, has "a loud voice." I think she means well, but she gets insulted easily.

Interspersed with all her criticism were songs of praise. She loves her building and her apartment. She has friends in the complex. She is glad that her income does not get checked every year. She thinks New Settlement is like a cooperative. She is happy and will never move. However, she told me to tell Jack to be nice to her. I told her that all the other people I had interviewed had nothing but good things to say about Jack, even the ones who were critical of other issues.

As I left, she walked out with me. She showed me the windowsill in the hallway that needed plastering and a new paint job. She pointed to the doorway where new cameras were needed. She told me that the building across the street, 1605 Walton, had dangerous tenants and poor upkeep. She wished that we would buy it. I felt as though I was with Susan Cole, walking the building and the neighborhood.

Ms. Abdul clearly cares about the maintenance of the building. She is passionate, proud of her apartment and loving toward her sons. She also has a good sense of humor.

I wrote thank-you notes to the twelve residents I interviewed. Jane Terry and Adjoa Julie Abdul called to thank me for the notes. Ms. Abdul sent a Christmas card that was over the top. I will never throw it out. I still hear from her each Christmas—and when something is wrong.

12
New Settlement Today

started this chapter right after returning from a visit to the Bronx. I was showing New Settlement Apartments to a global philanthropist, and he was impressed. It was a beautiful summer day. The buildings shone. As we walked around the campus, the tenants and their neighbors greeted Jack with enthusiasm. We also ran into a dozen or so employees, all visibly proud to be working at New Settlement.

We told the philanthropist that our goal is to help our residents and their neighbors become more upwardly mobile. With so much recent discussion about income inequality in the United States and its sometimes catastrophic impact on families, we believe that community development is one important line of defense.

Living in a clean and safe apartment gives young residents a fighting chance to stay in school and acquire the skills needed to earn a living. The programs at the community center give participants an awareness of their potential. The College Access Center has helped thousands of young people achieve important goals. The mixed-income nature of the buildings provides stability and role models.

Despite these benefits, New Settlement is not without problems. As I waited for the philanthropist on Townsend Avenue in front of one of the buildings, I overheard two women saying how they would never park their cars on the street. After apologizing for eavesdropping, I asked if there were many car thefts. No, that wasn't the problem. It was that teenagers liked to smash or steal rear-view and side-view mirrors.

More seriously, there had recently been two shootings up the street. Although neither was fatal, the situation is a source of urgent concern. Jack is also worried about renewed gang activity.

On the whole, New Settlement Apartments is thriving. In recent years Jack won a number of new grants to expand existing programs and to start new initiatives. Sometimes when he talks, I get dizzy trying to keep track of the new activities and accomplishments. One large new initiative is an after-school program for 150 middle school students. And in 2017 the state awarded New Settlement with a Twentieth Century Learning Grant. Supposedly this is a five-year commitment, but it depends on federal appropriations. The grant allows several new after-school programs, including one for high school students at the community center.

As a New Yorker, I feel comfortable saying that the $150 million that provided affordable housing for 893 families in 1990 was a great public investment for the city. Despite problems, the neighborhood keeps improving, and New Settlement remains in good repair and affordable for a mixed-income population. Nearly three-quarters of the apartments are still assigned to very low-income or formerly homeless residents at initial occupancy.

The buildings, which were rehabilitated twenty-seven years ago, needed capital repairs. The staff today consists of about two hundred individuals, including staff for the community center and part-timers. How do Jack, my successor Alexa Sewell, and the Settlement Housing Fund board sustain and expand the work that has been done so far? Not surprisingly, they have put an ambitious plan into effect.

The day after the Bronx visit described at the beginning of this chapter, there was a New Settlement Apartments board meeting at Settlement Housing Fund's office in Manhattan. It was interesting for many reasons. (Although I had retired as executive director of Settlement Housing Fund and did not join the Settlement Housing Fund board, I did stay on the New Settlement Board.)

Through the first half of 2014, New Settlement was in excellent financial shape. Even after increasing the allotment for community programs from $578,000 to $800,000, cash flow was over $250,000 for the first six months. There were practically no vacant apartments and almost no unpaid bills. In 2014, deposits to the reserve accounts were on schedule, and no funds had been withdrawn. I do not remember ever seeing such a good financial statement. It could not be happening at a better time, because the community center still needs significant cash to cover operating expenses.

Table 12.1. Rent ranges

Studios	$501–$1,201
One bedroom	$460–$1,423
Two bedrooms	$528–$1,577
Three bedrooms	$687–$2,008

Note: Annual incomes now range from public-assistance levels to about $75,000 at initial occupancy. In 2015 there were only two vacancies out of 893 apartments. No one had been evicted for nonpayment of rent.

But despite New Settlement's financial health, modest tensions have developed between the development and its parent organization. Some staff members at Settlement Housing Fund have always felt that the organization got too little credit for the work on projects like New Settlement.

For my part, I worried that Jack might one day want to sever ties with Settlement Housing Fund, especially because New Settlement is required to pay a significant annual fee to Settlement Housing Fund. In our original 1987 proposal for the project, the budget included a supervisory fee for Settlement Housing Fund, plus a budget line for what was described as "allocated services," which covered the cost of our oversight. Jack's salary is paid from that budget line.

Nevertheless, the relationship between the two entities has been a true partnership. Settlement Housing Fund created the mixed-income concept, wrote the proposal, established the project's board, oversaw management, started the community programs, and has monitored the buildings diligently. Today Settlement Housing Fund supports community programs, seeks development opportunities, and handles fiscal oversight. It is a partnership that has reaped many benefits and should continue to do so.

There have always been four levels of rent at New Settlement Apartments: one for the homeless (268 apartments), one for low-income families (357 apartments), one for moderate-income families (179 apartments), and one for market-rate units (89 apartments). Tenants pay between 20 and 30 percent of their gross income, from which money for utilities is subtracted.

Table 12.1 shows the rent ranges for three tiers at the end of 2014, not including those who receive federal subsidies. Lower-income families paid significantly less than did moderate-income families.

In creating New Settlement Apartments, our theory was that mixed-income housing and good community programs would promote upward mobility among families who lived there. From 1990 through today, 30 percent of the apartments are reserved for formerly homeless families. Initially, 70 percent of the apartments were allocated to very low-income families, a percentage that included the homeless. The highest income level allowed, for up to 10 percent of the families, was originally $53,000.

In 2016 the development remained mixed economically. The lowest annual income reported was $840 a year, and the highest was $196,058. Some 114 families earned more than $58,000. Thirty families earned over $90,000. The average income for a family of four was $40,000. In the larger community board area, the median annual income is $26,000.

Over the years, between 2 and 6 percent of the families moved out every year. Some were evicted; others bought houses. Given the available data, it's impossible to prove that a mixed-income environment leads to upward mobility. However, even at a moment when incomes have been stagnant for the so-called 99 percent, anecdotal information about rising family income among New Settlement families seems encouraging. By contrast, in the larger community board area, median income declined by $7,000 between 2000 and 2013. However, it is hard to be definitive about what these numbers mean because many long-term New Settlement tenants retired and now earn much less.

At New Settlement Apartments there are many impressive examples of success in this area. And, of course, providing low-income families with an excellent environment, including award-winning community programs, is a valuable outcome in itself.

Despite these benefits, in 2015 New Settlement faced the usual challenges for buildings renovated twenty-five years ago. Elevators need to be upgraded or replaced. The guarantee period for the roofs expired in 2006. Settlement Housing Fund hired a consultant to prepare an assessment of New Settlement's physical needs that included a cost estimate of repairs that could be anticipated for the buildings, with a timeline showing when the work would have to be done.

My optimistic guess in July 2014 was that at least $7 million worth of work would be required. The figure turned out to be over $42 million, which comes to about $48,000 per apartment. As of October 2014 our reserves amounted to about $800,000 for the initial fourteen buildings.

In July I had also thought that most of the work could be done gradually, using cash flow from rental income and operating reserves. But given the higher price tag, it became clear that major refinancing would be necessary.

There were several ways to finance the repairs. In 2015 the staff at Settlement Housing Fund came up with a scheme that will both preserve New Settlement Apartments and allow Settlement Housing Fund to refinance the buildings and take advantage of the dramatically increased property values, thereby securing the future financial health of both entities.

Another lurking danger involved the expiration of the project's real estate tax exemptions. Renewal of that exemption with no additional restrictions was part of the new proposal.

The refinancing plan involves a state tax-exempt bond and equity from the Low-Income Housing Tax Credit program, which was part of the 1986 Tax Reform Act. (Tax credits would be available for up to 70 percent of the apartments, the number occupied by eligible tenants.) The funds from refinancing would be used to upgrade common spaces in the buildings and provide new kitchen cabinets and other improvements in individual apartments. Most exciting, solar panels will be installed to provide electricity and thus make the complex more environmentally viable.

The one worrisome change is that program funding will come from cash flow, not from the operating budget. The numbers so far look good, but the situation could change. Funds from New Settlement Apartments are still required to operate community programs in the buildings and at the campus.

In July 2014 I had been opposed to refinancing with tax credits. We had used that program for other developments and were aware of its many complexities. I was also reluctant because annual income certifications for 70 percent of the tenants would be mandated. But that November I changed my mind after attending what was billed as a Solutions Conference sponsored by the National Housing Conference in Oakland, California. I visited some magnificent buildings that had been upgraded and preserved through the use of tax credits. The idea of protecting our buildings as affordable housing for the next sixty years while generating large amounts of money for Settlement Housing Fund and New Settlement was an enticing possibility. The financing was secured in June 2016, and renovation is underway.

In mulling the future of New Settlement Apartments, I asked Jack Doyle what pleased him the most about the complex and what kept him up at night. In response, he praised the existence of 1,022 units of safe, well-maintained, and affordable housing, along with the array of community programs and organizing initiatives that had helped to create a thriving

Figure 12.1. New Settlement Apartments before renovation. (Courtesy of the New York City Department of Housing Preservation and Development.)

Figure 12.2. New Settlement Apartments, 2017. (Photo by Ronald L. Glassman.)

neighborhood in what had been a devastated area. The challenge, he said, was sustaining and expanding that work.

"The needs are huge," Jack said, "given the high rates of poverty and the poor performance of so many of our neighborhood schools, and the resources are limited." "In the future," he added, "we want to keep the apartments permanently affordable. We will also want to add new community programs and expand existing ones." Our newest building will be ready for occupancy in 2017 or early 2018, and Settlement Housing Fund's staff is looking for other sites in the neighborhood.

For my part, I think that the buildings and the neighborhood will continue to improve. The staff and board members at Settlement Housing Fund and New Settlement Apartments will continue to monitor the development's physical, fiscal, and social life. New Settlement Community Campus will be an increasingly strong anchor for the neighborhood. Hopefully the schools at New Settlement Community Campus will provide high-quality education and will spark the improvement of other local schools. As mentioned above, the first high school class graduated in June 2016; out of 109 seniors, 89 will attend college.

Happily, we did not assume too much debt and were able to refinance the buildings in ways that maintain the development's income mix and quality of life. Despite the political tsunamis that have roiled our nation during the most recent presidential election and its aftermath, we can point to New Settlement Apartments as a potential model that should be replicated.

I remain hopeful.

PART III
A Tale of Two Bridges

13
Two Bridges
The Early Years

In 1955, a group of parents, settlement house directors, and clergy founded an organization known as the Two Bridges Neighborhood Council on the Lower East Side of Manhattan. The group's goal was to promote positive race relations in the neighborhood, comprising a service area that sat between the Brooklyn and Williamsburg Bridges, east of East Broadway. One of the council's first accomplishments was saving the Coleman Oval, the neighborhood's only playing field.

The successful preservation of this site led to the formation of a Little League in the early sixties. Local residents represented many ethnic groups and nationalities—Puerto Rican, Chinese, African American, Jewish, Slavic, you name it. Through the Little League the children and their parents got to know one another.

The council's first president was Geoffrey Wiener, executive director of Hamilton Madison House, a Lower East Side settlement house that had been founded in 1898 and located in a public housing project near the Two Bridges area. Through Wiener's efforts, Hamilton Madison began offering remedial reading classes in conjunction with the Two Bridges Neighborhood Council, classes that proved to be of great benefit to newly arrived young people who were struggling with English. Hamilton Madison also offered workshops for parents, designed to give them skills they could use to fight for better schools. Befitting the ethnic makeup of the local population, this program was trilingual, with workshops offered in Spanish and Chinese as well as English.

In 1963, the enthusiasm for the Little League displayed itself in the organization's banner, which read "Side by Side for a Better East Side." It was a time when news of riots and gang warfare dominated the headlines. Other parts of the Lower East Side were being roiled by rivalries among different groups, notably Hasidic Jews, African Americans, and Puerto Ricans. But in the Two Bridges area, despite the mix of ethnic groups, young people and families were getting along.

Many participants in Two Bridges programs lived in the area's large developments, including Knickerbocker Village, a middle-income development that was constructed in 1933, and the Alfred E. Smith Houses, a large public housing project that opened in 1953. Others, including Victor Papa, the current president of the Two Bridges Neighborhood Council, lived in tenements or smaller buildings that liberally dotted the neighborhood.

Natalie Sosinsky, who chaired the Two Bridges education committee in the sixties, remembers that period. She told me that all the churches and other organizations supported the Little League, and that other ideas emanated from there. Residents set up a sports committee, and then a housing committee. All these groups reflected the mix of residents from the neighboring public housing developments, as well as the older buildings nearby. All the committees were multiracial.

Paul Kurzman, who was staff director at Two Bridges from 1964 to 1967, started a local newspaper, *Two Bridges News*, that provided a forum for the heads of these committees and other neighborhood residents. Local Boy Scouts delivered the paper, door-to-door, free of charge.

All this was taking place in the mid-1960s, a moment when president Lyndon Johnson's Great Society vision was very much on the minds of Americans. In 1963 the Two Bridges Neighborhood Council sponsored a successful voter registration drive, in particular reaching out to local African Americans and Puerto Ricans.

In addition, the council sent busloads of community residents to the 1963 March on Washington for Jobs and Freedom. Michael (Mickey) Schwerner, a member of the Hamilton Madison House staff, helped with the bus rentals. The following year Schwerner would be found dead in a muddy ditch in Mississippi, one of the three young men murdered by the Ku Klux Klan after they went South to promote voter registration among African Americans.[1]

1. Two Bridges sixtieth anniversary booklet, published in June 2015 in cooperation with City Lore. The pamphlet's author was Molly Garfinkel, who conducted in-depth research, as advised by Victor Papa, president of the Two Bridges Neighborhood Council.

This was also a time when the Black Panthers were active in other parts of the country, and riots in big cities were shocking the nation and shattering the consensus of many civil rights advocates. By 1968, a stormy battle over local control of New York City's public schools would spark a citywide teachers' strike.

Importantly, in 1960 the council's housing committee created the "Two Bridges Self-Renewal Plan," calling for the development of mixed-income, integrated housing. There would be many iterations of the plan over the years.

In 1961 the city had approved a plan to build housing, stores, and community facilities on an eight-block site along the East River, between the Manhattan and Williamsburg Bridges. Because this onetime industrial area included mostly abandoned businesses, there would be no need to relocate residential tenants, a process that had become controversial when Robert Moses, the city's master builder, oversaw urban renewal.

The Two Bridges plan was one of many such urban renewal plans authorized by federal legislation in 1954. The U.S. government permitted a locality to condemn deteriorated properties, absorbing two-thirds of the costs of land acquisition through grants. New York State and New York City shared the remaining third of the cost. In New York, the land would be resold to housing developers for $500 per housing unit. Urban renewal made land a bargain, paving the way for development. In many areas of the country, properties were condemned, people relocated, and the sites sat empty. "Urban renewal is Negro removal" was a frequent complaint. That was not the case in New York, although delays became inevitable after Robert Moses was no longer in charge. I still tell potential developers or partners that it takes anywhere between six months and thirty years to complete a development initiative. In 2016, land prices in the five boroughs are astronomical. I often wished that the urban renewal program still existed.

In the 1960s a number of neighborhood organizations were designated as urban renewal sponsors, participating in all decisions about land use. There was Strycker's Bay on the Upper West Side of Manhattan, the Bedford Stuyvesant Restoration Corporation in Brooklyn, the Community Association of the East Harlem Triangle in Upper Manhattan, and many others. The Two Bridges Neighborhood Council was designated as an urban renewal sponsor in 1965.

As a first step, Two Bridges hired Edelman & Salzman, an architectural firm that had its offices in Greenwich Village. Their first plan for the area, developed in cooperation with city architects, envisioned a platform over the East River Drive featuring white concrete buildings that could have

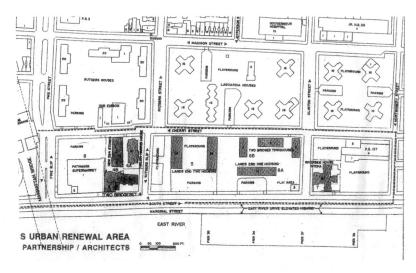

Figure 13.1. Urban renewal map. (Courtesy of Edelman Sultan Knox Wood.)

been designed by the modernist Le Corbusier. The various sites were co-ordinated. To the regret of the late Judith Edelman, a founding partner of the architectural firm, it soon became clear that the plan was unworkable. The cost of the platform turned out to be prohibitive.

A new plan was approved by the City Planning Commission on May 11, 1967, and by the Board of Estimate on June 9, 1967. The latter body, which comprised the five borough presidents and citywide elected officials, no longer exists (its functions have been taken over by the City Council).

The plan no longer included a platform. The new objectives included "demolition of structurally substandard buildings, removal of multiple ownerships, high-quality design, housing for varied income levels, commercial and community space, and a park."[2] Eventually there would be four separate urban renewal plans. There was also a large-scale plan that applied to most of the sites. Such a plan allows variations in some of the zoning rules if superior land-use patterns result. Urban renewal requirements can expire, but numerous government and other approvals are needed to change a large-scale plan.

The years kept going by with no action being taken. In 1971 the executive director of the Two Bridges Neighborhood Council was Dick

2. Certificate of Incorporation, Two Bridges Settlement Housing Corporation, March 13, 1972.

Duhan, a well-known leader of New York's antipoverty movement. John Lindsay was the liberal and idealistic mayor, and as a result, a visionary like Dick Duhan had considerable clout. The fact that council's board included settlement house leaders, neighborhood residents, and clergy, including a rabbi, sent an impressive message about the group's broad support.

Members of the Two Bridges board were advised by city housing officials to select a seasoned developer to participate in a new design plan. Settlement Housing Fund, formed in 1969, decided to compete to become the council's development partner. This move came at the urging of the fund's consultant and housing lawyer, Roger Schafer, who was my boss, although I was working exclusively for Settlement Housing Fund. Clara Fox, Settlement Housing's founder and executive director, made the final decision.

Roger kept telling Clara that she had to gain site control in key neighborhoods in order to achieve anything at all. Site control was everything. Clara would go on to quote that advice throughout her long career. Clara and Roger made a presentation to the Two Bridges board. At that time Settlement Housing Fund had access to a fund of $100,000, to be used for development seed money. Roger whispered to Clara that she should offer $35,000 to pay architects and engineers for new plans for the Two Bridges sites. Reluctantly, she did so.

Several private developers also competed to codevelop the sites with the council. Some had deep pockets and were looking for tax benefits. The outcome was uncertain.

Several months later the council selected Settlement Housing Fund as its development partner. The seed money plus Settlement Housing Fund's mission and professionalism carried the day. The game was on.

Martin Berger, the lawyer who represented Two Bridges, was a Lincolnesque figure. Marty rode around Greenwich Village on a bike and had at one time joined with Jane Jacobs to block the construction of a highway that would have bisected the neighborhood. He was part of the Village's liberal Democratic reform movement, and he wielded considerable political prestige. Together, he and Roger Schafer would craft a joint venture agreement that would set the project in motion.

In 1971 the Two Bridges Neighborhood Council and Settlement Housing Fund formed a new nonprofit organization called the Two Bridges Settlement Housing Corporation. Each group would appoint five board members, all of them members of the board of either the Two Bridges Neighborhood Council or the Settlement Housing Fund. An eleventh member would be officially "neutral." That member turned out to be Geoffrey Wiener, Jr., the son of one of the founders of Two Bridges. Both boards appointed diverse members as their representatives. The certificate of incorporation was approved by New York State on March 13, 1972.[3]

I came to the meetings of the joint board and thought it was taking way too long to work out the details of the certificate of incorporation and the bylaws. After all, we had housing to build. Both Settlement Housing Fund and the Two Bridges Neighborhood Council were slightly wary of one another. The Settlement Housing Fund Board members hoped that the council members would be practical and not too radical. The Two Bridges members thought that Settlement Housing Fund might be too tied to "the establishment." Happily, these tensions quickly disappeared.

One reason for this was that both groups shared a passionate commitment to ethnic and economic integration. The only issue I remember was a mild dispute between two Chinese board members, one whose family came from Hong Kong and the other from Communist China. After some initial nervousness, the two groups came to see eye to eye about everything for decades.

The Two Bridges Settlement Housing Corporation decided that the total urban renewal plan's goal would be to aim for a population that was 52 percent middle income and 48 percent low income. Reflecting the larger community, the ethnic makeup would be 30 percent Asian, 30 percent Latino, 20 percent African American, and 20 percent Caucasian.

The organization would sponsor developments on a redesigned site plan, using various federal programs as they became available at the time. The group would approve the designs, choose the builders and other professionals, and obtain government approvals. Edelman & Salzman (later the Edelman Partnership when Stanley Salzman left the firm) would be the architects for every site. Settlement Housing Fund's staff and consultants would figure out the financing and more. The Two Bridges Neighborhood Council would provide community programs. We did not believe that long-term ownership was necessary, mainly because of the tax considerations inherent to the financing requirements.

The two principals of the Edelman Partnership were Harold and Judith Edelman, a husband–and–wife team. Harold loved to draw. Judith, who taught at Columbia University, was both an architect and an advocate for planning. Harold and Judith would work with New York City housing and urban renewal agencies to create a new site plan that did not require a platform, which was preliminarily approved in 1966, with final approval in 1967.

3. Ibid.

14
Two Bridges Houses

The Two Bridges Settlement Housing Board decided to take advantage of the Great Society housing programs. During the 1970s, the city's housing agencies worked closely with the area office of the U.S. Department of Housing and Urban Development (HUD). City officials would decide about various urban renewal sites, the appropriate federal housing finance program for each, and the required next steps. After meeting with staff of the New York City Housing Authority and the City's Housing Development Administration, we decided to start with Site 7 at the northeast end of the Two Bridges Urban Renewal Area, consisting of four superblocks bounded by Clinton Street, Pike Slip, Cherry Street, and South Street. Because of available financing, the first site would be a public housing development. New York City public housing at the time won accolade after accolade in the press and among national and local housing professionals and advocates.

Because Two Bridges Settlement Housing Corporation wanted to participate as a developer, Site 7 would have to be a public housing "turn-key" development. Under that arrangement, we would join with a private contractor to build the project, using private financing. Then we would "turn the keys" over to the Housing Authority, the agency that still owns and operates the building.

The city's Department of Relocation would be in charge of relocating and demolishing the commercial properties that were on the site. As community representatives, we would be supportive, testifying before other agencies as needed. Relocation went relatively smoothly. The property owners were reasonably compensated. Then the empty structures were demolished so that a cleared and vacant site could be delivered to the developer. The Two Bridges Settlement Housing Corporation participated.

The Two Bridges Settlement Housing Fund board began its work by interviewing a number of potential contractor-developers. The staff and consultant then started to work with the architects and the selected contractor on a feasible design and would obtain the necessary community and government approvals. A fee, amounting to 2 percent of total development costs, would be shared by Two Bridges and Settlement Housing.

We chose the Raddock Organization initially, because of its access to private banking and because of a low cost estimate. Soon thereafter, M. Melnick & Co. became a partner, at the suggestion of the New York City Housing Authority's construction expert. Mike Melnick, coincidentally, was the contractor who had built the public elementary school that was adjacent to the site. He was known as a problem solver and had a good track record. Hal and Judy Edelman were pleased that Mike had joined the team.

The Two Bridges board insisted on construction jobs for local residents. The contractors agreed, on the condition that the workers were qualified. Vicki Amter, a member of the board, organized a successful local jobs program.

Working closely with the Housing Authority, the architects labored to produce a design that would meet the agency's standards. This involved a delicate balancing act. Several decades earlier, when the Housing Act of 1937 was first debated in Congress, real estate groups lobbied against it, claiming that socialism was lurking around the corner. The response was that housing for the poor would not be luxurious, to say the least. No doors on the closets, cement floors, and skip-stop elevators helped to keep the costs down and mollify the opponents. By the seventies, all that had changed. The changes were gradual. Robert Moses, champion of the superblock, believed that families needed light and air and livable apartments. Ira Robbins, a Housing Authority official, was an effective advocate. Both Robbins and Moses also believed that the buildings should be designed to last at least fifty years. They cared less about the exteriors. Moses's nemesis, Jane Jacobs, hated high-rises and hated Robert Moses. When John Lindsay became mayor in 1966, design became more important. Public housing in the later years of Robert Moses required full kitchens and larger rooms, compared to the standards of other government-assisted housing programs, including the Federal Housing Administration standards. Even though the Lindsay administration favored good design, cost constraints limited the overall design and building footprint. Federal regulations limited the per room costs of public housing. New York City had a budget line, HD 9, that added supplemental grants to allow feasible development.

Hal and Judy Edelman continued to work on the design, checking in with the builders, the Two Bridges Settlement Housing board, the city's Housing Development Administration, the Housing Authority, the City Planning Commission, and HUD. The approval process seemed to be going smoothly. We had a commitment to proceed.

And then everything stopped.

In 1970 the U.S. Congress passed the Environmental Protection Act. Although this was a significant accomplishment, enforcement caused problems in New York. HUD required environmental impact statements for all new projects. This could take a long time.

To help us move ahead, we hired Ethan Eldon Associates, an environmental consulting firm that was reasonably priced and had good references. The architects and the housing consultants had to provide what seemed like a lot of irrelevant information. We had to state, for example, that we would have no adverse effect on wildlife. However, during the process, it seemed that the project could be seriously endangered because it was located in a zone considered "absolutely" too noisy for public housing. This seemed silly, but we had to take the issue seriously.

We argued that every neighborhood in New York City was noisy. True, noise attenuation measures would be required, certainly in many areas of Manhattan. However, the Two Bridges Urban Renewal Area was adjacent to the East River Drive, an area where the decibel levels were so high that HUD ruled it would be inconceivable to allow residential development. Some of us thought that the argument was a subterfuge, a Nixonian dirty trick, using environmental concerns to block public housing. Still, we pored over the regulations.

One way to measure noise at the time was the "walk-away test." Two people would be involved. One person read poetry while the other walked backwards. The person walking backwards would stop as soon as it became impossible to hear the reader. Then the distance between the two people would be measured. I performed the experiment with my colleague Anne Lindgren. Our successful measurements did not convince the powers in charge that the area was sufficiently quiet. We hired Ostergaard Acoustical Associates to measure the noise.

Equally, if not more important, we alerted our elected officials, among them congressman Ed Koch and later congressman John Murphy. I also met with Charles Warren, head of the legislative staff for senator Jacob Javits. Chuck later became regional administrator of the Environmental Protection Administration, then counsel to the New York PBS station Channel 13, and today is considered one of the best environmental lawyers in the country. He became a great friend and has headed Settlement Housing Fund's board for over twenty-five years.

Many people thought that the noise regulations were ridiculous. If luxury buildings abutting the East River Drive on Sutton Place and East End Avenue thrived, how could anyone say that locations on the Lower East Side along the same road were too noisy for housing for poor people? I was able to persuade Cyril Harris, the acoustical expert retained by Lincoln Center, to write a letter stating that with the proper windows and other noise-attenuation measures our location could be acceptable.

In November 1972 Clara Fox submitted a guest article about all this to the *New York Times*, and it landed on front page of the real estate section. I had written it for her, and she thanked me profusely for "putting her on the map." Everyone at the different housing agencies and in the real estate community applauded her.

Senator Javits's staff members contacted the appropriate people at HUD. Congressman Murphy wrote a letter. Congressman Koch called others. The city and state officials pleaded with the local staff at the HUD area office. The Ostergaard sound report emphasized that double-glazed windows and either air conditioners or noise-reducing electric fans (called hush machines) could be installed at the units' front windows. No one would ever have to open a window. It would be possible to block the noise from the highway. We duly installed the air conditioners, which also helped the residents in the hot months of summer.

Noise attenuation measures were expensive, using up most of the project's construction contingency. Fortunately Mike Melnick, the contractor, had many ideas about how to save money. At first he suggested eliminating floors, thereby reducing the number of apartments from 250 to 225. Clara Fox wouldn't hear of it. Every apartment was urgently needed. The waiting list for public housing consisted of more than two hundred thousand families, all in need of shelter. That idea went by the wayside.

Then the contractors, along with construction experts at the Housing Authority, came up with another idea. The building would be occupied in two stages—first the lower floors, and then the upper ones. That allowed a favorable payment schedule while the interiors of the top floors

were being fitted out, painted, and completed. As it turned out, by following this schedule, the entire job was finished in fourteen months, well
ahead of its projected time frame of twenty months. Mike Melnick still remembers that he made more money in savings from interest and carrying
charges during construction than from his contractor's fee. After that experience, I always tried to have an incentive clause in construction contracts so that contractors could benefit from finishing early.

The Two Bridges board formed a committee to work with the Housing Authority to select tenants. We reached our goal of racial and ethnic
diversity, with Asian, Latino, African American, and Caucasian populations all included. Because until 1983 the income limits for public housing were 80 percent of the metropolitan area median income, there was
no concentration of extremely low-income tenants, although the income
mix was less diverse than we had planned.

Two Bridges Houses opened officially in 1975 on Clinton and South
Streets. It is a turnkey project operated by the New York City Housing
Authority. The twenty-six-story building provided 250 apartments in a
simple brick building.

At first there was an office for the Housing Authority Police headquarters located on the ground floor of the building. Then, in 1995, mayor
Rudy Giuliani merged the unit into the New York Police Department.
The police headquarters was replaced by a community center, eventually
to become a cornerstone branch of the Chinatown YMCA.

In order to learn more about the current residents of Two Bridges
Houses, I spoke to several people who had lived there for a number of
decades. The group included Norman Lee, who had been the vice president of the Two Bridges Houses tenants' association.

Norman lived at Two Bridges Houses from infancy through early adult-
hood. His father, a wealthy man in his native China, had lost his money
after the Communists came to power. He then moved to the United States.
Although poor, he managed to obtain two degrees, one from NYU and
the other from Fordham. He was a strong role model for his son, who
spent thirty-five years living in Two Bridges Houses.

As an adult, Norman decided to become active on the tenants' association board in deference to his father, who had been the president. Norman graduated from the University of Buffalo and is currently a national
sales manager for Fox TV in Chicago. He owns several properties. He and
his wife and three children had moved to Chicago for this job opportunity (though his wife also grew up in that area, which also influenced
their decision).

Figure 14.1. Two Bridges Houses. (Courtesy of Edelman Sultan Knox Wood.)

Norman said that Two Bridges was "a great place to raise a family," although he acknowledged that there had been problems. The population included what he described as good people, many of whom now have high-profile jobs, as well what he called "bad eggs." He felt that it was good to have a mix of incomes. The problems came from those who were not educated, as well as those who "did not try." Drugs remained an issue.

In the seventies, the effects of the recession were apparent. People had a hard time finding work. Then things got better. The building was kept well most years, but in some years the boiler broke down and repairs were slow. The tenants' association was active. Norman followed in his father's footsteps and was on the board for eleven years. Eventually his parents moved to Queens, but he stayed and raised his family at Two Bridges: "To me, Two Bridges was home."

He thinks that the YMCA on the ground floor is good for the area's young people. His daughter also took music lessons offered by the Two Bridges Neighborhood Council. Now that she is in Chicago she misses her music teacher.

When moving to Chicago, Norman told the manager at Two Bridges to keep the new air conditioner and the improvements he had made in the apartment. It was one more way to give back. He learned to care for his home and neighborhood at Two Bridges Houses. As he spoke, he seemed proud of his participation in the community. He said that he hoped young people would continue to create communities like Two Bridges.

In the meantime, I tried to make an appointment with Chi Yung, the director of the Two Bridges YMCA. I walked into the office and there he was, a young man with a phone in one hand and a mop in the other. The facility was very clean. The walls were painted bright yellow. A full range of programs were listed on the bulletin boards. Yung said that he needed permission from the district manager in order to grant an interview. I obtained that and we scheduled another meeting.

Because of a difficult schedule, he did not show up for that meeting, and I waited in front of the door for an hour. It turned out to be a good investment of my time. It was a beautiful day. I spoke to over a dozen tenants and to the superintendent as they went in and out of the building. I wandered inside and saw that the first floor and the elevators looked pretty good.

I spoke to Craig Rogers, who functions as the super. His job is to coordinate repairs and to assure that the halls are clean and that everything works. The Housing Authority has a central unit for heating issues, painting, and other large works. Craig confirmed that the residents of the building are still diverse—Asian, Latino, African American, Caucasian, and now even some Indian families. The residents who walked by confirmed the diversity. "We have everything," one of them remarked.

I also spoke to a young woman named Glenda, whose grandmother was born in Puerto Rico. She showed me a picture of her two children.

Figure 14.2. Tamar Lopez. (Courtesy of Tamar Lopez.)

She grew up in the building and now is the tenant of record. Her children go to the adjacent school, and her rent is affordable. She feels safe "most of the time." Her children participate in programs at the Y. They take Mandarin lessons in addition to speaking English and Spanish. I asked about the worst problem she deals with, and she told me that for a while there was no hot water. Another tenant, who did not give me her name, complained about the smell.

I had a longer interview with Tamar Lopez, a tall, attractive young woman whose business card identified her as an actress and model. As I entered the building, I noticed for the second time that the lobby and elevator were clean. There was a sophisticated intercom system, but one of the residents showed me how to buzz up to Tamar's apartment. She let me in, and I could see that she had been working at the computer on her desk. She explained that she had to go to a photo shoot later in the day. Tamar lives in a one-bedroom apartment that she shares with her mother. She moved there when she was five years old, eighteen years ago. Her mother, the tenant of record, has been on the waiting list for a two-bedroom unit for years, but there is little turnover and priorities for larger families. Tamar's mother had worked as a housekeeper but now is disabled.

Tamar said that the best thing about the apartment is the neighborhood, especially the mix of people. The worst thing is that there is still crime, although personally she feels safe. She is worried about gentrification and does not want to see displacement of existing residents. She also thinks that the management does not treat her mother with enough respect. Her mother did not benefit from a good education and struggles with English. Still, she still is dignified and deserves respect. According to Tamar, some of the managers need sensitivity training.

Repairs could be better. It takes a long time after leaving a ticket requesting repairs to get the work done. On some cold days there is not enough heat. From time to time there is no hot water.

Tamar said that when she was young she used the programs at the community center, which was there before the Y took over. She went to the after-school programs and on trips. Today she has no time for programs. Her acting career and modeling take up most of her time. She completed her undergraduate work and is now applying to graduate school. She wants to be a psychologist.

Tamar would not want to live anywhere else. "This is my home," she explained. She likes the diversity, the tenant patrol, her friends, the East River Park, events at the local Educational Alliance, and the Henry Street Settlement's Abrons Arts Center. She wants to live in this neighborhood for her whole life.

Everyone to whom I spoke seemed to be proud of the diversity.

Finally I returned to the Y to meet with Chi Yung. Yung and two assistants work full-time, and there are between eight and twelve part-time employees. He was working on a grant application but took time out to speak to me. He described the classes for all age groups. There are basketball tournaments, chess lessons, after-school programs, leadership development, computer classes, games, and more. Half of the classroom spots are reserved for residents, and the rest are open to the wider community. Adult classes include Mandarin, cooking, and salsa dancing. All classes are free. Chi Yung, who grew up in the community, seemed to take great pride in the programs.

Two Bridges Houses has provided clean, diverse, and affordable housing since 1975. Hopefully repairs will continue, and it is almost certain that the development will remain affordable.

15
Lands End I

While the public housing on Site 7 was under construction, we were also working on Site 6A. Frances Levenson, deputy commissioner of the Housing Development Administration in the 1970s, gave us the green light to start planning the so-called Mitchell-Lama/236 development. The Mitchell-Lama program, named after the late state senator MacNeil Mitchell and the late assemblyman Alfred Lama, provided bond financing with low interest rates, amortization periods of up to fifty years, and tax abatement in order to create middle-income housing. Developers were required to put up 5 percent of total development costs as an equity investment. Then, annual profits from rents were limited to 6 percent of that initial investment. Section 236 of the Housing Act of 1968 could be used to subsidize part or all of a development that was financed with state or city loans. The federal subsidies lowered interest rates to 1 percent. At the suggestion of clients of Roger Schafer, I approached Senator Javits's staff and the House Banking Committee staff to include three words in the 1969 Housing Act to allow part of a building to be subsidized instead of the entire project. I also helped to persuade lawmakers to draft an amendment that allowed Section 236 projects to include deep subsidies for up to 40 percent of the apartments in a building, a move intended to make these units affordable for families earning very low incomes. The original bill allowed such subsidies for only 20 percent of the apartments; the final version allowed a better mix of incomes.

The Two Bridges Settlement Housing Fund board approved the plan for Site 6A that would involve building a Mitchell-Lama development, assisted with federal 236 subsidies and deep subsidies for 40 percent of the units. Hal and Judy Edelman, our trusted architects, got right to work on the zoning analysis. The site would include 252 apartments, including studios and one-, two-, and three-bedroom units.

Deputy Commissioner Levenson had assembled a brilliant group of young people on her staff. The Two Bridges project was given priority status because of the community involvement and the success of the public housing turnkey development on Site 7. Relocation and demolition moved forward with some difficulty. Among the site tenants were owners of dilapidated commercial facilities, some of which were occupied by artists, who tried to protest. They were not legal tenants, but some nonetheless hired lawyers and tried to block demolition. They were not successful.

The environmental review process was easier than it had been on our first site. In fact, everything seemed amazingly smooth—until it wasn't.

Some of the HUD programs were in trouble, including Section 236. In many cities, public housing was mismanaged and politically unpopular, to say the least. Senator William Proxmire of Wisconsin, chairman of the Appropriations Committee, described all HUD programs as wasteful. He was shocked that it cost over $50,000 to build a two-bedroom apartment in New York City.

In January 1973 HUD secretary George Romney called for a moratorium on all new commitments for housing assistance. Shortly thereafter President Nixon reaffirmed the moratorium in his 1973 State of the Union address, announcing a study of federal housing programs to be released nine months later.

Right after the announcement, Clara Fox and I were summoned to a meeting at the city's housing agency. Private and nonprofit developers, state and local officials, and others assembled in a crowded meeting room to learn the horrifying details of the moratorium. I kept whispering to Clara that she should stand up to organize a committee to protest. She responded to the nudges, which led to the creation in 1973 of the New York Coalition to Save Housing, later the New York Housing Conference. Our New York groups made a lot of noise. Nixon was far from popular, and the moratorium seemed to embody "tricky Dick" at his worst. We organized busloads of advocates to travel to Washington, D.C., and a press conference was held on the Capitol steps, during which Senator Javits promised to save as many New York projects as possible. The Two Bridges Neighborhood Council organized a demonstration of placard-waving protesters on one of the empty lots in the urban renewal area.

New York officials kept negotiating with HUD. With the help of Senator Javits's staff, I was able to get a meeting with the deputy assistant secretary for housing production, Dan Kearney, who seemed much more sympathetic than I had expected. I remember sitting outside his office, waiting for our meeting to start, and listening to his secretary as she told people who called that "Mr. Kearney is out of the office." That experience encouraged a lifelong tendency to be persistent. I asked for an exception to the moratorium for four New York projects, one of which was Site 6A of the Two Bridges urban renewal area. All four eventually got built, each under a different pretext.

The one program the Nixon administration would not sacrifice was an initiative called Operation Breakthrough. This was an experimental program that promoted factory-built housing, which was seen as a way to save money. HUD Secretary Romney had been the president of American Motors, and then governor of Michigan (as well as father of presidential candidate Mitt), so an assembly-line-based housing solution appealed to him.

A few years earlier, at Montreal's Expo 67, I had seen a stunning housing development called Habitat by the architect Moshe Safdie. This was an almost sculptural project that made ingenious use of modular, factory-built apartment units. I started to dream about something similar for Two Bridges.

To learn more about factory-built housing, our team examined the work of a New Jersey organization called Shelley Systems that was building apartments using factory-constructed units. The city approved our plans for the site on June 21, 1973, specifying that we were to use, as the approval put it, "the Shelley System or something similar."

Although we weren't able to negotiate a price with Shelley Systems that satisfied HUD and the city officials, we found another system that met the Operation Breakthrough guidelines. A Westchester-based company manufactured panels that could be used for the facades of high-rise apartment buildings.

The company was controlled by the Starrett Corporation, a large New York City contractor owned by Paul and Seymour Milstein. Starrett's majority stockholder was National Kinney, the organization that owned parking facilities throughout the city. Starrett and National Kinney formed a partnership to work with us at Two Bridges.

Although the various parties distrusted one another, the Milsteins seemed to respect Clara Fox, who, with her articulateness and charisma, proved a strong negotiator. Harold Grabino, vice president of National Kinney, had the day-to-day responsibility for the development, although he was visibly skeptical about a partnership with nonprofit organizations that represented the community.

Grabino had a gruff personality that was not atypical of developers or contractors. When we explained that we required a fee for our work, he was far from pleased. I learned from an anonymous source that some of his own team members had problems working with him.

We met quite a few times. An active Two Bridges board member, Kai Liu, was at a key meeting. At the time Kai was a young lawyer, slight in stature and reluctant to speak up. Grabino, who was tall, loud, and domineering, seemed larger than life. He kept emphasizing the urgent need to protect National Kinney's investment. He repeatedly said that the surrounding area was such a mess, and that the main problem would be how to unload the property when the tax benefits expired seventeen years later.

To our astonishment, Kai Liu stood up, leaned over the table, and glared as he said, "Fuck National Kinney," and then quietly sat down. Grabino was appropriately silent. Eventually he gave in to our relatively modest demands.

In 1974 we signed an agreement to work with National Kinney on Site 6A, which became Lands End I, as well as on Site 5, the larger adjacent site. At that time the Two Bridges Settlement Housing board did not want to be permanent owners. We wanted to assure that the building got built according to our guidelines. We agreed to provide our expertise in development, to use our connections and goodwill to obtain HUD and city approval, to select the residents, and to stay involved with other community development activities. We did not want to be landlords. We had hoped that in seventeen years, when tax benefits expired, we could assume ownership or convert the building to a cooperative.

In those years developers were unpopular in many communities. We were accused of consorting with the enemy as we embarked on a co-venture with a private developer. We tried to explain that only such a co-venture would help provide the housing so desperately needed in the community. Although not everyone was persuaded by our arguments, today this is the rule rather than the exception.

The contract with National Kinney required weekly meetings during the development period. A plan was worked out under which the Edelman Partnership would be retained as architects, and National Kinney would pay all fees and other predevelopment costs. Although we continued to battle with Harold Grabino, the relationship improved. We even became friends with Grabino as he grew to respect our knowledge.

The total development cost was $11 million, or about $43,000 per unit for 252 apartments. Some of the fees were never received. However, this was still a good deal, helping our organizations to sustain themselves for years. One provision called for sharing the 6 percent return on equity. Harold Grabino had once told Clara Fox that as a landlord, he would make more money from losses than profits because of tax consequences. "Losses are good," he told Clara, and she never forgot. That was certainly true when marginal tax rates were 90 percent on the highest income groups. We did not pursue those funds for years, assuming there would be no cash flow. Years later our efforts were rebuffed. Tax rates went down, and cash flow became a good thing.

Still, we kept hearing that National Kinney would want to get rid of the project after seventeen years. However, the contract could not explicitly require a sale to Two Bridges. The tax laws stipulated that real estate deals could not be made for tax benefits alone. There had to be a genuine business investment, according to the "hobby rules." The contract included a provision that, "subject to the advice of tax counsel," the project would be sold to the tenants or a nonprofit organization formed for the benefit of the tenants. National Kinney and its successors supposedly would be obligated by the contract. That did not happen.

Construction started in 1975 and was complete by the end of 1977. The white panels and terraces above the third floor looked good and complied with the requirement to use prefabricated components. Vicki Amter, an active Two Bridges board member, worked to assure that residents from the neighborhood were hired as construction workers. In addition to caring about jobs, Vicky hated red brick, and at least for this development she was happy with the building's appearance.

Susan Cole, Settlement Housing Fund's marketing expert, oversaw tenant selection. She worked with a committee from Two Bridges, including Vicki Amter and Goldie Chu. Goldie was on the original Two Bridges education committee in 1958. She was passionately pro-integration and therefore did not want the building to become dominated by Chinese residents alone. She was also an early feminist. Goldie was a board member of Two Bridges Neighborhood Council and eventually joined the Board of Settlement Housing Fund. Later she would become the "neutral" member of the joint board. The committee achieved its goal: ethnic and economic diversity. Harold Grabino started to respect our work but continued to be sporadically gruff. He seemed to like Susan Cole, possibly because she could be equally gruff. Still, Grabino somehow convinced National Kinney that his brother-in-law should become the on-site manager.

Susan Cole was our asset manager as well as our tenant selection expert. Even though we were not owners, she regularly "walked" the building to assure that it was well maintained. Susan was not satisfied. She thought the brother-in-law was incompetent. The tenant files were a mess. The manager had no rapport with the residents. Susan sat down quietly with Grabino. Starrett had its own management company, Grenadier Realty Corporation. The president was Robert Rosenberg, an attorney who had been deputy commissioner of the city's housing agency. Bob passionately believed in integration. The Grenadier staff, which was both competent and integrated, included engineers, accountants, an insurance specialist, and a labor relations expert. Later they would add an energy maven who knew about green energy before the term was even invented. The executive vice president, Natalie Weinthal, watched every detail of management and maintenance. Grenadier could afford all this because the firm managed tens of thousands of apartments. Susan told Grabino to replace the brother-in-law with Grenadier. Amazingly, he listened.

Lands End I was formally dedicated on October 29, 1978, at a ceremony in which City Council president Carol Bellamy presented four tenants with gold keys. "The fact that this development was built," Bellamy said at the dedication, "is proof that a determined community effort, coupled with the support of private industry and government, can succeed even in the midst of a federal housing moratorium and serious city fiscal constraints." All the elected officials were there. The press release for the event noted that Lands End I was the final project to be financed under the city's Mitchell-Lama program.

As it turned out, during the decades that Grenadier was in charge of Lands End I, the company kept the building in great shape both physically and financially. The facade and some terraces were repaired, and the lobby was improved. Rents remained affordable.

All this was possible because of a favorable refinancing and because of large reserves that had been mandated by HUD and the city. National Kinney and its partners restructured the ownership entity. Starrett, and its management arm, Grenadier, were in control. Then there were additional refinancings and an exit from the Mitchell-Lama program.

A new, complicated group became the owner. This was Pembroke, an affiliate of DVL, a division of Blackacre, which was the real estate arm of a large conglomerate called Cerebus.

Because the Section 236 subsidy agreement for Lands End I would soon expire, Settlement Housing Fund assembled a team to try to buy the development. By that time we owned developments throughout New York, and the Two Bridges Neighborhood Council owned a housing development for the elderly. We had to sign a confidentiality agreement in order to make an offer. The principals at DVL were polite, but they refused our bid. They wanted to keep the building. "We do not like to sell," said Larry Cohen, one of the principal owners.

DVL exited the Mitchell–Lama 236 program in 2004. In response, the tenants organized and hired a lawyer. HUD provided what were called Section 8 "enhanced" vouchers at a higher than ordinary rent to protect the lower-income families. Existing tenants with higher incomes would be protected through a "landlords' assistance plan," essentially limiting annual rent increases. When apartments became vacant, rents could be increased to market-rate levels.

New elevators, windows, and other upgrades were promised. Part of the motivation, according to Peter Gray, one of the owners, was to attract market-rate tenants. The existing tenant leaders were nervous that the George W. Bush administration would not provide the vouchers. Luckily, the vouchers have remained in place. At least at first, the market-rate units were rented to young single people who, as roommates, shared the rent, which climbed to over $2,000 a month.

In February 2015 a large for-profit real estate group called CIM bought Lands End I, in partnership with L+M Development Partners and Nelson Management. The principal of L+M, Ron Moelis, had been a consultant for the tax equity financing of another site that Two Bridges Settlement Housing Corp., developed in 1997. (This time we retained ownership.) According to Peter Gray, also a principal of the seller, the price was over $100 million, or about $396,800 per apartment. The principals of L+M are committed to affordable housing. Eben Ellerston, director of acquisitions, told me that the new owners have signed a regulatory agreement requiring that half the apartments remain affordable for forty years. The other half can be rented at market rates as units become vacant. Real estate tax abatement was part of the deal.

However, a glitzy advertisement on the Nelson Management website in 2015 referred to the units in a way that sounded very much like the ads for new luxury developments. "Stunning river views, designer kitchens and baths, hardwood floors, dishwashers, a twenty-four-hour doorman, and a fitness center" were among the amenities listed. Plans for the future included a glass-enclosed deck, which will be a Wi-Fi lounge. There was no mention of affordability.

In 2015 I met with Ana Lam, who had worked as a manager for Grenadier, first for Two Bridges Tower and then for all the Two Bridges sites. When L+M Development Partners and Nelson Management bought the Two Bridges sites, their management subsidiary hired Ana to oversee Land

End I and II (the latter will be discussed in the next chapter). She confirmed that the Section 8 tenants were protected, as were the tenants whose incomes were too high (through a landlord assistance plan). In September 2015 the typical "landlord assistance" monthly rent for a one-bedroom unit was $1,027, for two bedrooms $1,164, and for three bedrooms $1,400. By contrast, the market-rate units rented for $4,100 for three bedrooms.

Hiring Ana was a smart move. Ana knows every tenant, and she said that many of them need help, especially with the paperwork. According to her, the Section 8 tenants and those with the landlord assistance plan pay their rent on time. She has more trouble with the market-rate tenants. The young people who share the apartments are the most difficult. Sometimes they fight with one another. Then they stop paying rent and leave, often owing a lot of money. Caesar Jines, who used to be superintendent at Lands End I, said that some of the market-rate tenants met those with subsidies and learned about Section 8. "Do you think we could get some of that?" they asked.

Had Two Bridges Settlement Housing Corp. retained ownership, all the units would have remained permanently affordable. Grenadier Realty maintained the buildings well for forty years, allowing the owners to make a huge amount of money when the developments were resold. I realize that private owners need incentives to create and sustain subsidized housing, and forty years is a good run. However, our group worked hard to make the building a reality. Forty years ago National Kinney staff members had been worried about their exit strategy. And although the neighborhood improvements benefit everyone, it seems a shame that our effort ended up enriching private developers.

Was Lands End I worth all the effort? Debbie Leung, who lived in the building from 1977 until 1998, would say yes. Debbie is a tenant advocate, working for the Two Bridges Neighborhood Council, but her office is at Hamilton Madison House, one of the settlement houses that joined forces to form the Two Bridges Neighborhood Council. She is also on the Two Bridges Settlement Housing board. She thinks that the area is much safer than it had been, and that it was never too bad in the first place. However, just a few people can cause great damage. She spoke of an unreported rape right outside the public housing building in the aftermath of Hurricane Sandy.

Debbie and her husband raised four children in a three-bedroom apartment at Lands End I. Until her husband finished school and got a good job, she was the main wage earner.

Figure 15.1. Debbie Leung. (Courtesy of Debbie Leung.)

The building, she said, was always clean, safe, and in good repair. But what pleased her the most was the value. The initial rent was only $300 a month. The building was near her job. Her children did well at the local schools, and they all graduated from college and now support themselves. Eventually Debbie's parents moved to Lands End II, the building next door. Asked to name the worst thing about the building, she shrugged and said, "Really nothing."

Debbie and her family, who are Chinese, were able to save their money, and they bought a house in Queens in 1998. But she returns to the neighborhood for her job and for her volunteer work at Two Bridges. After Hurricane Sandy, Debbie came back to Lands End I to see if everyone was safe and to find out what was needed.

During that visit she knocked on the door of the apartment where she had lived for twenty-one years. The new tenant, a white woman, was friendly. Eventually, Debbie asked about the rent. To her astonishment, she was told that the rent was over $3,500 a month.

About 70 percent of the building's residents still benefit from Section 8 or the landlord assistance plan. Their rent is relatively low for now. However, the rent for up to half the units will rise to market rate once they become vacant. Debbie estimates that most of the market-rate tenants today are white.

Lands End I benefits from a strong tenants' association, headed by Aaron Gonzales. His wife, Daisy Echevarria, is active and had been a former chairperson.

Both Aaron and Daisy have good careers. He is a mechanic for the Metropolitan Transportation Authority and takes great pride in his ability to repair things. She is a lawyer. The couple were responsible for enlisting the support of elected officials to protect the residents of Lands End I when the owners left the Mitchell-Lama program. Council member Margaret Chin, who represents the area, negotiated the plan under which half the building would remain affordable for forty years, in contrast to the original thirty years originally proposed. Aaron and Daisy also represent Lands End I in an organization called TUFFLES (Tenants United, Fighting for Lower East Side), whose goal is to preserve the neighborhood and keep it affordable.

Aaron and Daisy have lived at Lands End I for over thirty years. They had both grown up in public housing and remember destructive tenants, drugs, shootings, and dirty diapers thrown out of windows.

For them Lands End I was a significant step up. The apartments were attractive and the buildings clean. The neighbors, representing different ethnicities and income groups, respect one another. Friendships have developed and endured. Their apartment is immaculate and beautifully decorated.

Security at Lands End I has always been good, they said, and repairs are made promptly. However, the plumbing has caused some problems. Aaron and Daisy believe that the washing machines in the laundry room are horrible. They were generally positive about the new owners and have met with the principals several times. They tell me that the new owners are responsive and respectful.

Many of the market-rate tenants have joined the tenants' association. Some, but not all, are good neighbors. Still, Aaron and Daisy have mixed feelings about the market-rate conversion and about gentrification on the Lower East Side. They are sad that 50 percent of the apartments will no longer be affordable.

Similarly, gentrification on the Lower East Side had its pluses and minuses. It's nice to have amenities, new stores, and upscale restaurants. Security will inevitably improve because of new people with resources. Things would be better if there were more police in the neighborhood. Aaron and Daisy have met with the officers at the local precinct, who are cooperative but often limited in how much they can do. Like most of the residents of Two Bridges sites, Aaron and Daisy are incensed about losing the local Pathmark supermarket (discussed in Chapter 17).

One of the best things about the new management is that they kept Ana Lam on as site manager. One of the worst things about the arrangement was that some tenants could not afford the new rent. Ana intervened positively for a frail tenant named Betty, whose voucher did not allow an increase in her subsidy. With Ana's help, Betty successfully moved to the building next store, Lands End II.

Residents at Two Bridges Tower at 82 Rutgers Slip are also part of TUFFLES. Aaron and Daisy hear about problems at "82" and have concerns. However, they think the community programs there are very good.

They also thought that the Two Bridges Neighborhood Council and Settlement Housing Fund had not worked hard enough to stop the sale of the Pathmark to Extell Development and to prevent Lands End I from losing affordability for half the apartments. "Why did you sign that gag order?" they asked me, referring to our attempt to purchase the building. I did my best to explain that I could not negotiate to buy the building unless I signed. We all agreed that sometimes we have to compromise.

Aaron and Daisy are passionate about making the Two Bridges area a great, inclusive environment for everyone. Much of the success of Lands End I can be attributed to the residents.

16
Lands End II

As Lands End I was nearing completion in 1977, we started the serious planning process for Lands End II, which would be built on Site 5 of the urban renewal area. Lands End II would become the first newly constructed Section 8 project for families in New York City.

True to the promises made by President Nixon and HUD Secretary Romney in March 1973, HUD released its recommendations late in the fall of 1973. By then James Lynn had replaced George Romney as HUD secretary.

At an early briefing on the program in Washington, D.C., Secretary Lynn described the new Section 8 rental program that would replace both public housing and the Section 236 interest rate subsidy program. The Housing Act of 1937 would be amended to provide a flexible rental program, allowing private developers, nonprofits, and in some cases local housing agencies to participate as owners. The program would provide funds to local housing agencies that could be used as rent subsidies in existing private housing. Section 8 Housing Assistance Payments Contracts could also be pledged to secure private financing for new or renovated buildings. Fair Market Rents would be established for metropolitan areas throughout the country. There would be one level of rents for new buildings and another for existing housing. Tenants would pay 15 to 25 (today 30) percent of their income for rent. HUD would pay the difference between the rent needed to operate the building (including debt service on the mortgage) and the tenant's payment.

I had been invited to the briefing, during which I asked whether the Fair Market Rents would be high enough to cover the true cost of op-

Figure 16.1. Lands End I and II. (Courtesy of Edelman Sultan Knox Wood.)

erations. The answer was affirmative. One of the problems with the 236 program was that the subsidies weren't deep enough to reach the rents that the eligible tenants could afford.

I came back to New York as a true believer. I told Clara Fox, our executive director, that to my amazement the Nixon program was great. She threw me out of her office.

Eventually I was able to convince her and others that the program was not only feasible, but worth supporting. She became a staunch advocate.

Although the legislation passed in 1974, it took time for HUD to publish regulations. Then HUD had to establish Fair Market Rents, based on local surveys and indices. The first Section 8 allocations were used for existing housing and for recently completed new housing.

The city's housing staff and the staff at the local HUD office decided that the first new Section 8 buildings should be built on the remaining urban renewal sites. The development team for Site 5 of the Two Bridges urban renewal area was the first team to make a proposal for a Section 8 contract that would finance newly constructed family housing.

Our proposal called for 490 apartments in two twenty-six-story brick and concrete buildings, with open space and parking between the buildings.

The development would be financed with a loan insured by the Federal Housing Administration (FHA) pursuant to Section 220 of the National Housing Act of 1949. The statute authorizing most FHA-insured loans mandated mortgage limits for various sized apartments that were too low to work in New York City. Construction costs in New York have always been high. However, through the efforts of Senator Javits, the act was amended to establish higher limits in "high-cost areas."

We used a few additional tricks to increase the amount of the mortgage that could be insured. For example, HUD allowed a dining alcove to be counted as a bedroom. As a result, a two-bedroom unit with a dining alcove would have the same mortgage limit as a full three-bedroom unit. The dining area was called an "other habitable room" (OHR in FHA-speak). The Section 220 insurance program was available only in urban renewal areas and had a higher per-unit mortgage limit than did the other programs. The program also had a more generous allocation of costs for nonresidential uses than did other programs, allowing an additional increase in the mortgage.

In housing development, at first it always seems that construction and operating costs are too high to qualify for a government program's parameters. One goes through several estimates, shaving off this and that, and somehow an absolutely unfeasible budget becomes one that miraculously works. It should not have to be so tricky. Over the years, however, developing a workable project has become harder and harder. Today things are much more complex and difficult than had been the case in the late seventies.

For Lands End II, Section 220, with the "other habitable rooms" and the allowance for commercial and office spaces, was feasible. Or so we thought.

After HUD made its commitment, the attorneys in Washington noticed a provision in Section 220 that required conformance to a comprehensive "workable program" as part of an urban renewal plan. However, the Housing Act of 1974 replaced the urban renewal program with Community Development Block Grants. So it would seem that the "workable program" provision would be moot. The HUD counsel disagreed. I called Chuck Warren, Javits's legislative chief, in a panic. I did not think he actually heard my request. Ten days later he called, saying that he could tag a clause on another bill that was coming to the Senate floor within a few days. The new clause would simply eliminate the Section 220 "workable program" requirement. It went through Congress and was signed into law. At that time it was sometimes easier to enact a technical amendment in Congress than to get the HUD counsel to change his mind. Nevertheless, when I called the New York HUD counsel he was pleased. He said he was about to cancel twenty-five commitments for Section 220 insurance, including Lands End II. Whew . . .

Once again, Two Bridges Settlement Housing Corp. had to make a deal with National Kinney and Starrett. It was easier to agree on a fee structure this time around. The developers continued to respect our expertise. I recommended Huntoon Paige as the mortgage lender, and the team was happy to have them. The loan officer, Lee Goodwin, had been an excellent state housing commissioner in the Rockefeller administration. We also brought in an investment company, the National Housing Partnership Corporation, a national organization that had formed to provide equity for public-private partnerships.

The Settlement Housing Fund staff members were rather shocked at the cost: $30 million, or about $60,000 per apartment. This seems minuscule today, but the government agencies gave our partners a lot of grief. Furthermore, the developers insisted that rents would be set at the maximum that HUD would allow, $643 a month for a two-bedroom apartment. Although it seems more than reasonable now, we thought that was excessive at the time. However, the state law that provided real estate tax exemption limited the profit that could come from rents. Setting the rents at a "high" level meant that it would be possible to accumulate reserves for repairs, which could prove useful as time went on.

We obtained the approval of the community board and the city agencies relatively easily. HUD approved the proposal and issued commitment letters for mortgage insurance. The project was completed in 1979. By then Settlement Housing Fund, the Two Bridges Neighborhood Council, and the managing agent, Grenadier Realty, had established a great relationship. We jointly selected the tenants, adhering to our diversity goals of 30 percent Asian, 30 percent Latino, 20 percent African American, and 20 percent Caucasian.

We also wanted economic diversity. Until 1983, tenants earning up to 80 percent of area median income were eligible for the Section 8 program; 30 percent of the apartments in each locality had to be reserved for tenants earning less than 50 percent of median income of the metropolitan area. Usually that happened through the Section 8 voucher program for older housing. The secretary of HUD could establish waivers to allow higher or lower income limits in high-cost areas or in areas where incomes were very low. However, the secretary did not make it easy to obtain waivers. We went to the HUD secretary, cited the urban renewal plan for diversity, and obtained the waiver. Up to 10 percent of the tenants could earn up to 110 percent of the median income of the metropolitan area. That was quite a coup.

The Two Bridges Neighborhood Council, Susan Cole, and Grenadier Realty, the managing agent, worked very hard to select the tenants. The process involved office interviews, credit checks, and home visits. At the same time, National Kinney and Starrett were pressuring us to fill the units quickly. There were thousands of applicants for the 490 apartments. The job got done, although it is never easy.

Sheila Hart, cochair of the Lands End II tenants' association, remembers her own home visit. She was fourteen in December of 1979, when she moved into Lands End II. It was two weeks before Christmas. She had been living with her mother on West 156th Street. Her brother was working at Gouverneur Hospital, which was near the Two Bridges site. When he saw the buildings under construction, he urged his mother to apply for an apartment.

The woman who conducted the home visit was impressed because Sheila's apartment was clean, although there were three large, noisy dogs living in the unit immediately above. Even worse, no one walked the dogs. They would urinate into the pipes, which spilled into the apartment where Sheila and her mother were living. The smell was terrible. Sheila's mother recounted this tale of woe to the home visitor. To their delight, they were accepted as tenants at Lands End II.

Sheila Hart, who is African American, is busy as the cochair of the tenants' association. She helps management in coordinating repair schedules, assuring that someone will either be home or leave a key. She does not want to see cases in which contractors cannot get access to apartments to make important repairs. The Asian tenants are good about attending meetings, but sometimes they do not want to speak up, even if their units need work. Sheila tries to help them.

Until recently she had worked as a police officer, assigned to a hospital. What Sheila likes best is that the buildings are kept clean and in excellent repair. She feels safe there. I pressed her to say what she thought could be improved. Reluctantly, she said that that heat could be turned up a little. She said that the new owners reach out to the tenants. They are always available to discuss issues. They even provided backpacks and school supplies for the children. And, "Ana Lam, the on-site manager, goes overboard—she is so helpful to everyone."

Sheila is happy to live in a diverse building. She said that during Hurricane Sandy, everyone came together. She and her cochair met with the

Lands End I tenants' association, and management was able to get portable generators quickly.

At first Sheila and her mother lived in a two-bedroom apartment. After her children were born, the family was able to transfer to a three-bedroom unit. Her son is now in college and working, living on his own. Therefore she transferred back to a two-bedroom unit. When I visited her, the apartment was immaculate and nicely furnished.

I asked her about the Two Bridges Neighborhood Council. She said, "You mean Victor Papa?" She started to laugh. "Sure, I know Victor." The Lands End II tenants joined in the kite festival and other programs. Her daughter liked the science, technology, engineering, and math classes. She had nice things to say about the teacher, Roxie. However, she said hesitantly that she wishes the program were at Lands End II, not at "82," meaning 82 Rutgers Slip, where the last site was built. She thinks that some of the some of the young people there are "a little too rough."

She is enthusiastic about living at Lands End II. She was glad her mother was accepted, which allowed her to live most of her life in the development. Everyone in management treats the tenants respectfully. She hopes that her children will raise their families there as well. She keeps telling them that they should stay in the building, although sometimes they groan. Sheila is happy that the new owners have made a forty-year commitment to keep the Section 8 program. She gives credit for the arrangement to City Council member Margaret Chin. Sheila said she is glad that the building will still be affordable, "not for the rich and famous."

Tanya Castro is the tenants' association cochair for community relations. She is also head of the local PTA. Her grandmother was the third tenant to move into Lands End II. Tanya was three at the time. There was a fire in the building where her family had been living. It was the days of slumlords on the Lower East Side, especially in the area around Avenues A, B, C, and D known as Alphabet City. Several adjoining buildings were burned to the ground. Tanya's family was forced to live in a shelter after the fire. They applied to Lands End II and made it through the tenant selection process.

Tanya has lived at Lands End II for thirty-five years. Residents of the building became close friends. Neighbors would take care of one another. One parent would provide childcare when others were working.

Her five children, two of whom are now in college, enjoyed the access to local parks, playgrounds, and basketball courts. Tanya also liked the small grocery store on the first floor of the building. The owner would extend credit, offered discounts to local residents, and even gave away food rather that see anything spoil.

But it was the neighbors whom she really liked best and still does. "We are all family," she says.

She thinks that Ana Lam is a great manager. And so far there are no complaints about the new superintendent. However, some of the porters do not work hard enough. Maintenance could be better. Sometimes things are patched over when they should be replaced.

I asked about the worst things at Lands End II. She said that it was terrible when people had to be evicted. She was concerned about some of the older residents who forgot to pay or were having a hard time stretching their social security payments to make ends meet. She understood the need to make timely rent payments.

Tanya's job as cochair involves community outreach. She has worked with the tenant leaders at the other sites in the Two Bridges area. She is actively working to improve local schools, some of which are in poor shape. Shootings and robberies have occurred on the surrounding streets, and she is concerned about safety in the neighborhood. Sometimes she feels safe only in her own development, where security is good. She has positive relations with the local police precinct, but there is not enough law enforcement presence.

Tanya is a leader of the group that wants to preserve opportunities for lower-income families in a gentrifying neighborhood. She was sad to see the demolition of the Pathmark supermarket (discussed in Chapter 17). Section 8 is essential for affordability. However, many residents have increased their earnings, and sometimes the new rent is a burden.

Luckily for tenants with modest incomes, over the years none of the owners of Lands End II ever tried to leave the Section 8 program, although there were refinancings and changes in the ownership entities, each time bringing profits to the owners and sometimes improvements to the buildings. Starrett bought most of the general partnership interest from National Kinney. A company called Aimco bought the limited partnership interest from the National Corporation for Housing Partnerships. In the late nineties DVL became the next owner. The relationships were not always warm and cozy.

In 2014 DVL sold their interest to L+M Development Partners, one of the city's largest developers of affordable housing, who now have a majority interest in the project. L+M principals confirmed that the building would not be converted to luxury apartments. The city required a twenty-year commitment to affordability for the project. Then, City Council member Margaret Chin asked for a forty-year pledge, and L+M agreed. The city's housing agency administers the Section 8 agreement, adjusting the rents every five years to reflect changes in operating costs and debt service. As part of the new arrangement, real estate taxes were cut in half.

The commitment to forty years of affordability is a great achievement. However, I almost fell out of my chair when I learned that the purchase price was $279 million, over $569,000 per apartment. No wonder DVL agreed to sell. According to Eben Ellerston of L+M, the financing came from private equity. The city did not use its limited bond authority to finance the acquisition. There were no tax credit investors, making management and regulatory compliance easier. L+M will probably build another development on the parking lot. At least 30 percent of the units will be affordable, maybe more. The principals at L+M, which is an employee-owned corporation, have confirmed that the building will not be converted to luxury apartments.

In the lobby at Lands End II, a security guard sits at a desk and asks visitors to sign in. The lobby is spotless, the elevators look new, and the halls are perfectly painted. Lands End II looks like a new building, not one that is thirty-six years old. Ana Lam, the on-site manager, has her office on the first floor. She is enthusiastic about the new ownership arrangement, even though she remains loyal to Grenadier Realty, where she had worked for fifteen years. "Everyone gets along very well," she said about the change in ownership.

She has a great relationship with the tenants. According to Ana, most have very low incomes, and many original tenants are now senior citizens. Some of the Asian tenants have trouble filling out the necessary paperwork. She is able to find translators as needed.

Overall, she said that the tenants are great. It is rare to hear managers who actually praise tenants. Nearly all residents pay their rent on time. The only complaint occurs when someone's music is too loud. She remembers only one court case for nonpayment of rent in the last ten years, and now the tenant pays on time.

As we were talking, Caesar Jines, the superintendent, came by. Caesar has worked at Two Bridges for decades, at both Lands End I and Lands End II. He started as a porter before advancing to handyman and then superintendent. In my opinion, the superintendent is the person determining the success or failure of a property. I asked him about problems, and he had to think a while. He suspects that some of the older Asian tenants might rent out rooms illegally. However, the new rules require that tenants transfer to smaller apartments when family members leave. Both Ana and Caesar confirmed that the families are upset that the adjacent supermarket has been demolished.

Ana, Caesar, and I took the elevator to the roof. It was a beautiful, sunny day. We could see the Lower Manhattan skyline, the Williamsburg, Manhattan, and Brooklyn Bridges, and the East River shining in the sunlight. I walked around and looked at all the Two Bridges sites. Then I saw the demolished supermarket site and became less happy. Each of the sites had their struggles during development. But I felt good knowing that Lands End II will remain affordable, at least for the next forty years.

17
The Pathmark

At almost every board meeting of the Two Bridges Settlement Housing Corp., we heard complaints about the lack of local stores. Board members of the Two Bridges Neighborhood Council who lived in the neighborhood invariably mentioned the lack of supermarkets within walking distance. There was a Sloan's supermarket about a mile away, but it was dirty and expensive. The co-op market was not conveniently located and offered little variety in food products. There would be a convenience store in Lands End II, but it would be small.

In response to these complaints, in the early eighties board members of the Two Bridges Neighborhood Council formed a subcommittee to see whether a supermarket could be included as part of the urban renewal area. Goldie Chu was the chair, Vicki Amter was a member, and the Two Bridges staff member, Larry Silver provided support. The committee members drove around the five boroughs, Long Island, and Westchester, visiting all the supermarkets. They determined that Pathmark offered the best prices and the greatest variety, including ethnic food. Furthermore, all the Pathmark supermarkets that they visited were clean.

When the committee reported back to the Two Bridges Settlement Housing board, I mentioned that my uncle, Louis Rosenberg, was a builder-developer who works exclusively with Pathmark in the five boroughs. He was always ready to sing at our family dinners, a wedding, or a bar mitzvah. I knew he could put over a song, but I had no idea whether he was a good builder or whether he would work well with community groups. I was aware that he lost patience with the City Planning Commission when he needed a zoning variance or other kinds of approvals. I hesitated but then told the group about him.

Board members suggested inviting Lou to a meeting. They did so, and he agreed to explore the possibility of building a supermarket. He had just completed a Pathmark in the Bronx near Co-op City and a Key Food supermarket in in the Greenpoint area of Brooklyn. He said he would contact the president and vice president of Pathmark. Everyone was enthusiastic, especially Clara Fox.

In the late sixties Lou had built the very first Pathmark, on Albany Avenue in Flatbush, Brooklyn. His son still owns the property, although it is now a Key Food, soon to become a Food Town. According to his son, Lou never liked to sell anything. He thought his properties would all increase in value.

Lou told the group that Pathmark could not build a small store. They needed scale. We had to find a site that measured at least forty-five thousand square feet. Parking would be essential to make the supermarket profitable.

The only available remaining large site in the Two Bridges urban renewal area was Site 8, which had been designated as a park. Local residents thought there were enough parks along the river. However, once land is designated as a park in New York, it takes state legislation to change the use. To our surprise, however, that was relatively easy to accomplish.

Settlement Housing Fund had a good relationship with the city's housing agency. When the agency staff wanted to create the first community gardens in the late seventies, they had no budget authority to pay for insurance. It was the era of fiscal crisis. Nonetheless, Clara Fox found a grant to cover the cost, about $30,000.

Clara called Barry Zelikson, the deputy commissioner of the Department of Housing, Preservation, and Development. Zelikson thought the supermarket was a great idea. The department was about to submit its legislative package to the state. The new designation of Site 8 as a supermarket was included in the package. We met with the late senator Roy Goodman, a Republican who cared about community development. The legislation passed easily.

Lou Rosenberg and Arnold Pearl, the vice president of Pathmark, drove around the neighborhood. They liked what they saw. Multifamily housing developments abounded in the immediate area. The tenants were all potential customers. The two men confirmed what the community members had complained about. There was no decent place to shop. They figured that there would be a lot of people who would walk to the site. In addition, the location adjacent to the East River Drive would be convenient to people who would drive from Brooklyn or other parts of Manhattan. When city officials asked to see Pathmark's market study, Lou described how their drive-by observations precluded the need to hire market consultants. "First comes the drive, and then the hand shake" was Lou's mantra. He hated spending money on consultants, studies, lawyers, and complicated leases.

The city's appraiser determined that the forty-five-thousand-square-foot site was worth $1.62 million. Through urban renewal write-downs, city officials could reduce the price to $6 dollars a square foot, or $270,000. Lou and his partners agreed right away to pay that price. Buying urban renewal land from the city was a difficult process. However, the city mothers and fathers in the later years of the Koch administration learned that selling land at attractive rates resulted in buildings that would thrive. The bargain paid off in the long run. This benevolent practice went out of fashion and came back in again with most administrations. At first a new administration wants a lot of money for land. Then they come to their senses. If a lot of money is charged for land, other subsidies are needed to make development feasible.

Marty Berger, the Two Bridges Settlement Housing Fund attorney, negotiated a joint venture agreement with Sherilu Construction (named for my Aunt Sherry and my Uncle Lou). The Edelman Partnership would prepare a site plan, and Sherilu would build to Pathmark's specifications. The team would also include Lou's partner, the contractor Sam Feinerman. He was somewhat gruff but good at handling negotiations.

Pathmark would sign a forty-nine-year lease with Sherilu, which would eventually form another company to own the property. Sherilu would employ qualified community residents during construction, and Pathmark promised two hundred permanent jobs for the community.

Neither Settlement Housing Fund nor Two Bridges Neighborhood Council wanted to own the property or participate in running the store. That was not our area of expertise. Our job was to win approval from the local community board, the Planning Commission, and the Board of Estimate. We would receive a development fee of $200,000 when construction began. As usual, Two Bridges and Settlement Housing would split the fee, fifty-fifty.

As it turned out, Independence Saving Bank provided a construction loan. The bank was a member of the Federal Home Loan Bank of New York, and I was a member of the Community Advisory Committee. The Home Loan Bank had a new initiative, the Community Improvement Program, that was used to provide loans to member banks, which in turn would offer ten-year mortgages for commercial establishments in lower-income neighborhoods. That was a good fit for a row of small stores, eventually to be constructed on an adjacent site, and would benefit the Home Loan Bank's portfolio.

On August 6, 1981, an affiliate corporation, Cherry-Pike, signed the lease as landlord with Supermarkets General Corporation, the company that owned Pathmark, as tenant. The lease was forty-seven pages long, plus exhibits. A developer of commercial properties can access financing much more easily when a signed lease is in place before construction starts. Rent payments would start when the supermarket was open for business. The landlord would need to provide a temporary certificate of occupancy before receiving rent. The term was twenty-five years, but the tenant had options to renew every five years, providing an additional thirty years before the need to negotiate a new lease. The rent would be a flat amount of $478,640 a year for the first twelve and a half years ($10 per square foot). Rent would increase to $512,145 for the next twelve years. Rent would increase again by 10 percent each time the tenant exercised its option. At the time of the lease, Lou had expected the interest rate to be 14 percent. The lease allowed for adjustments if interest was higher or lower than the 14 percent projection. Pathmark had the right to sublease or assign the lease to a third party.

Pathmark would specify its preferred layout, and the Edelman Partnership would create the exterior design and handle the engineering. The tenant would need to approve. There would be underground parking and a parking lot. The building would cost $2.3 million, or $50 per square foot.

The lease required close collaboration between Lou Rosenberg's team and Pathmark. There would be weekly meetings during construction with both parties. Pathmark had to approve the prime subcontractors. Mutual sign-offs were required at various stages of construction. Luckily the parties trusted one another and had a long history of working together. There can be so much tension during construction that it is key for all the team members to get along internally.

The lease satisfied the lender.

The next hurdle was negotiating the city's Uniform Land Use Review Procedure, the infamous ULURP process. Numerous steps are required. First a developer or city agency submits a proposal to the City Planning Commission, which determines whether the proposal is complete. This should take weeks, maybe months, but it often takes years, especially if there are environmental issues in contention. Once "completeness" is determined, the proposal goes to the local community board, which has sixty days to consider it.

Next comes a formal hearing at the City Planning Commission, again taking place sixty days after the community board vote. In 1981, the final approval was that of the Board of Estimate. Today, in 2017, the mayor approves such matters, followed by the City Council. The fastest ULURP review in my experience took six months, when the political support was alive and well. Most of the time it takes a year or two. Controversial projects can take what seems like forever.

Despite all the community support, the Pathmark became controversial. A lobbyist named Richard Lipsky organized some of the owners of small stores to protest the sale of the site to the Pathmark developers, which generated negative publicity. Clara Fox and I went to see Howard Rubenstein, the powerful publicist whom Lipsky had hired to oppose the Pathmark. We told him about the Two Bridges partnership with Pathmark and explained the store's importance to the urban renewal effort. Rubenstein dropped Lipsky as a client and disassociated himself from the anti–Pathmark campaign. (Decades later Lipsky was convicted of bribing a New York State senator.)

As for any possible negative impact on the small stores, the supermarket's supporters argued that just the opposite would be the case. They and others predicted that the small stores would prosper as a result of the new supermarket. The explanation was that shoppers who make a large purchase at Pathmark but forget to buy one last item then will go to a small store to get it.

We advocated aggressively for the Pathmark, first with the Planning Commission staff. The initial review by City Planning staff was difficult. We had a coach inside the Planning Department staff, Marcy Anhouse. She liked affordable housing and community development. She would tell us the exact language to use in our requests, and we would follow blindly. It always worked. I was not happy the day she retired.

Then we testified before the local community board, the Planning Commission, and the Board of Estimate in favor, while Mr. Lipsky and his group protested. At first the Planning Commission objected to the parking. However, Pathmark insisted that the parking was key to its operations, and the commission gave its approval, parking and all. The developer, Louis Rosenberg, said that he could not have succeeded without the support of the Two Bridges Neighborhood Council and Settlement Housing Fund. We were fortunate that the Planning Commission saw the light. The local community board and the Board of Estimate approved the proposal as well. The opposition persisted even after construction started and claimed that there was a technical issue with ULURP relating to the parking. Once again, Marcy Anhouse figured out a way around the issue and a minor change was approved, making everything comply with zoning rules.

Construction proceeded smoothly. Some two hundred local residents were hired, as promised. The building was completed on time and opened to great fanfare in 1983. Two Bridges residents were delighted to have an affordable place to shop. As the years went on, city employees shopped there as well because of the supermarket's proximity to City Hall. Pathmark made money, and Lou Rosenberg was happy with the outcome. For thirty years, the Two Bridges neighborhood had an excellent supermarket.

Only recently did we come to regret that we did not have an ownership interest in the property. We also came to regret that the lease allowed Pathmark to sell or sublet. In 2000 Pathmark sold its lease to A&P, another large supermarket chain. Operations seemed to continue under the Pathmark name. There were secrets, bankruptcies, litigation, and more. It was hard to get information.

Louis Rosenberg had died in 1998, but his son, Michael, remained active in his father's properties. In 2004 Sam Feinerman, now Michael's partner, called and asked, "Are you sitting down?" As it turned out, a group of three partners offered to buy the supermarket building and the lease on an adjacent row of small stores. They were willing to pay $7.5 million for the small stores and many millions more for the supermarket building. Michael was flabbergasted.

Because Two Bridges Settlement Housing Corp. owned the small stores, our approval was needed for the sale of the leasehold. We agreed, subject to approving any subtenants.

A few years later, Extell Development, a huge Manhattan developer, entered the scene and bought A&P's lease for $87 million. Because city approval was required, litigation dragged on for years. The supermarket was still in business, but we were worried. The urban renewal plan expired in 2007.

Then came the economic crash in 2008. The various parties fought with one another endlessly, and nothing seemed to be happening. Years went by, but the supermarket was still in business.

Protests were mounting. It all seemed wonderfully ironic that there were protests against building the Pathmark in the 1980s, and then there were protests about its closing, starting in 2007. Pathmark had become very popular in the community and all over Lower Manhattan.

In October 2012, a letter was sent to Sam Martin, the head of A&P, and to Roy Schoenberg, one of the partners who had bought the supermarket. The letter, signed by assemblyman Sheldon Silver, state senator Daniel Squadron, Manhattan borough president Scott Stringer, and City Council member Margaret Chin, read as follows:

> We are writing to you to express our deep concern about the planned closure of the Pathmark store at 227 Cherry Street on the Lower East Side of Manhattan. As the elected officials who represent this area, we know that Pathmark plays a crucial role in the lives of thousands of residents of this neighborhood, many of whom are elderly and low income.
>
> The Lower East Side community is already underserved when it comes to full-service supermarkets offering fresh, affordable food. Our constituents would face a significant burden if they lost a grocery store in this location, which is the only affordable food option within a reasonable distance. . . .
>
> If there is to be a new development at 227 Cherry Street, it is imperative that it include a low-cost, full-service supermarket of comparable size to the current Pathmark. Further, we ask that Pathmark's closure be postponed until such a development is shovel-ready to prevent the unnecessary creation of a food desert.

In 2013 Schoenberg and his partners sold the property to Extell, and the store was closed soon thereafter. The Two Bridges Neighborhood Council had no legal means to prevent demolition. The only thing the council could do was publish a grocery guide listing local bodegas, small food stores, and markets that local shoppers could use in the absence of the supermarket.

Demolition was complete by June 2014. Construction is underway for a luxury condominium tower that will be eighty stories high with eight hundred apartments. There are also plans to build a smaller affordable building next door in order to get zoning bonuses for the condominium. Construction has caused many problems for Two Bridges Tower, the nonprofit affordable building adjacent to the former Pathmark. The noise has been unbearable, and there has been structural damage as well. So far, Extell has repaired the damage promptly.

On October 14, 2015, *Crain's New York Business* published an interview with Gary Barnett, Extell's CEO. According to Barnett, the building will be known as "One Manhattan Square." Initial marketing will be exclusively to wealthy individuals from China, Singapore, and Malaysia. The initial sales prices will range from $1 million to $3 million.

On October 26, 2015, when I was heading to the subway after a meet-ing at one of the Two Bridges buildings, I saw a diminutive Asian woman passing out fliers calling for a "March against Displacement." The flier was in English and Spanish and featured a photo of people protesting, holding up posters written in Chinese. It called for the mayor to "stop the racist Extell luxury development."

In the magazine section of the December 4, 2016, issue of the *Wall Street Journal*, a glossy two-page advertisement described the project as "Extell's Next Big Thing." Residents of the Two Bridges buildings are not happy. They had enjoyed shopping at Pathmark for thirty years.

18
Two Bridges Townhouses

T wo Bridges Townhouses, a cluster of three low-rise buildings with fifty-seven condominiums for moderate-income families, broke every conceivable rule. The development budget was too low. The financing was iffy. The contractor failed to perform. We had many sleepless nights in planning and execution. But somehow we managed to pull it off.

After the dedication in 1979 of Lands End II, the large Section 8 project on Site 5, the next step was to start planning the smaller Site 6B. We knew that the city had federal money that could be used for home ownership programs, including condos, through what was known as the Section 235 program. The program, originally authorized as part of the National Housing Act of 1968, lowered mortgage payments by providing interest rate subsidies for moderate-income home buyers. New York City provided construction grants and tax abatement to make the program feasible, given the high costs of construction.

We decided that Site 6B would be ideal for a condominium financed through this program. At the time interest rates were high and inflation was rampant. The program lowered interest rates on mortgages from double-digit levels down to 4 percent. Other for-profit and nonprofit groups were developing condos on other sites with Section 235 subsidies. And because lower- and moderate-income families had few opportunities to buy new homes, especially on the Lower East Side, we thought the demand for such housing would be high.

We first contacted Briarwood, an experienced Queens condominium developer. But their price was too high (or so we thought), and the city officials required us to seek bids from other contractors. We then contacted an African American contractor named Jim Francis, who was working with a prefabricated superstructure called steel studs, which resembled Tinkertoys. His price was low, and his presentation was persuasive. The city officials liked Jim, as did our board members. Hal Edelman, the architect, was intrigued with the steel stud system. We had chosen Citibank as the construction lender and Intercounty Mortgage for permanent loans. The bankers were also impressed with Jim's presentation. However, his financial statement was less impressive than his proposal. The bankers required an escrow deposit and a completion guarantee by the adjacent Pathmark supermarket developer, Louis Rosenberg.

Lou had taken a liking to Jim Francis, as had the rest of us. We had our team.

In September 1982 we signed a joint venture agreement with Jim Francis. Jim waived his contractor fee to reduce the equity requirement. We would split profits from savings and from sales of the condo units.

We were required to presell 80 percent of the units before we could start construction. But while selling the units, we could also begin the process of buying the land from the city. That meant obtaining approvals from the community board, the City Planning Commission, and the Board of Estimate.

Things were proceeding smoothly. Our initial survey resulted in a list of five hundred potential home buyers. The initial zoning analysis estimated that the site would accommodate a maximum of sixty-six units. Harold Edelman designed a cluster of three rows in a U-shaped configuration. The buildings were three stories tall, each with a simple red brick facade. There were skylights for some of the apartments. There would be a total of fifty-seven apartments—four one-bedroom units, twenty-two two-bedroom units, and nineteen three-bedroom units, all priced at $57,000; along with twelve four-bedroom units priced at $66,000. Even in the 1980s, this was affordable.

Next came two significant meetings. The first was an evening meeting called to inform community members about the plans and to generate interest among potential purchasers. Susan Cole, then Settlement Housing Fund's associate director and marketing specialist, gave the main presentation. Kai Liu, a member of the Two Bridges board, translated everything Susan said into Chinese. At one point Susan turned to Kai and snapped, "You are *not* translating what I said." How she knew, no one ever figured out. In any case, the meeting was successful, and presales could begin.

We got hundreds of inquiries. Susan oversaw sales, with a lot of help and support from the Two Bridges board and staff. Larry Silver, executive director of Two Bridges at the time, did yeoman's work. But finding qualified buyers who had good credit and met the Section 235 income limits took time. In addition, Susan had her own requirements. For example, she turned down the occasional Chinese couple who arrived carrying bags of cash to cover the down payment. Her explanation was that the cash might have come from money launderers. She also wanted both the wife and husband as signatories on paperwork (instead of just the husband).

In order to obtain binding commitments and to take deposits for condominium units, the New York State attorney general would need to approve an offering plan. Our lawyer, Marty Berger, made that happen.

We presold the units to a diverse group. The purchasers deposited their down payments in an escrow fund, controlled by Marty Berger. Now construction could begin, and we had our closing with Citibank.

The second significant meeting was held to inform the qualified purchasers about their units, the plans, the timetable, and the general process that would take place. The meeting was held at the community room in the adjacent building, Lands End I. Again, Susan was the main speaker.

As it turned out, she had arranged to meet some of the Two Bridges staff for dinner at a nearby Chinese restaurant. During the meal she heard a loud rat-a-tat, followed by someone yelling "Hit the decks." A shooting had taken place, and the police wanted Susan, who had been a witness, to come to the precinct. She informed them in no uncertain terms that she could not do this because she had an important meeting. She then persuaded one of the officers to drive her and the Two Bridges staff to the meeting because she could not be late.

The design was beautiful. The three buildings looked good, even on the site plan and elevation drawings. The top-floor units had cathedral ceilings, room sizes were generous, and there were plenty of closets. We were pleased.

The development process had the usual ups and downs. Construction began in 1983. Jim Francis planned to build the project in three stages, allowing families to move into their apartments as each section was completed. We were still fascinated with the steel stud system, which was prefabricated. Then just as the foundations were being dug, there was a building collapse in Brooklyn involving a site where the steel stud system was being used. We amended the plans to require welding the steel rods where they connected in order to prevent something like that from happening on our site.

Work resumed at the end of 1983, but our troubles continued. Workers excavating the site discovered rubble and debris, none of which had been detected by the test borings. We ended up using 70 percent of our contingency fund to excavate more deeply, using piles. This was expensive but unavoidable, given that excavation is often the riskiest part of construction. All the sites at Two Bridges had problems with the foundations. We applied successfully to the city for additional funds, about $4,000 per unit, bringing the total cost per unit to $76,000—not bad, even then.

In the spring of 1984 we started to get letters from lawyers, demanding payments to some of the subcontractors. The first claim was from the lawyer representing the excavation contractor, stating that he was owed a payment of $6,740.50. Jim resisted, saying that the work had not been done correctly and that he promised to handle everything. Construction seemed to be crawling along.

The bank required lien waivers before making advances, and Jim somehow satisfied or argued around the requirement. We were horrified to receive a second notice that the steel subcontractor was also about to place a lien on the property because of unpaid bills. We disputed this, and we bonded the lien.

The next crisis came when we learned that the Section 235 program was going to expire in September 1985. HUD then sent out a notice that granted a year's extension to all existing projects that had reservations. There would be other extensions. This "exciting" project was getting a little too exciting.

At the same time, the construction lender was becoming increasingly nervous. Citibank was the lender for a number of Section 235 projects in various stages of development, most of which were experiencing difficulty in controlling costs.

Shirley Bresler, vice president of the Citibank division in charge of community development, was a city planner turned banker and a careful lender. She was diligent in reviewing every document, including the details of the insurance policy.

Shirley started raising questions about the requisitions. Jim Francis was often glib and gave lengthy explanations that were hard to follow. At the same time, the buyers wanted to move in. Some had children and were worried about having enough time to register them for a new school. Others had told their current landlords they'd be ending their leases. It was a tense time.

In November 1985 Jim wrote a memorandum stating that "the West and North buildings were approved for Certificate of Occupancy, pending some paperwork." The site plan needed an amendment. The Home Owners Warranty, a special insurance program, was in place. We felt somewhat reassured. Still, Shirley did not think we had enough funds to complete construction. We approved change orders to eliminate some of the amenities. For example, there would be no cathedral ceilings in the third building.

Troubles continued to mount. Questions were raised as to whether Jim had inappropriately spent funds from the construction loan. Meanwhile HUD gave us a deadline of March 1986 to begin moving in residents.

Even as we were getting the units ready for occupancy as quickly as possible, some of the buyers banded together and hired an attorney, who in turn threatened to sue us. We met frequently with the attorney and the purchasers in an effort to explain the delays and problems. Predictably, the meetings were brutal.

We called an emergency meeting of the Two Bridges Settlement Housing Corp. board, and Louis Rosenberg, the Pathmark developer who had provided a guarantee for Jim. Although Lou had guaranteed completion, we did not know what would happen. He agreed to finish the project and would spend up to $300,000. However, both the Two Bridges Neighborhood Council and the Settlement Housing Fund would each have to contribute $25,000. In January 1986 we deposited our checks in a special fund. That arrangement assured that we would work as a team.

In our struggles with the Section 235 program we were hardly alone. The other Section 235 condo projects throughout the city were in even worse shape. Most of the others became rentals. We were determined to keep our commitments to the purchasers. We told the purchasers we would not raise the prices for their units. Some of our nonprofit colleagues in other neighborhoods cancelled their 235 reservations and contracts in order to sell the units at market rates. Some of the bankers and other advisers suggested that we do the same thing. We refused. We could have made money that way, but we thought that it would have been wrong.

We still weren't particularly popular with the buyers, who were angry and wanted to occupy their units as quickly as possible. Finally, in 1986 the work was completed and the residents moved in. Some were happier than others. Some had read the original offering plan and complained that we had not provided outdoor tables and elaborate landscaping. In response, we explained that the plan had been amended to save costs wherever possible so that the buildings could get built.

There are punch list items after construction in most developments, but some are less serious than others. We made repairs from the small amount of funds left in the construction loan. Some of the subcontractors had

Figure 18.1. Two Bridges Townhouses. (Courtesy of Edelman Sultan Knox Wood.)

guaranteed their work, and the ones still in business came back to take care of defects. For other problems, there was the much-vaunted Home Owners Warranty program. The owners, often with our help, had to chase the insurance company, which was a struggle. Jim Francis hired an attorney, trying to make claims. We made counterclaims, and Jim was nowhere to be found.

As recently as 1991 we were fielding complaints about leaks in some of the skylights, as well as problems with subflooring and boilers. But as the years passed, we stopped hearing from the residents. This was a good thing.

In the event of a sale, for the first fifteen years after occupancy any profits from resale were required to go to New York City to repay the part of the subsidy that had been used to write down the cost of the units. Occasionally we would get a call requesting information about how to make the repayment.

After the problems eased, the Two Bridges Settlement Housing Corp. was pleased with the development. Although Judith Edelman, one of the principal architects, thought that the three-story building was out of place in the high-rise neighborhood, the rest of us liked the way the buildings looked.

The repayment requirement for resales expired in 2002.

In 2015 we learned that one of the owners had just sold an apartment for $1 million. To those of us who had struggled to make the development happen, that was astonishing. Susan Cole thinks that selling a subsidized unit at market value is wrong, and that the units should be permanently affordable. Personally, I'd rather see a resident pocket the money than a for-profit private developer.

According to Debbie Leung, a Two Bridges Settlement Housing board member who advocates on behalf of the residents of the area, there is some dissension among the owners of the townhouses. This is not unusual in the world of New York City condos and co-ops.

One of the owners has lived with leaks and cracks in the ceiling for years. Debbie showed me photographs that document the problems. The management company hired by the condo (not Grenadier) hasn't been responsive to Debbie's calls. Condominium owners often get into arguments about whether owners should make their own repairs or whether the responsibility belongs to the condominium association. Debbie believes that some of the owners want to see some of the lower-income families move out, hoping that future sales might produce huge profits, hardly what we had in mind when we struggled to keep the initial prices affordable.

It's possible to argue both sides of the issue. Whatever one might think, for all the drama the Two Bridges Townhouse development was not a failure.

Nor was the Section 235 program, which was officially ended in 1987. In my opinion, the legislation should have been amended by increasing the mortgage limits and the income limits. Hundreds of thousands of homeowners could have benefited.

19
Two Bridges Senior Housing

At the dedication of Lands End II in 1979, city housing commissioner Anthony Gliedman promised to support an application to HUD to build housing for the elderly on Site 4A of the urban renewal area. At the time, we had our hands full with the Pathmark and the condos, but we began planning. The following year, however, we were told by city officials that housing for the elderly would have to wait until a new citywide development plan was finalized. That took a while.

We'd be applying to HUD for money under Section 202, the federal program for housing for the elderly and handicapped, a popular initiative that offered loans and operating subsidies. Enacted in 1959 during the Eisenhower administration, it was at first just a 3 per cent loan program. Then, in 1974, with considerable lobbying by skilled professionals from the American Association of Retired Persons (AARP), operating subsidies were added, making the program able to reach very low-income residents. Tenants would pay 25 per cent of income for rent (30 percent after 1983).

The program provided loans for 100 percent of construction and soft costs, including fees, inspections, insurance, and even initial operating costs during the first months of occupancy. Only experienced nonprofit groups could apply. These groups had to escrow $10,000 during construction and in the first three years of operations to guard against cost overruns. There were no development fees. However, a consultant fee of $40,000 was allowed.

We decided that the Two Bridges Neighborhood Council should form a new corporation that would own the property. Settlement Housing

Fund would be the consultant. It turned out eventually to be a much better deal for Two Bridges than for Settlement Housing Fund, which must have spent much more than $40,000 in time and energy to get the building to construction and occupancy.

We had been consultants on five other projects for the elderly, all constructed within budget and on time. None of them were easy. Still, we liked the program. It provided safe, secure housing for independent older people. We included as part of the operating budget a service coordinator who would link the elderly to health, education, and recreation programs. This was counter to early HUD policy. Somehow we got away with it, and years later HUD accepted the policy. Seniors needed a social service coordinator. The atmosphere in all the buildings that I have visited indicated that the 202 projects were great places to live.

The initial application for Section 202 fund reservations consisted of some thirty documents plus schematic plans. We had to demonstrate that Two Bridges was experienced in programs for senior citizens; to do that, we pointed to the track record of Hamilton Madison House. Over the decades, all the former executive directors of this turn-of-the-century settlement house had played major roles on the board of Two Bridges. Frank Modica, Hamilton Madison's executive director, eventually became chairperson of Two Bridges Neighborhood House and Two Bridges Settlement Housing Corporation.

The new corporation formed to build housing for the elderly, Two Bridges Senior Housing Development Fund Company, had to apply for federal tax exemption pursuant to Section 501(c)(3) of the Internal Revenue Code before applying to HUD for Section 202 funding. Federal tax exemption would allow local sales tax exemption, mortgage recording tax exemption, and real estate tax abatement. At first HUD disapproved of Settlement Housing Fund as consultant because Goldie Chu, a member of the new Two Bridges Senior board, was also on the Settlement Housing Fund board. She promised not to vote on specific issues relating to senior housing, and all was okay. The initial application was approved in 1985.

Then the fun began. We needed to apply for a firm commitment for HUD financing. We did so as we went through the ULURP gauntlet to buy the land from the city. The first roadblock, as was the case for other Two Bridges sites, was the environmental review.

But this time there was a new challenge. The environmental staff of HUD determined that the proposed building, being near the East River, was in what was known as the hundred-year floodplain, meaning that it would stand where the worst flood anticipated in a century could strike.

In 1985 such a threat seemed ridiculous. There had been so much construction along the East River Drive, and no one had ever worried about flooding. (Little did we know.) The architects and local HUD officials figured out a way to go forward. The building would contain no basement, and we would need the entrance to the first floor to be constructed ten feet above the floodplain height, which referred to an elevation in Sandy Hook, New Jersey. The first-floor ceiling would also need to be several feet higher than normal. We were allowed to carve out below-grade space for the boiler room, which seems strange today. (At the time, government officials were not too worried about what would happen to the boiler during a flood that happens once in a hundred years.) It took a year to get the final "negative declaration," which is the name of the wonderful government document assuring that there are no environmental concerns that would prevent construction.

The problem with complying with the floodplain rules was one of costs. The Section 202 program was subject to federal statutory cost limits. Luckily, we were using urban renewal land, which was priced much lower than appraised value. We managed to squeak by.

Settlement Housing Fund was experienced as a consultant to projects for the elderly. We knew, for example, that it was hard to interest seniors in studio apartments. They preferred one-bedroom units because they offered room for their old furniture as well as space for a guest or potential caretaker. However, HUD insisted that nearly a quarter of the 109 apartments be studios.

In the Reagan years, HUD's policy mantra was "cost containment." No architectural frills or generous room sizes would be allowed. The approved architectural style became known as the Velveeta box, named after the popular cheese spread's rectangular product packaging. HUD's cost containment rules also precluded community rooms that exceeded two thousand square feet. Still, Harold and Judy Edelman, our esteemed architects, managed to design an attractive building despite all the constraints.

We usually like to have our contractor as part of the team from the beginning of the design stage. We save money that way. HUD required competitive bidding, but only for nonprofit sponsors using the 202 program. Bidding often results in getting stuck with an unsavory or unqualified contractor who "lowballs" (bidding is no longer necessary, for precisely this reason). Although we were required to obtain bids, we were happy to choose Glick Construction as the general contractor.

The Glick organization was a family business. We had worked with them on two other projects and were highly satisfied. Reuben Glick, president of the company, cared about the quality of his buildings. For example, he would call, delighted that he had negotiated a great price for ovens (in fact, they were very same model he had at home, about which his wife was poetic in her praise). Reuben's brother, Daniel Glick, liked to be out in the field, supervising construction. He paid attention to details.

Even though we had received a firm commitment, some vacant buildings remained on the site, and it took months to clear the land. Only then was it possible to perform test borings and design the foundation. HUD extended the firm commitment until September 30, 1985. That would not be the last extension. Between local and HUD deliberations, there were years of delays.

Finally, in 1987 we scheduled the initial closing. It started in the morning and took all day to complete. The final approval of the team's disclosure forms had not been received from Washington. They were needed for all members of the development team. We had submitted them years before, and updated them a few months prior to the closing. Finally, at about 5:00, we received confirmation by fax that all was well.

Construction proceeded with few problems. The development cost $8.4 million, or $77,147 per apartment. At the end of the project we asked for an additional $56,000 to cover the cost of damage to the parapet during construction, redesign of the first floor, and emergency lighting at each staircase. HUD approved our request. The project was completed in 1988. The permanent mortgage closing took place a year later. The mortgage carried a 9.25 percent interest rate. The Housing Assistance Payment contract covered the costs of operations and debt service. Tenants would pay 30 percent of income for rent.

As with the other sites, Susan Cole supervised tenant selection, along with management and a committee from the staff and board of Two Bridges Neighborhood Council. Timing was not in our favor.

Our original marketing plan reaffirmed our requirements: 30 percent Asian, 30 percent Latino, 20 percent African American, 20 percent Caucasian. "Nothing doing," we were told by the HUD official in charge of marketing. We could have "goals" but not "quotas." Applicants were chosen by a random lottery. We could not skip over applicants to achieve an integrated population. Victor Papa, the current president of the Two Bridges Neighborhood Council, remembers a meeting at which a HUD official said we could go to prison if we skipped over anyone on the applicant list in order to achieve a racial balance.

The rigorous HUD regulations were a response to a racial-discrimination lawsuit the U.S. Department of Justice had brought against the owners of Starrett City, a government-assisted complex with 5,880 apartments in the Spring Creek section of Brooklyn. The case was argued in the United States Court of Appeals for the Second Circuit on July 16, 1987, and decided on March 1, 1988. The court ruled in favor of the Department of Justice.

Starrett's owners had wanted an integrated development in a predominantly white neighborhood. The first goal was a population that was 22 percent African American, 64 percent Caucasian, and 14 percent for other minorities. Earlier a group of African American applicants had also sued the owners, but settled when the owners promised to select thirty-five additional African American tenants every year upon turnover.

The Court of Appeals ruled two-to-one in favor of the government. Judge Jon O. Newman dissented. He did not believe that the intention of the Fair Housing Act was to prevent integration in privately owned housing. The Supreme Court did not accept an appeal, and HUD was strict in enforcing its new policy.

Fortunately, Alan Wiener was the director of HUD's New York office, and he was responsible for vastly increased productivity there. At that time he sustained the idealistic approach he had when he worked as a young lawyer for Legal Aid and then for the Lindsay administration. He is now an important banker and real estate leader: he oversees a huge New York banking arm of Wells Fargo. It is fun to remind him that in the sixties he wore a ponytail.

In 1981 Alan had written a memo approving New York City's policy that allowed 50 percent of the units in a development to be reserved for residents who lived within the local community board boundaries. We liked that policy. Residents of the community who walked by a construction site had at least a slightly better chance of living in a new building than did those from other neighborhoods. The Two Bridges area is located within Community Board 3, one of fifty-nine community board areas in New York City. The neighborhood always had a diverse ethnic mix, with many Latino residents as well as Asians. Our marketing staff also reached out to local churches and community organizations to spread the word about the new building for the elderly. We did manage to achieve integration, though we fell short of our goals. About 50 percent of the tenants at initial occupancy were Chinese, throwing off diverse ethnic balance for which we had hoped. Over the years, more and more of the units were rented to Asian applicants.

Most important, the building, with 109 apartments, provides excellent housing for seniors and for people with disabilities. Very few need to go to nursing homes. The residents can live independently. Operating subsidies assure affordability. If a tenant's income goes up, he or she pays more, up to 30 percent of adjusted income. Similarly, if income goes down, the resident pays less. The tenants' rent plus the operating subsidies are sufficient to keep the building in excellent repair.

Grenadier Realty was and remains the managing agent. Hamilton Madison House Settlement House hired Ben Silver as the social service coordinator, and he was effective in working with seniors. I remember visiting the building when some of the tenants were doing tai chi: a group that included Jewish, Latino, African American, and Chinese men and women who were exercising together.

The lobby is decorated with beautiful landscapes, still lifes, and murals depicting the Lower East Side, all painted by the residents.

Starting in 2003 Two Bridges Neighborhood Council was fortunate to be able to refinance the mortgage. That was the year I met Niall Murray, a vice president of Allied Irish Bank. He outlined a plan for refinancing older Section 202 projects—those funded before 1990, when the statute was amended to change the funding mechanism from loans to grants. There were also recent changes in Section 202 to allow syndication of these developments, using Low-Income Housing Tax Credit investments.

Under the plan, a local finance agency could issue bonds to upgrade Section 202 buildings, bring in investors, and provide a 15 percent development fee for the nonprofit sponsor. The Section 202 program had originally provided no development fee whatsoever, and many nonprofit sponsors were struggling to stay alive. I immediately contacted five nonprofit groups that had Section 202 projects, including Two Bridges. "Should we do that?" asked the late Frank Modica, who chaired the Two Bridges board at the time. "Absolutely," I answered. "You can get a fee of several hundred thousand dollars, maybe even a million. And you can make the building even better than it is now." I suggested that Niall Murray should be the consultant. We would help. Indeed, there were meetings from time to time with HUD where I attended to explain the ramifications of program and advocate for approvals.

Niall was successful. He left Allied Irish Bank to become a full-time consultant. The Edelman Partnership developed a plan that called for replacing kitchen cabinets, upgrades in the apartments, a canopy, new outdoor seating, and a complete expansion and refurbishing of the first-floor community rooms. The work on the first floor included the construction of a large new wing that would be attached to the existing community room.

Figure 19.1. Housing for seniors. (Courtesy of Edelman Sultan Knox Wood.)

As usual, there were problems. Although the soil was better than on other sites, it was still necessary to drive piles. This could create noise in addition to the possibility of structural problems. The solution turned out to be what were called "mini-screw piles," a solution that seemed innovative at the time.

The work was beautifully done. The large community room was named for Frank Modica. The Two Bridges Neighborhood Council made some money, which is a good thing. The group ran for several years at a deficit while waiting for other income-producing ventures.

The programs for the elderly keep expanding. One of the back rooms is now the music room. There is a piano and a part-time teacher, who is passionate about giving piano lessons. Children in all the Two Bridges buildings participate in music programs. There have been very good reviews for the recitals.

Although the building was constructed to be higher than the ten-year flood plain, there was flooding and damage to the boiler room during Hurricane Sandy. However, the central management at Grenadier Realty was able to obtain a portable boiler, and the damage was repaired promptly. Insurance and reserves covered the costs of repair

Over the years, the programs kept expanding. In 2003 Ben Silver retired and was replaced as Philip Li, and Amy Kam joined the team. The arts programs remain strong. There are computer classes as well as English as a second language programs. There are physical fitness classes every day. The goal, according to the director, is to assure that the residents become engaged with one another, as opposed to staying confined, alone in their apartments. For fun, there are bingo programs. Most popular of all are the poker games.

Because of the strict HUD regulations, on turnover, the population is now about 80 percent Chinese. Still, there are Latino and African American tenants who participate in all the programs. Philip Li believes that "the multicultural atmosphere is beautiful."

20
Two Bridges Tower

As we were completing construction of Two Bridges Senior Housing, we thought the adjacent site would be perfect for a complex of small stores. This was Site 4B, the last in the urban renewal area. Because the property was near the Manhattan Bridge, we did not think the government agencies would permit residential construction there. In October 1987 we wrote to housing commissioner Paul Crotty, asking for site control of 4B to work with the Pathmark developer to build the stores. We never heard back, and at the time we were busy with other projects.

By 1990, the Dinkins administration had new ideas for the site. At that point we had won the "noise" battles, and the use of soundproof windows and air-conditioning made residential construction environmentally possible. The initial environmental assessment mandated commercial or community use for the first three floors. Apartments could be located on the higher floors.

The city had run out of large rehabilitation sites and decided to focus on the few remaining vacant sites in urban renewal areas. Mayor David Dinkins had appointed Felice Michetti as commissioner. She decided that the urban renewal sites should be completed as the next stage of creating 225,000 new or preserved apartments.

In 1992 the city gave us seed money to begin planning Site 4B. Our architects, the Edelman Partnership, got right to work. On the other sites, they would work for years without payments until the start of construction. They had faith in our ability to get to a construction start. This time we were relieved that we actually had money from the city to pay them for their initial work. The seed money also covered the cost of a Phase II Environmental Assessment and for test borings.

The design called for 198 apartments in a twenty-one-story tower, with commercial space in the front and three floors of nonresidential space, including a large community room overlooking the East River. A row of small stores would be built as part of the development. This supposedly would be the final building to be constructed in the urban renewal area.

Because Two Bridges Settlement Housing Corp. was the urban renewal nonprofit sponsor, we did not have to compete for site control. However, the city's staff was concerned about the row of stores, which we considered essential. We wanted to work with Sherilu, the developer that had done a great job on the Pathmark site and had also helped to rescue the condo project. The city's solution was to request that we merge the two tax lots so that the stores and the tower could be considered a single development. Two Bridges Settlement Housing Corp. would own both the tower and the stores. Sherilu would have a forty-nine-year lease and sublet spaces to other businesses. We hoped for a dry cleaner, a pharmacy, and other service shops. We had the right to approve subtenants—for example, no liquor stores. After construction, we would be required to split the lots again in order to qualify for tax exemption. The process was extremely difficult both times.

The next job was to choose the contractor. I knew that we would require a reinforced concrete superstructure because of the height and because the test borings revealed the need for ninety-foot piles. This would not only be expensive, but would require a contractor who was experienced with reinforced concrete. The Two Bridges Settlement Housing board interviewed four contractors and was torn between HRH and the Gotham Organization. We had good experience with both companies. We went to look at some of their recent work and checked references.

In December 1993 the presidents of both HRH and Gotham happened to attend a luncheon for the New York Housing Conference, an advocacy organization for which I was staff director. During the event, each man asked me whether we had selected a contractor. I said that we liked them both and might have to flip a coin. The two men promptly huddled together and decided to form a joint organization. The city officials approved the selection.

Development Issues

In the last days of the Dinkins administration, the city issued a commitment letter to provide $17.5 million in a deferred interest loan to subsidize the cost of construction. The Edelman Partnership and its consortium of engineers completed working drawings. We were required to do extensive environmental exploration in order to get the City Planning Commission to approve the application for Uniform Land Use Review Procedure (ULURP) and the Land Disposition Agreement. Soundproofing was part of the design. The first three floors would be devoted to nonresidential uses. The building would be structured so that the ground floor would be higher than the hundred-year floodplain. There would be no basement. However, both the city and the construction lender, Dime Savings Bank, were almost paranoid about the soil because of possible contamination or, even worse, toxicity. Irving Fisher, president of HRH Construction, had an idea that saved the day. His excavation contractor, for an extra $150,000, would guarantee the price for excavation and soil removal. "No runs, no hits, no errors" was the baseball metaphor they used describe the guarantee, which to me was like an extra insurance premium. Since the cost of site preparation was estimated at $1.8 million, this seemed like a worthwhile expense.

The environmental review was torture, but we were eventually successful. After we thought we were home free, however, the environmental specialist at the City Planning Department informed us that the site might present archeological issues. There was a possibility that during excavation we would discover logs and remnants of barges that were the only surviving examples of Dutch-British cooperation during the early colonial era. After a few gasps, we promised that an archeologist would be on the site to monitor excavation.

A Witches' Brew of Financing

The next task was always my favorite part of the work (really)—figuring out how to finance the project. One of the reasons for the initial city approval was that we had agreed that 30 percent of the apartments would be reserved for formerly homeless tenants, a population many other groups were reluctant to accept. Our agreement was subject to the assurance that the city would allocate Section 8 vouchers for the homeless units, making the project reasonably feasible. Dime Savings Bank insisted that the city provide a letter confirming the availability of Section 8 vouchers and relieving us of the requirement to house homeless families if for any reason Section 8 was not available. Without Section 8, public assistance rents were so low that even the operating costs would not be covered (to say nothing of debt service).

Our goal, as always, was to achieve economic and ethnic integration. We decided that 50 percent of the apartments would be for upper-moderate-income families, 30 percent for the formerly homeless, and 20 percent for low-income families, those who earned less than 60 percent of the metropolitan-area median income. City officials approved the plan.

We applied to New York State for an allocation of Low-Income Housing Tax Credits for 50 percent of the apartments and obtained preliminary approval. That allowed us to seek additional funding sources.

In January 1994 Rudy Giuliani was inaugurated as mayor of New York City. We had hoped that he would continue the pro-housing policies of Mayors Koch and Dinkins. In fact, his deputy mayor, Fran Reiter, claimed that the two previous mayors had devoted too much money to housing and not enough to job creation. The first housing commissioner, Deborah Wright, and her staff thought that our costs were too high, about $105 per square foot for construction. In 2016, the cost for high-rise construction averages $350 per square foot.

We advocated for good design, especially because we wanted to attract higher-income families to live in a mixed-income building. Although city officials fought most of the amenities, we ended up with nice apartments—lots of light and beautiful views. The rooms seemed small at the time, but today they qualify as spacious.

The Giuliani administration did not like new construction projects. They emphasized transferring ownership of bankrupt developments from the city to small owners. This would encourage small business. It seemed to me that the city officials would have liked to see our project fail to reach construction. The cost would end up being almost $40 million, about $200,000 per apartment.

Luckily, the previous assistant commissioner, Barbara Leeds, had written the commitment letter for $17.5 million in the last month of the Dinkins administration. This was to be a "soft loan," with a 0.25 percent annual fee. Another 0.75 percent would accrue and be payable in thirty years. It was also forgivable under the right circumstances, and we were pretty sure that the loan would in fact be forgiven. It would be hard for the next administration to wiggle out of the commitment, especially because city seed money had already been spent for the plans. The Giuliani team claimed that it was impossible to provide more than $14.6 million because there was not enough money in the capital budget. We fought for a while but then decided to accept the $14.6 million, and we launched our quest to find additional funds. My advice is always to compromise but never to sell out. Sometimes it is hard to make the distinction.

Dime Saving Bank was the first to come to the rescue. The Dime chairman at the time was Richard Parsons, a prominent "Rockefeller Republican," who later held many high positions in the corporate and nonprofit worlds. He approached Al DelliBovi, president of the Federal Home Loan Bank, to request an affordable housing, zero-interest, forgivable loan of $1.4 million, the largest ever provided to a single development. Shirley Bresler, who had helped us with the condo, had moved from Citibank to Dime, and she was an important booster for the project. The bankers did not want to be in charge of compliance with the terms of the Federal Home Loan Bank loan, so they assigned it to Settlement Housing Fund. Dime Savings Bank was the construction lender, and the city's housing finance agency, the Housing Development Corporation, agreed to provide permanent financing. This would be a thirty-year mortgage, with interest at 8 percent, reasonable at the time. We could prepay with no penalty after ten years. The Housing Development Corporation also provided a second mortgage of $700,000 at 1 percent from a special fund used to house homeless families. Now we had to find the rest of the money.

Settlement Housing Fund's board treasurer, Howard Mendes, asked me to meet Ron Moelis, a young developer who supposedly had new ideas. I thought Ron was smart. Today he heads one of the largest development companies in New York, L+ M, which bought the large buildings on the other Two Bridges sites. However, at the time I already knew about all the ideas he suggested. I also knew all the bankers and investors he knew, plus a few others. However, I liked him and thought he would be a good team member. He became a tax partnership consultant. As it turned out, he negotiated with the investors and obtained much more money that I would have dared to ask. Thank you, Ron. We closed the gap.

The original investor was National Westminster, a national bank that was subsequently taken over by Fleet Bank. In 1996 Fleet asked our permission to sell their shares of the partnership to the Bell Atlantic telephone company. We consented. Bell Atlantic became Verizon soon thereafter. All this happened during construction.

However, the investors would only put up part of the money during construction. This is typical of investors in the tax credit program. We were able to obtain a below market bridge loan from JPMorgan (this was prior to the merger with Chase).

The sources of funds for construction, fees, and interest were as follows: $1.4 million from the Federal Home Loan Bank, $14.6 million in a "soft" loan from the New York City Department of Housing Preservation and Development, $700,000 at 1 percent interest from the New York City Housing Development Corporation, $15 million from investors, and a construction loan from Dime for $7.5 million. JPMorgan provided a below-interest bridge loan of $8.9 million because the investors' funds were to be provided over a five-year period. The Housing Development Corporation provided permanent financing as a "takeout" for Dime's construction loan.

Tax exemption became a difficult issue. Most of our projects were 100 per cent exempt from real estate taxes for up to forty years. There was a new, generous real estate tax exemption program (known as 420-c) for projects financed with Low-Income Tax Credit investments. The exemption was automatic, and we thought our project qualified. However, "coincidentally," while we were in the development phase, the city issued a new regulation to limit eligibility only to projects in which 70 percent of the apartments benefited from the tax credit investments. Two Bridges Tower had tax credits for 50 percent of the units. This was to be a mixed-income building. We had to use another program (known in real estate circles as 421a), typically used for luxury developments. The total tax exemption would last only ten years and then would gradually phase out. We knew we would need to refinance, because we would not be able to raise the rents to cover the new tax bills. Even worse, the row of small stores was a roadblock to obtaining 421a. The city's solution was to require separating the tax lots that we were originally required to merge. We grunted and with a lot of effort split the lots. One of the city officials wrote us a letter stating that the residential mortgage would be removed from the stores. That never happened, a fact that would come back to haunt us.

"Will that project ever start construction?" was the consistent, nagging question of the Two Bridges Settlement Housing board. The last piece of the puzzle involved showing how the rents would cover the operating costs and the mortgage payments. There were income limits for residents attached to all the sources of financing, and the tenants could not pay more than 30 percent of income for rent (nor did we want them to). The rents for initial occupancy were set in three tiers.

TWO BRIDGES TOWER

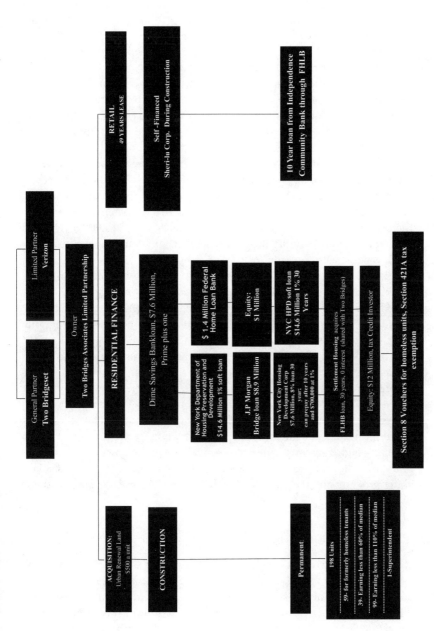

Figure 20.1. Complicated financing. (Based on the author's files.)

The fifty-nine formerly homeless families would have Section 8 rents at $566 for a one-bedroom unit, $660 for two bedrooms, and $837 for three bedrooms. The part of their rent that exceeded 30 percent of their income would come from Section 8 payments.

The thirty-nine low-income families would pay $471 for one bedroom, $566 for two bedrooms, and $657 for three bedrooms.

The upper-moderate-income families would pay $750 for one bedroom, $850 for two bedrooms, and $1,000 for three bedrooms.

Annual residential rental income would come to nearly $1.8 million in the first year of occupancy. The bankers required a vacancy reserve, reducing projected residential rental income to $1.7 million. However, operating costs, taxes, and debt service coverage was estimated to cost $2.182 million. We had a significant gap that had to be covered by commercial rent. The rental income from the small stores, $40,000 a year, was earmarked for community programs. Sherilu agreed to rent the first floor for $18 per square foot, for a total of $46,800.

The rent for the first three floors of the tower was another problem. Luckily, the late Frank Modica, executive director of Hamilton Madison House, was president of the Two Bridges Settlement Housing Corp. board. He promised to move several of Hamilton Madison's programs from Queens to that space. Included was a large-scale program, the only one of its kind on the East Coast, for Asians who were addicted to drugs or alcohol.

Modica signed a lease obligating his agency to pay rent of over $400,000 a year. That agreement closed the gap and got us to a favorable feasibility analysis by the banks, investors, and government agencies. This was the final step toward achieving a go-ahead. And while we were worried about attracting higher-income families to a building with a substance-abuse program, that did not prove to be an issue. The entrance for the substance-abuse program and the entrance for the residents were far apart, and there was no problem.

The Dramatic Closing

If we did not get to a construction loan closing by October 31, 1995, the tax credit allocation would expire. We closed on the last Friday in October at the offices of the bank's attorneys. We needed three conference rooms. The initial payment from the investors of $1 million was to be the first money in. That presented no problem because the investor had advanced the funds to Settlement Housing Fund, and we simply wrote a check.

There were last-minute arguments about the construction contract that dragged on and on. After the disputes were settled, other funds from the investor, National Westminster, and the bridge lender, JPMorgan, were to be wired. However, by the time we agreed about everything, it was 2:00 on a Friday afternoon. When we tried to get the money, the federal wires were down. That was unheard of. We were struggling to find a messenger to go to the investors' offices in New Jersey to pick up a check. This would not be easy. We came close to losing the project. Miraculously, at four o'clock that day, the wires came back into service. Over the next week all the funds started to flow and construction could start. Nevertheless, it was a real squeaker.

Most of the participants had never witnessed such a closing or such a concoction of financing sources for a single project. However, ten years later, when housing had grown ever more complicated and byzantine, this would become the norm. Every agency brags about leveraging all the other sources. Excel spreadsheets ease the pain, but at that time everything was done with a good calculator.

Another problem had to do with bookkeeping and accounting. Some of the lenders and government agencies wanted their funds used only for construction, not for fees, interest, insurance, or development fees. The investors' funds could pay for these items, as could the bridge loan. Our assistant comptroller, Sheila Carpenter, was in charge of loan drawdowns and had to allocate the expenses carefully. The audits and reports at times were overwhelming.

Construction

Now that the closing was over, it was time to start digging, literally. The contractors had to prepare quickly, because it was already November. Soon the weather could delay things.

During excavation, we had to test the quality of the soil. Everyone was worried about finding illegal gas tanks or toxic earth that would have to be carted far away. Even one of the young bankers, Diane Khuzami, put on hip boots and went to the site to check on how everything was going.

We were glad that the excavator had guaranteed the price. Luckily the soil was just contaminated, not toxic. Instead of removing the soil, which was ninety feet deep, the soil was encapsulated and covered with clean fill. The other good news was that no one found anything archeologically significant. Usually, once the foundation is complete, construction proceeds with few surprises. Finishing the job, however, is often problematic.

Indeed, construction went smoothly at first. Susan Cole and/or Ann Loeb, Settlement Housing Fund's assistant director, attended the weekly job meetings. The architects were there, as was the representative for Dime Savings Bank. At least once a month the representatives of the investors and the city and state agencies attended. This seemed to be the most supervised construction project in history. The concrete superstructure managed to get built expeditiously despite concerns about the weather. The joint venture between two contractors was occasionally dysfunctional. Each would blame the other when something went wrong. Keeping the costs under control was challenging.

There was only one major change order, costing about $85,000, though we had a contingency allowance of about $1.148 million. The contractors were elated about finding a relatively inexpensive elevator contractor. Although I do not believe in the aphorism "You get what you pay for," this time it happened to be true. Over the years when something went wrong, we had to order spare parts from other countries. Eventually the elevator company went out of business, and the maintenance contract from different vendors became difficult. We spent a lot of money on repairs in 2012 after Hurricane Sandy. At the end of 2015 we had to replace all three elevators used by the tenants.

The most difficult problem involved getting the building finished and taking care of punch list items. The contractors obtained a temporary certificate of occupancy, claiming that tenants could move in. We did not agree. This is often the case. The contractors want to move on to the next job, and the owners of the property want all the punch list items completed.

One meeting I attended made me laugh. Ann Loeb, Settlement Housing Fund's diminutive, soft-spoken assistant director, ordered the two presidents of the contractor organizations to go inside one of the closets. Both men were over six feet tall. They towered over Ann, who was about five feet two. "Look," she said, "the closet shelves have not been painted. We cannot stand for this." Although one might sympathize with the contractors, this is the kind of passion that makes a building succeed. Other punch list issues included missing appliances, no lights in the bathrooms, and a host of other small but important items. We fought it out and began selecting tenants

However, one serious problem remained. Hamilton Madison did not have funds for furnishing and equipping the nonresidential space, even though the various social agencies had approved the rents. There was almost $1 million remaining in the contingency. Clara Fox, our founder,

Figure 20.2. Two Bridges Tower. (Courtesy of Edelman Sultan Knox Wood.)

and I were able to convince the new commissioner, Lillian Barrios Paoli, that the contingency should be used for these purposes. I wrote a letter outlining the problem, and the commissioner said that the contingency funds would serve as "reparations." The contractors were upset, because they thought they would be able to keep the remaining funds. Everything worked out in the end.

The Lottery

The next job was to select the residential tenants. We were worried about whether anyone would apply to the higher-rent apartments. Would higher-income people be willing to live on the infamous Lower East Side in a building in which homeless and low-income families occupied half the apartments? Apparently the answer was yes. Some twenty-two thousand families applied for the 139 apartments not reserved for the formerly homeless.

Susan Cole supervised the selection process with a group from the Two Bridges board. As always, the process involved review of applications for eligibility, office interviews, credit checks, and home or shelter interviews. The applications are thrown on the floor and then entered on a list from which they would be selected randomly. We reviewed the first five thousand applicants on the list in order to select 197 residents. (One two-bedroom apartment was reserved for the superintendent.)

Someone in the community was selling applications fraudulently. Lucky for us, our applications were printed on special paper that could not be duplicated. We eliminated the fraudulent applications.

We achieved a diverse tenant population as well as economic integration. Every floor would be economically integrated. On some floors the formerly homeless had the best views.

As people moved in, they seemed happy with the apartments. We received some favorable press. In 1998 a reporter for *National Mortgage News* visited the site, looked at the building, and interviewed a formerly homeless woman. The interviewee had suffered two strokes but talked proudly about her daughter, who was working, and her granddaughter, who was in school. The three African American women lived together in an immaculate, airy two-bedroom apartment. The reporter was appropriately impressed. In his article, he compared the building to Chartres and Notre-Dame.

A conference attended by bankers used the project as a model for combining sources to create affordable housing. The title of the gathering was "Scrambling for the Crumbs."

The final agonizing task, which took over five years, was obtaining the final certificate of occupancy. Usually that's the job of the contractor, but the group had finished their work years before. Various inspectors kept postponing their inspection, and the delay was annoying. We had to pay $500 to extend the temporary certificate every six months. Ann Loeb came to the rescue, and we received the certificate in 2002.

The Next Years

Over time the building succeeded. We had a large reserve fund of well over $1 million, which we used for various capital improvements. We put in place twenty-four-hour security, a good manager, and a good superintendent. There were some issues involving drugs, and for a few years we had an arrangement with the local police precinct. Officers patrolled the stairways, and things quieted down.

Although Hamilton Madison ran some community programs, attendance was not that great, perhaps because the community offered other programs. There was a social worker on staff, who worked well with management.

Despite the rigorous selection process, we had problems with a few of the formerly homeless tenants. Several units were badly maintained by the residents. There was domestic violence. Our social work staff intervened, but there were serious difficulties.

Incomes Go Up

Because of the Low Income Tax Credit legislation and the affordable housing loan, we are required to monitor the incomes of 107 of the residents, and in 2002 the income report was quite interesting, Although there were a few cases in which very low incomes went slightly down, twenty-eight tenants had significant increases. Some had doubled their earnings. One family's income went from $26,000 in 1997 to $81,000 in 2002. Housing is not an automatic path to upward mobility, but living in a clean, safe place can help.

Trever Holland

As with Settlement Housing Fund's other projects, I wanted to interview longtime residents of the building to see how they had fared over the years.

I interviewed Trever Holland, an African American tenant leader who moved into the building when it opened in 1997. His wife, Christina Geigel, said that she had "won the lottery." The couple had met when Trever was at Columbia University and Christina was at Barnard College. Trever had been a lawyer but now spends most of his time now advocating for the community. Trever likes the neighborhood. Christina's family lives nearby. The location of the F train is convenient. The waterfront is a great

Figure 20.3. Trever Holland. (Courtesy of Trever Holland.)

amenity. The area was relatively quiet until Extell started construction next door at the former Pathmark site. Trever feels safe in the building but believes that the twenty-four-hour security is essential. He is aware of a number of tenants who are drug offenders. Still, the neighborhood is much safer than it had been. One seldom hears car alarms and there is absolutely no graffiti, which is good evidence of success.

When I asked him about the worst aspects of living in the building, he immediately asked me, "Besides Extell?" Although he hopes that Extell will build a new supermarket as part of their new development, he hates all the construction noise and the damage to the building (although it has been repaired).

Trever is also concerned about the illegal dogs that a few of the tenants have somehow "hidden" from management. There is one resident who needs a dog legitimately, but there are supposed to be no others. The tenants do not clean up after their dogs, creating quite a mess.

Most of all, Trever worries that low- and middle-income people will "have nowhere to go" as higher income residents keep moving nearby. There are no units where families can move as they have more children.

When Trever first moved to the building, Hamilton Madison had social workers to help the lower-income and formerly homeless residents learn to take care of their units and adjust to living in a mixed-income building. Some of these families had never lived on their own before. He regrets that the social workers have been replaced by others who staff community programs. Many of the programs are geared toward those who can afford to pay for piano lessons, after-school programs, and other activities. Although "the music lessons are nice," the very low-income families cannot afford them.

Ironically, in his early years in the building, Trever had suggested building a gym on the first floor as an attractive amenity and an alternative to the "social work programs." His suggestion was dismissed as a luxury. Now he wishes for the social workers he had originally questioned.

Trever's eyes lit up when we discussed smoke-free buildings. He thinks that prohibiting smoking would be a great policy for Two Bridges Tower, but he admits it would be hard to achieve.

Overall, Trever was positive. He said he was "proud to live in the building." He would never consider living in a less diverse neighborhood. He believes that diversity is good for a community. He added, "Not only am I proud to live in the building. I am proud of the building itself."

Helen Ong

I also interviewed Helen Ong, who moved to Two Bridges Tower with her parents and her brother, when she was nine years old. She is now a dental student at Stony Brook University, and her brother is a pharmacist at NYU Langone Medical Center.

Her family had lived in a walk-up building on East Broadway, in Chinatown, not far from Two Bridges. The apartment was too crowded for the family. Her mother applied for an apartment at Two Bridges. She was on that list of twenty-two thousand applicants and was successful in the lottery. The family was surprised and elated to have been selected.

Helen especially enjoys the spectacular view of the East River and the bridges from her twentieth-floor apartment. Her family feels fortunate. One of the best things for the family is to live in an elevator building, especially having lived in a walk-up before.

Although the elevators are among the best things about the building, they are sometimes also the worst things. Recently there have been times when one elevator was out of service because of the need for repairs. People become impatient. She also remembers a few years ago when some of the apartments were infested with roaches. The staff of the building called in exterminators and took care of the problem. Her brother, who is home during the day, is concerned about the construction at the Pathmark site. There is noise and shaking at times. Everyone in the building was sad that the supermarket was demolished.

Helen feels safe in the building. She appreciated the security guards, who patrol the stairways and the entrance. She says that the building is clean and in good repair.

Although Helen did not participate in after-school programs, she did enjoy the holiday parties. She has noticed that new programs are listed on the bulletin board.

Helen and the members of her family feel lucky to live at Two Bridges Tower.

Refinance

The overall project began to hit cost constraints. Although we were able to use the reserves for major repairs, operating costs kept increasing. We knew that the tax exemption period was about to expire and that real estate taxes would start to phase in.

I was aware that some early federal projects had been refinanced by for-profit developers with huge distributions to the development partners. Even at the initial closing in 1995, one of the underwriters had said that refinancing would be a good idea after the initial tax exemption period expired.

We were paying $908,000 in annual debt service. By 2006 we had the right to prepay the mortgage from the City's Housing Development Corporation. Coincidentally, in 2007 a friend had joined a new company that underwrote FHA-insured mortgages. He tried to convince us to use his products, and I was intrigued. At the time interest rates were 6 percent for thirty-year mortgages. We could have reduced our debt service cost to about $500,000. Victor Papa, president of the Two Bridges Neighborhood Council, thought this was a good idea. At that time there was tension between Settlement Housing Fund and the Two Bridges Neighborhood Council. This was the first time in our thirty-year collaboration that there was any disagreement whatsoever. Still, we all decided to refinance, using an underwriter known to both organizations.

We contacted the City's Housing Development Corporation. Staff members were agreeable but wanted us to prepay not only the first mortgage, but also the small loan of $700,000 at 1 percent interest. We said okay. The City Department of Housing Preservation and Development had a second mortgage of $14.6 million, with interest that had accrued to over $1 million. We had always expected the city's mortgage to be forgiven. The only reason for the second mortgage format was that grants could not benefit from the federal Low Income Housing Tax Credit program. We met with the commissioner, who would not allow any distribution to Settlement Housing Fund or Two Bridges Neighborhood Council.

However, he said we could take the funds from cash flow that would result from the savings on debt service.

We applied for a mortgage to be insured by HUD pursuant to Section 223(f) of the National Housing Act. It was a long process. Oppenheimer Multifamily Housing & Healthcare Finance acted as the bankers. HUD required minor repairs, and we were planning facade work, using our large reserves. The funds were transferred to Oppenheimer as a reserve. We needed the approval of our investors at Verizon. Their staff did a lot of due diligence. Their reviews were impressive but time-consuming.

In the meantime, city officials kept adding new requirements. The accrued interest of about $1 million had to be added to second mortgage of the Department of Housing Preservation and Development (HPD). The new total was now about $15.6 million. We could use half the remaining reserves for development fees that we had never received, but the other half would be used to reduce the HPD mortgage. We could increase the community program budget to $200,000 a year. However, at the last minute, city officials demanded that in 2016 we would start to pay significant debt service to the city.

We closed on the refinancing in February 2012. Luckily, by then interest rates on the HUD loan were low, 3.9 percent for a thirty-five-year term. We borrowed $3.325 million. The loan was used to prepay two loans from the Housing Development Corporation, and to cover title insurance, reserves, and various fees.

The good news is that debt service was reduced from $908,000 to $307,400. The unfortunate news was the need for debt service on the HPD loan. This requirement was added at the last minute. Hopefully my successors at Settlement Housing Fund will be able to renegotiate this requirement or find other solutions that will improve cash flow without hurting operations and programs.

Current Events

In 2014 Two Bridges and Settlement Housing Fund formed a new corporation and bought out Verizon for $10. That was a good deal. Verizon had been a good partner.

In 2004 the adjacent row of small stores and the adjacent supermarket had been sold to an organization called Little Cherry, named for Cherry Street, where the stores were located. We met with the three principals of the corporation and started to plan for a housing development over the stores. There were many iterations, but the plans did not work out.

Today there is a proposal to sell our air rights from the tower and from the adjacent building for the elderly. This will be complicated but hopefully feasible.

As with all the buildings, this one was worth the effort. I reviewed the 2015 income re-certifications for ninety-four tenants who moved to the tower between 1997 and 2014. The news was even more impressive than it had been in 2002. These were all residents who had either been homeless or had low incomes at initial occupancy. Incomes for seventy-three of the tenants increased, many dramatically. Eight families have incomes over $100,000, including two who had been formerly homeless. The incomes of thirty-five tenants were more than twice as high as when they moved in. The incomes of the other twenty-one families either went down or stayed the same. Many of those whose incomes went down were on fixed incomes or received government support. Some of the family members had either retired or lost their jobs. For example, one of the formerly homeless families saw a decline income from $22,800 to $11,500. Fortunately, she had a Section 8 voucher to protect her. Others were not so lucky. Still, the news was great for a large majority of the families.

Some people argue that tenants with higher incomes should move out of affordable building in order to make room for lower-income tenants. I disagree strongly. First of all, the mix of incomes provides stability and role models. Second, there are no available apartments that these middle-income residents can afford. The income mix was and remains a great idea.

21
The Future for Two Bridges

It appears that the tale of Two Bridges has no clear ending in sight. Still, the outlook is positive. In 1997 we celebrated completing Two Bridges Tower, the "last" vacant site in the urban renewal area. However, as the ownership and leadership at the various sites have changed, new plans have emerged.

Site 7, the public housing turnkey known as Two Bridges Houses, will almost certainly remain as public housing for decades to come. Although repairs are slow and problems with heat persist, the building looks much better than do other nearby projects. The tenants participate in programs at the local YMCA and at Two Bridges Neighborhood Council sites. There are few vacancies.

At Site 6A, Lands End I, 70 percent of the apartments are currently affordable. At least half the apartments will remain affordable for forty years. For the other half, the sky will be the limit. The building is in excellent repair and in good financial shape. Luckily, the on-site manager is skilled, and the numbers work. A new building is planned for the parking lot.

Site 5, Lands End II, will remain as a Section 8 project (100 percent) for at least forty years. Again, resources and management are stellar. The current owners plan to build a new building on the parking lot. The income mix for the new site is uncertain.

On Site 8, the Pathmark supermarket has been demolished. In order to obtain zoning bonuses, the new owner, Extell, is building two hundred affordable apartments. Right now they say that they will build a supermarket on the site as well. They are also building a tall luxury condominium.

The community is protesting, probably to no avail. The developer has the legal right to construct the condominium and the affordable building, with or without a supermarket.

The condominium units on Site 6B, Two Bridges Townhouses, are going for very high prices. Many of the original residents or their children are still there. All restrictions have been removed.

Two Bridges Senior Housing on Site 4A is a beautiful residence for seniors, who enjoy physical fitness classes, mah-jongg, poker, and more. The building is in great repair and sound financial shape. There are even music lessons for the neighborhood children offered at this site. The building is a home run. However, plans to build over or on part of the site could disrupt the current tranquility. The result could be worth it, and the residents seem pleased. The plans call for a new mixed-income structure, which will candelabra on top of this development. Included will be amenities for the residents of the senior development and for others in the community. Two Bridges Settlement Housing Corp. would be a partner. There are many complications to this plan, however, including litigation.

Two Bridges Tower on Site 4B is always close to 100 percent occupied. The building looks great, though there is some tension with a few of the residents. The great unknown is the future of the row of small stores. Our new nonprofit, Two Bridges Settlement Housing Development Fund Company, owns both the tower and the site of the stores.

In retrospect, the founding leaders of the Two Bridges Neighborhood Council would be pleased to see the activities of the council today. I became a member of the board in 2014. Victor Papa, the organization's president, is determined to lead the council to new achievements, both in collaboration with Settlement Housing Fund and in creating new programs for the community. This was the goal of Clara Fox, founder of Settlement Housing Fund. Victor always reminds the joint organization about Clara. Today he collaborates well with Alexa Sewell, the current president of Settlement Housing Fund.

Victor Papa and the Staff

I interviewed Victor on January 14, 2016. He was proud that the Two Bridges Neighborhood Council, in collaboration with Settlement Housing Fund, created a diverse neighborhood from scratch. Even better, in the last few years, high-quality community programs have been added to the mix. However, he is worried about how the neighborhood has changed over the last few years. He said, "We can't stem the tide of new development geared to the taste of higher-income young professionals who are moving to the Lower East Side in droves. The challenge involves using new models to create opportunities for lower-income residents as the pressure for expensive housing and commercial development continues. We need to learn all the new language so that low-income families can continue to live in this community."

Kerri Culhane, originally a consultant, was associate director of the Two Bridges Neighborhood Council from 2011 until 2015. She breathed new life into the organization. Under her leadership, the city's Department of Environmental Protection provided a grant to create a rain garden on the tower site. She and the staff helped to organize other leaders and property owners in order to require the city to assure sustainability along the waterfront. She also obtained grants for various nutritional and health programs geared toward the needs of neighborhood residents. Kerri worried that the staff might not be able to contend with all their obligations without burning out, a concern shared by many effective nonprofit leaders.

Wilson Soo is also a smart young leader, who kept the organization going for many years. He understands administration, grants, and budgets. Unfortunately, he resigned in 2017. Francine Gorres is creating new programs for the larger community. Debbie Leung, the housing referral advocate, is a Two Bridges board member and former original tenant at Site 6B.

July Yang, who was in charge of the new music program, is replacing Kerri Culhane as associate director. She is both a concert pianist and recently was first in her class in the Pace University MBA program. There are waiting lists for the music classes and accolades for all the programs.

Concluding Thoughts about Two Bridges

It is personally gratifying to see new young leadership both at Two Bridges Neighborhood Council and at Settlement Housing Fund, individuals who are passionate about community development and fostering upward mobility for low-income New Yorkers. Although housing problems and poverty are severe in at the time of this writing, many talented people are searching hard for solutions.

Settlement Housing Fund and the Two Bridges Neighborhood Council did not anticipate that this neighborhood would become gentrified. We just thought the views were great and were pleased to create high-quality affordable housing. However, the gentrification that has taken place makes it hard to argue that subsidized housing ruins surrounding neighborhoods by bringing about a decline in property values.

PART IV
Looking Ahead

22
Lessons and Recommendations

In 2014, more than 7.2 million renters in the United States either lived in dilapidated housing or paid more than half their income on housing, according to a 2016 report by the National Low Income Housing Coalition.[1] It was also estimated that in November 2016 more than 549,000 Americans were homeless.[2] This is disgraceful in a wealthy country like the United States.

More Resources and Flexible Programs

To address the problem, more than anything else we need money. We never had enough. Federal housing funding levels were much higher in previous decades, but not nearly high enough to create affordable housing for everyone who needs it. Rent subsidies should be an entitlement. A news program on public radio described the shortage of housing assistance in West Hartford, Connecticut. The reporter noted that we do not hand out food assistance or health care by lottery, and that housing is equally important.[3]

The goal is to make sure that no one has to pay over 30 percent of their income for a decent place to live. Actually, 20–30 percent would be

1. National Low Income Housing Coalition, "The Gap: The Affordable Housing Gap Analysis, 2016," 2.
2. U.S. Department of Housing and Urban Development, "2016 Annual Homeless Assessment Report to Congress," 1.
3. "The Long Way Home," *Planet Money*, April 29, 2016.

even better, which was the original New Settlement Apartments formula. Between 1937 and 1983, housing programs required that tenants pay no more than 25 percent of income for rent. In the 1974 act, congressman Ed Koch introduced a successful amendment lowering the limit to 20 percent for large families (i.e., those with more than three children) and 15 percent to large, very low-income families. In the initial 2019 federal budget proposal, rents would rise to 35 percent of income for all assisted families. This is both unconscionable and impractical. If tenants cannot afford the rents, they will stop paying, be evicted, perhaps become homeless.

In addition to rental assistance, we need programs to encourage home ownership for people with good credit and the ability to keep their homes in good repair. Home ownership helps build neighborhood pride. It is also a way for low- and moderate-income families to build equity.

Federal grants should be available to create new buildings in regions where the market does not provide an adequate housing supply. Federal programs should be flexible to allow regional variations. A user-friendly system would also make a lot of sense. We need to retain federal mortgage insurance and a secondary market to assure that housing can be financed. State and local governments should augment federal assistance, creating great neighborhoods as well as decent housing. Most of this can be accomplished with a few revisions to Section 8 of the Housing Act of 1937 and to the Community Development Block Grant Program, enacted in 1974. We also need to assure those in charge have a vision and know what they are doing.

There are two major reasons why the buildings at New Settlement Apartments and in the Two Bridges urban renewal area have thrived for decades. First, we had excellent financing, thanks in part to excellent government housing programs, many of which no longer exist. Second, we had highly competent people managing and caring for the buildings. The principals and staff at Grenadier Realty, the management company for New Settlement Apartments and most of the Two Bridges sites, are competent, cooperative, and detail-oriented. Settlement Housing Fund is an excellent asset manager that watches over the buildings with loving care. None of us are perfect, but we are conscientious and can do great work.

Management Expertise

To further explore my theories about resources and competence as key to effective programs, I spoke to Felice Michetti, a true housing expert. Early in her career she worked in various Bronx neighborhoods and in a multitude of capacities for different New York City administrations. She was the visionary who created and implemented the Koch ten-year housing program, and she served as the housing commissioner under Mayor Dinkins. She is currently president of Grenadier Realty, managing over twenty thousand apartments, including most of Settlement Housing Fund's properties.

I asked what she would do to address the nation's housing needs. After hesitating for a few moments, she said that few people want to face the fact that it's about money. "Nobody wants to recognize the cost," she said. "Subsidies need to be deeper," she continued. "It does not help a lot of people when you build apartments that rent for $2,400 a month." She favors mixed-income housing. She admires "housers," those who understand buildings, finance, mechanics, and communities. She and I did not always agree during our negotiations when she worked for the city, but she was always fair and knew the housing business inside and out.

Politicians often advise against "throwing money" at a problem. I disagree. I hope that the government allocates enough funds to create high-quality affordable housing, with enough resources left over to sustain the buildings over their lifetimes.

Competent management is also essential. One of the top people in the world of management is Natalie Weinthal, executive vice president of Grenadier. Natalie likes the management business. She wouldn't be doing it for over thirty years if she did not find it interesting. "You never know in the morning what to expect later in the day," she once said. "There's always a problem to solve. There are always surprises. It is not a nine-to-five job."

There are also emergencies. Thanks to Natalie's efforts, emergency generators were delivered to the Two Bridges buildings immediately after Hurricane Sandy. She has even used her own personal credit card to buy supplies that are needed immediately for emergency repairs.

Natalie started her career helping to rent affordable buildings. She tells me that it was always satisfying to see people get decent housing. At Lands End II there were eight thousand applications for 490 apartments, and the process had to move fast. Working with Susan Cole and a committee from the Two Bridges Neighborhood Council, the difficult job got done. The result was a diverse population. Sometimes it was necessary to show the tenants how to use the appliances in their units and to explain the culture of living in a high-rise building. "One should not go to the laundry room in pajamas," for example, was something several tenants needed to be told.

She tells me that one of the most important aspects of management is good communication. Grenadier hires people who speak several languages— Spanish, Chinese, even Russian—so that they can communicate with tenants. The staff needs to listen to the tenants and hear their complaints and issues, even if the tenants are doing something wrong. The Grenadier staff is diverse at all levels. It is important to hire honest, competent individuals. It is also important to respect the residents. If one of the tenants calls Natalie's assistant with a complaint, the assistant calls the on-site manager with the tenant on the line to solve the problem.

Of course not all the complaints are legitimate. For example, sometimes people go to all lengths to get an apartment. One applicant knew that some apartments were reserved for disabled individuals, so she showed up in a wheel chair. However, after leaving the building, she was seen folding the wheelchair and walking briskly away.

The superintendent is the key person in assuring that a building runs well. The super must know how to care for the physical plant and how to communicate with the residents. That person needs to be on call twenty-four hours a day.

The work can be challenging. Dealing with a fire or, even worse, a shooting is extremely difficult. When tenants do not pay their rent, when there is not enough money to pay the bills—these are among the worst aspects of the job.

Natalie tells the managers to buy products with care, as if they're spending their own money. Sometimes the owners are reluctant to spend any money at all on the buildings. Natalie understands their viewpoint, but she is sometimes frustrated.

Natalie emphasized the importance of security and having your own staff to supervise security guards from an outside company. She takes satisfaction from the condition of the buildings in the Two Bridges area as well as the diversity of the population.

Natalie's mother grew up in one of the New Settlement buildings in the Bronx. She said, "New Settlement has everything—good housing, excellent programs, activities for young people, college access." Jack Doyle calls her at 11:00 at night and finds her wherever she is. I guess that's what Natalie means by communication.

Public Housing

Edward Goetz, in his 2013 book *New Deal Ruins,* writes that "although the discourse of disaster dominates discussions of public housing, the reality is that in most places it worked and still does work."[4]

---

4. Edward G. Goetz, *New Deal Ruins* (New Brunswick, N.J.: Cornell University Press, 2013), 2.

Newspaper articles today tend to focus on issues like broken elevators or shootings in the stairwells. In the 1970s we would read about garden contests and the New York City Housing Authority Symphony Orchestra.

Public housing in New York City provided good, safe housing for hundreds of thousands of families between 1937 and the late 1990s, when the federal government reduced operating and capital funds, and the state and city stopped providing subsidies. It makes me sad to see the current articles that describe the "projects" as places of danger and despair.

There are over four hundred thousand of the 8.4 million New Yorkers living in public housing. The New York City Housing Authority owns 328 developments with about 178,000 apartments, and employs 11,700 staff members.[5] This is a huge operation. During the 1970s and 1980s, competent professionals could be found at all levels of the agency. As they retired, both institutional memory and commitment were lost.

Public housing was not a priority for Mayor Giuliani. Less attention was paid to hiring managers who understood the importance of maintenance. During Giuliani's administration, the special public housing police force was eliminated and the Housing Authority had to pay the city for security, an approach that left less money for repairs and maintenance.

Mayor de Blasio has eliminated these payments, and the agency's current chairperson, Shola Olatoye, is an experienced professional who is using new tools to address the problems facing public housing. For example, she is using the HUD Rental Assistance Demonstration (RAD) program, which involves public–private partnerships. The Housing Authority was slow to use this program, but it is now on board with several new initiatives. Initially, some of the tenant associations opposed involving the private sector. After careful negotiations, most of the associations were convinced that this is the only way to achieve improvements without substantial increases in rent.

Public housing rarely wins architectural awards. Still, the interior layouts are good, and the buildings resemble such acclaimed middle-income buildings as Stuyvesant Town or Peter Cooper Village. The waiting list for public housing in New York contains more than 270,000 names. It is urgent to find the funds to renovate Housing Authority buildings and make them safer. Public housing is a resource that should be cherished, not neglected.

5. See the New York City Housing Authority website, http://www1.nyc.gov/site/nycha/index.page.

In January 2015 I visited James Weldon Johnson Houses, a large public housing complex in East Harlem. The Fund for the City of New York was bestowing its Sloan Award, given for excellent public service, to Michael Johnson, the project's assistant manager. The tenants attended the ceremony and cheered wildly. The buildings shone inside and out.

Michael Johnson seemed an exemplary manager. He gives his cell phone number to tenants so they can contact him in case of emergency. At the time of my visit there was no backlog for repairs. The complex includes attractive landscaping and a first-floor community center. Good management at James Weldon Johnson Houses clearly made a difference.

As mentioned above, one federal instrument being used to repair and preserve public housing, the Rental Assistance Demonstration (RAD) program, converts publicly owned developments to Section 8 buildings in partnership with private investors. This is a good short-term solution for a few public housing developments, but it saps money from overall resources appropriated for Section 8 and tax credit deals. This is worrisome because the federal Section 8 budget, already inadequate, is threatened with new cuts. Other cities have used RAD effectively, and in 2017 New York is starting its first RAD building in Far Rockaway, Queens.

When good financing is available and competent people are in charge, public housing has worked well. I would like to see adequate federal funds designated specifically to repair and preserve government-owned public housing, at least in New York City. Even though the city's public housing gets bad reviews in the press, over the decades the New York City Housing Authority has played an important role.

There are currently plans to build new mixed-income housing on many of the parking lots and other plans to build commercial facilities there. These plans will take time to achieve but will have a positive effect on the image and economics of public housing in New York City.

According to Denise Muha, executive director of the National Leased Housing Association, "Most public housing authorities in medium and large cities have long waiting lists. I know of no housing authority in these markets with short waiting lists." Despite the critics, people need public housing.

Housing experts and the public in general can also learn from the way urban areas around the country have approached the challenge of developing affordable and sustainable housing, as I discovered in visiting several cities and consulting their housing leadership.

Troubles in Chicago

In 1943, a prosperous African American business leader named Robert R. Taylor was elected chairman of the Chicago Housing Authority. Although Taylor and his board favored a large commitment to racially integrated public housing, the city's politicians were hardly supportive. The members of Chicago's Board of Aldermen once took a bus tour and recommended locating sites for public housing in the communities represented by their political enemies. Chicago public housing became the poster child for crime in high-rise buildings, a sad distinction that lasted for decades.[6]

Cabrini–Green in Chicago was notorious, and in the nineties it was demolished to permit a new mixed-income community. I visited the site right before demolition and thought that some of the buildings didn't seem that bad. Perhaps they could have been renovated. However, the new buildings have worked out well.

I also visited Chicago's Robert Taylor Houses and was horrified. The windows were broken. There was debris all over. The storefronts were burned out. Gangs of young men were hanging out on the property. I didn't stay long. It is sad to remember that the buildings were named after an inspirational African American Chicagoan. Robert Taylor Houses has now been demolished to make room for new development.

Similarly, the descriptions of Henry Horner Homes in Alex Koltowitz's book *There Are No Children Here: The Story of Two Boys Growing Up in the Other America* provide a manual for how *not* to run public housing.[7] There were rotted doors stashed in the basement, reflecting a history of disrepair and danger. There was little or no security. Graffiti was left on the exterior and interior walls. The complex has been replaced by mixed-income housing.

Chicago's relationship with HUD has been thorny, involving an agency takeover of the Housing Authority to resolve a 1966 civil rights lawsuit, *Gautreaux et al. v. Chicago Housing Authority*. Although Chicago has some excellent new developments, and the worst problems have been addressed, the early public housing was hardly a success.

6. Edward Banfield and Martin Meyerson, *Politics, Planning and the Public Interest: The Case of Public Housing in Chicago* (New York: Free Press, 1955).

7. Alex Kotlowitz, *There Are No Children Here: The Story of Two Boys Growing Up in the Other America* (New York: Knopf Doubleday, 1992).

A Voice from Yonkers

Joseph Shuldiner is one of the most experienced professionals in the world of affordable housing. He was deputy commissioner of the New York City Department of Housing Preservation and Development and general manager of the city's Housing Authority. He then went to Chicago and dramatically improved troubled buildings there.

One of his greatest successes was in Los Angeles, where public housing was revitalized and reimagined under his watch. After the Watts riots in 1965, some ten thousand of the city's public housing apartments were destroyed. After the protests in 1991 following the brutal beating by the police of Rodney King, the total damage to public housing amounted to only $27,000. Shuldiner credits that to the fact that the residents respected their buildings, which were well maintained. Today there are few publicly owned units. The use of Section 8 vouchers is more prevalent. But still, Shuldiner did good work there.

After his success in Los Angeles, Shuldiner was recruited by the Clinton administration as an assistant secretary of HUD, serving between 1993 and 1995. He is now executive director of the Yonkers Housing Authority, which oversees 5,649 apartments, including 2,400 units in traditional public housing and 3,249 units of Section 8 housing in privately owned buildings.

The newer buildings are in reasonably good condition. The older buildings, which are forty to fifty years old, are, in Shuldiner's words, "okay, but they are a ticking time bomb." Systems need replacement, and no federal money is available to pay for the work. The physical needs assessment of the buildings showed that $160 million would be required for repairs of the worst units over the next decade, which comes to about $80,000 per apartment. HUD has committed capital funds amounting to only $3 million annually.

Shuldiner and his staff have been using every tool available through various HUD programs to keep the buildings intact. In 2016 the Yonkers Authority was poised to begin its first project with the RAD program.

The best thing about public housing in Yonkers is that the agency preserves sound housing and provides good service less expensively than would be possible by the private sector alone. The projected government subsidy for a RAD apartment is $550 a month, compared to $850 for a private-sector apartment using a Section 8 voucher. The worst problem is trying to cope with deteriorating public housing stock using totally inadequate federal support.

The buildings are safe. Security guards are stationed in the buildings designed for families. The authority pays for extra police protection. There have been no fatalities since 2010, despite gangs and other problems in the surrounding neighborhoods.

Shuldiner believes that it is important to keep public housing authorities intact, whether the buildings are publicly or privately owned. In some cases the private sector achieves cost savings by paying low wages, which he does not consider a good solution. He believes that housing authorities should assure that decent, safe housing is available for all local residents and that affordable housing should be located in viable neighborhoods. I reminded him that his vision matches the goals of the National Housing Act of 1949.

The Landscape in Seattle

Stephen Norman was assistant commissioner at the New York City Department of Housing Preservation and Development in the Koch and Dinkins administrations. In that role, he was the city official in charge of the development and construction of New Settlement Apartments between 1987 and 1990. He left city government to work for the Corporation for Supportive Housing, an organization that provides investments and technical assistance to groups creating housing for the homeless. He then moved to Seattle, where in 1997 he became executive director of the King County Housing Authority. In that role Norman oversees housing projects and initiatives in the regions surrounding Seattle, excluding the city itself.

The agency has an ownership role in about ten thousand apartments, including four thousand that receive federal assistance. The King County Housing Authority has used all programs in the public housing tool kit, among them Hope VI, a program that replaced some developments with mixed-income housing, and the Moving to Work program, which allows regulatory flexibility. The rules enabled the authority to pay higher rents for better areas. Some of the developments in King County were converted to project-based Section 8 assistance, some with Low-Income Housing Tax Credits.

The buildings are in good shape. Using the system under which HUD inspects projects and rates their physical condition, the average rating for the King County buildings was 97.5, the equivalent of an A plus. There is little crime.

Norman is especially pleased that many housing developments are located in what are known as "high-opportunity areas." Nearly a quarter of the young people receiving federal help live in communities where higher-income families live, and the neighborhoods are considered safe.

Although he has taken advantage of HUD's Moving to Work flexibility, Steve still works to improve the less fortunate communities. He is also acquiring buildings that are near the expanding light rail corridors, planning for the future.

The worst problem is that local rents are escalating dramatically, and federal assistance has not kept up. Support for Section 8 rents, for example, has not increased since 2012, even though costs keep going up.

There is also a large unmet need. Many low-income families pay up to half of their income for rent. Seniors on fixed incomes face severe difficulties. Families are forced to move out to peripheral areas, where there are fewer jobs and no mass transit. Homelessness is increasing. Local school districts reported that six thousand public school children were homeless in 2015, living in cars, on borrowed couches, or five-to-a room in motels. Additional problems involve the challenges of dealing with the thirty-nine jurisdictions comprising King County.

Norman has been able to use innovative programs to keep the Housing Authority buildings in good shape. The Moving to Work program has helped, although "it is not primarily about moving or work." It clears the way to pooling traditional public housing funds with Section 8 payments. This allows the authority to allocate the money to the buildings that need the most repairs. It is the equivalent of a block grant. Furthermore, the authority can leverage private equity and debt to finance repairs. The program, although renewed this year, was in doubt for a while. HUD was imposing unworkable requirements. Although the agencies that had Moving to Work designations were recently able to negotiate a new, favorable ten-year contract, the process was difficult. Senator Patty Murray has been a staunch supporter.

The King County Authority has been successful in acquiring Class B apartment buildings and upgrading them to qualify for federal assistance and/or Low-Income Housing Tax Credit, bond-financed developments.

Norman believes that public ownership is important to assure long-term affordability. He doesn't recommend reviving traditional public housing, because the financing depends on annual congressional appropriations. (This was not the case before the Budget Act of 1974.) He does, however, advocate mixed-income developments and a less intrusive regulatory environment. He believes in a business model combined with a community service mission.

Public Housing in Cambridge, Massachusetts

The Cambridge Housing Authority oversees a portfolio of some 2,500 apartments. In addition, about a thousand Section 8 vouchers are used in privately owned buildings. All the public housing buildings have either been upgraded or have contracts for upgrading through HUD'S RAD program. The buildings will be controlled by nonprofit organizations that are affiliates of the authority. The Cambridge Housing Authority also controls the buildings by owning the land through ground leases. The affiliates are general partners in partnerships that benefit from the federal Low-Income Housing Tax Credit program. Most have project-based Section 8 contracts. The Cambridge Housing Authority benefits as well from HUD's Moving to Work program.

None of the buildings are distressed; some are just old. All the buildings needed repairs. For many, the cost was moderate, $50,000 to 60,000 per apartment. One building had to be replaced, and the cost was $500,000 per apartment, making a strong case for the repair of older buildings. New construction required infrastructure, new streets, and more. The authority is required by law to bid the projects competitively, which can be costly and time-consuming.

Greg Russ, the housing authority's executive director, is proud of his board and staff. He has enjoyed his work for other authorities, but he finds that his team in Cambridge is exceptional. "They have a great ethic" and are very competent. Working at the Cambridge Housing Authority has been one of the best experiences in his long career. His admiration for his staff was palpable.

His worst problem, he said, involves dealing with Washington, D.C., which he describes as "regulatory torture." Obtaining the renewal of the Moving to Work contract was an example of an effort that took far too long to achieve.

Of course, renovating buildings with tenants in occupancy is difficult by its nature, especially in buildings occupied by the elderly. Relocation is usually required, which is expensive and difficult. But the results have been worth the trouble.

The buildings are generally safe. The Cambridge Housing Authority works closely and cooperatively with the police. A former member of the local police department is a staff member at the authority. Compared to other areas, Cambridge has little crime. There are few gangs, although from time to time Greg worries about young "wannabe" gangsters. Security cameras can be found in most of the buildings.

In some senior buildings, federal legislation requires that younger disabled individuals be admitted as tenants, and that does not always produce the best socioeconomic mix. Massachusetts law permits limiting such occupancy to 13.5 percent of the units in a senior building.

Greg believes that public housing authorities should have a role in controlling affordable housing, involving the private sector as needed. He is concerned about the transaction costs for the Low-Income Housing Tax Credit program. He explained that it would be better to establish a fund of credits at the U.S. Treasury Department. The credits would be available as of right to investors certified by a local agency. Transaction costs would be a fraction of what they are now. Greg would also take housing program administration from HUD and give it over to localities. Regional variations are so significant that central administration becomes practically impossible. HUD would retain fund allocation and equal opportunity law enforcement.

Public housing is the only affordable housing in Cambridge, where efficiency apartments now rent for $3,000 a month. Even though the city of Cambridge and the state of Massachusetts provide funding, the need for more federal money cannot be overstated.

Federal Cutbacks from 1995 to Today: What to Do

On the cover of the October 20, 1996, issue of the *New York Times Magazine*, there was a huge picture of a house. The headline read, "The Year That Housing Died." The article inside, titled "Slamming the Door," was written by Jason DeParle, one of the leading writers on social issues. He lamented the fact that President Clinton's budget for 1997 included no new money for Section 8 vouchers, compared to other years when money for four hundred thousand new vouchers had been appropriated. Even President Reagan had included forty thousand new vouchers in his last budget.

DeParle outlined the gap between the cost of market-rate housing and what people could afford, using dramatic examples from Charlotte, North Carolina. Although new funds were provided in the last years of Clinton's second term, there was never enough money to meet more than a small portion of the need.

Fast-forward to the present, and everything is worse. The 2013 budget "sequester" meant that over one hundred thousand families were actually stripped of their Section 8 housing at a time when rents were spiraling. The "sequester" was the response of Congress to balancing the budget at a time when the administration and Congress were at loggerheads. The number of tenants who lost their assistance for 2014 was projected at one hundred thousand. The initial Trump administration budget is even worse.

The Section 8 program enacted by the Nixon administration in 1974 and implemented under President Ford came close to having all the qualities that would result in the creation of effective buildings. Large and very low-income families paid only 15 percent of income for rent. The program was beneficial for tenants, owners, bankers, and the government. Led by Secretary Carla Hills, HUD made commitments for over 450,000 new apartments in 1976.[8]

In subsequent years, the Section 8 program would be criticized for its supposed great expense. But the critique was not accurate. Most effective housing programs cost the same amount, because they involve bridging the gap between operating and finance costs, on the one hand, and what lower-income residents can afford to pay, on the other. Some programs seem less expensive because costs are beautifully obfuscated. The fact that so many Section 8 properties have increased in value over the decades is a testament to the effectiveness of the program, although it is also presents a problem. In New York City, it costs much more to build and operate housing than anyone other than the super-wealthy can afford. The basic components of rent are the costs associated with mortgage financing plus utilities, taxes, staff, insurance, audits, legal fees, and management. Government aid programs can subsidize one or more aspects of these costs so that rents can be reduced accordingly.

If I were in charge of providing affordable housing for the nation, I would start by quadrupling the federal Section 8 budget. Today only one out of every five eligible families receives government housing assistance of any kind.[9] Everyone in need of affordable housing should be able to get a federal rental assistance voucher. The tenant would not pay 30 percent of income for rent, but rather 15–25 percent, with the balance of the rent paid by the federal government. As a result, families would have more funds for food, education, medical costs, and other expenses. In many cases, they would pay their rent more promptly, saving the owners the costs of eviction. The rent-to-income ratio for New Settlement Apartments ranged from 20 to 30 percent, and the formula worked well. It will

8. Erika C. Poethig, "Urban Wire," *Urban Institute*, May 28, 2014.
9. Ben Austen, "After the Towers," *N.Y. Times Magazine*, February 11, 2018.

change soon, after refinancing with programs that require that rent equals 30 percent of a resident's income. Given the choice, I would calculate rent based on after-tax income, providing an incentive for people to earn more money, thereby rewarding the taxpayer. When I mentioned this to a city official right after the fiscal crisis, he said, "What a great stimulus that would be for the economy."

The Lindsay Years and Section 8

The first time I heard a proposal of this sort was in 1972 from mayor John Lindsay's housing czar, Albert A. Walsh. He was a Rockefeller Republican and had worked in state government, private practice, and as the head of several city housing agencies. He was the chairman of the housing authority when New York's public housing buildings were thought to be the best in the country, maybe the world.

Walsh called for a "single, variable subsidy" to cover the difference between the rent a person would pay with 25 percent of his or her income and the rent needed to cover the cost of operating and paying debt service on a building. Everyone who could not afford market-rate housing would be eligible. Some families would receive five dollars a month, and others $1,000. He did not think that localities could afford this kind of subsidy, but he believed that the federal government was obliged to assure that all Americans could live in a decent home in a suitable neighborhood. He thought that including a large range of beneficiaries would generate political support. Mayor Lindsay testified in favor of this program before the House Banking and Housing Committee (later renamed the Financial Services Committee) of the House of Representatives in 1972.

The Section 8 program established by the Nixon administration in 1974 resembled Walsh's idea. However, although exceptions were possible, in general no one earning more than 80 percent of area median income was eligible. Section 8 vouchers can still be used in private housing. Until 1983, Section 8 contracts could be pledged to finance new or substantially rehabilitated buildings. Hundreds of thousands of apartments a year were built, and a few million families still receive aid through this program.

However, amendments over the years reduced (in fact, they practically eliminated) the amount of new Section 8 assistance and limited eligibility to very low-income families and individuals. The Reagan administration made dramatic changes between 1981 and 1983. New construction and substantial rehabilitation could no longer be financed through pledges of Section 8 contracts. Income limits were lowered from 80 to 50 percent of area median. Instead of paying 15 to 25 percent of income for rent, families had to pay 30 percent.

I believe that the Section 8 program should be revised and funded with significant new appropriations. Income limits should be set locally. That was the practice for public housing before the Brooke Amendment to the Housing Act of 1969, which established operating subsidies so that tenants would not have to pay more than 25 percent of income for rent. This, too, went to 30 percent under Reagan.

In addition to creating mixed-income developments, I wish it were easier to achieve ethnic diversity. One way to do that would be to revisit the Starrett City case, examining the potential of explicitly creating diverse housing. This would be a great undertaking for the pro bono department of a law firm.

Settlement Housing Fund had sponsored three early Section 8 developments in which the income limits were adjusted to allow a mixed-income population. The National Housing Act of 1968 and the Housing and Community Development Act of 1974 allowed the secretary of HUD to make exceptions to income limits in high-cost areas and/or very low-income neighborhoods. After a lot of effort and persuasion, we were able to take advantage of that part of the statute in several buildings in the Two Bridges area.

As consultants for Manhattan Plaza on West 42nd Street, which provides housing primarily for performing artists, we obtained a viable Section 8 income mix, reflecting the needs of the artists and the community. Forty years later, this development and the projects at Two Bridges and the Bronx are all beautifully maintained. Because there were adequate development and maintenance budgets, the buildings lasted. The original investment was a good one. Unfortunately, Settlement Housing Fund did not retain ownership of some buildings, and these have been sold for enormous profits. In a way, it is a compliment to the program that the big worry is conversion to luxury use. But compliment or not, it's a problem.

More about What to Do Now—and What Not to Do

Housing should become an entitlement. Everyone who cannot afford market-rate housing should qualify for aid. In May 2017, the average rent in New York City for a two-bedroom apartment was $3,100, according to RentJungle.com. A family would need an income of $124,000 a year to afford that rent while paying no more than 30 percent of their income. If we want to create mixed-income neighborhoods, rent subsidies should be available for everyone who cannot afford the HUD Fair Market Rent for an appropriately sized apartment. Middle-income families could justifiably resent housing assistance for their low-income neighbors while they are stuck in overcrowded, substandard units. Furthermore, we do not want to drive middle-income groups out of urban areas. Politically, a larger constituency for housing assistance would result if a broader band of the population benefited.

Housing as an entitlement seems to be catching on. Matthew Desmond of Harvard University, in his best seller *Evicted: Poverty and Profit in the American City*,[10] as well as the Bipartisan Policy Committee, both recommended that Section 8 become an entitlement for extremely low-income tenants.[11] In *$2.00 a Day: Living on Almost Nothing in America*, Kathryn J. Edin and Luke Shaefer emphasize the benefits of Section 8 for families barely able to survive.[12]

Very recently, James Stockard, former curator of Harvard's Loeb Fellowship Program, said, "It's time to ensure that no American has to worry about where they and their families will sleep tonight. . . . The U.S. needs to declare a basic right to affordable housing, and then deliver it to the people." He quotes a study finding that "$10,000 in public funding covers ten-plus months of permanent affordable housing—but only six-plus months in a shelter or one week in a hospital." He cites Scotland as a country where everyone assumes that housing is a civic responsibility.[13]

Many advocates recommended limiting assistance to extremely low-income families. I understand where they are coming from. The expectation is that there will be almost no resources available in the years to come. The idea is to take care of all the families at the lowest income levels.

Still and all, who is to say that the lower-income family's needs are more serious than those of a two-parent working family who cannot find an affordable apartment? Doesn't it send the wrong message to deny housing to moderate-income families? Many earn a lot more than the proposed income limits but cannot come close to affording market-rate housing. A curve is better than a cliff. And there are many advantages to

10. Ibid.

11. Bipartisan Policy Center, "Housing America's Future: New Directions for National Policy," February 2013.

12. Kathryn J. Edin and Luke Shaefer, *$2.00 a Day: Living on Almost Nothing in America* (Boston: Houghton Mifflin Harcourt, 2015).

13. James Stockard, "Opinion: Why Affordable Housing Needs to Be a Right, Not a Privilege," *TED Ideas*, May 19, 2017, https://ideas.ted.com/opinion-why-affordable -housing-needs-to-be-a-right-not-a-privilege/.

creating mixed-income communities like New Settlement Apartments and the Two Bridges projects.

Federal rental assistance should be available to help house the homeless, the elderly, mobility-impaired, low-, moderate-, and middle-income families and individuals. Rental assistance payments should be funded either directly or through federal tax refunds. I prefer the direct route, which is easier to understand. Most of these recommendations could be accomplished with a few revisions to Section 8 of the Housing Act of 1937 and the Community Development Block Grant program, both enacted in 1974.

State and local programs should expand and augment federal programs. In my tweaked Section 8 program, the federal government, as it does now, would establish "fair-market rents" for modest housing that would meet standards acceptable to localities. The housing owner would check incomes at initial occupancy only. Fair-market rents and assistance payments would increase automatically to reflect cost indexes in the locality. Owners could raise their rents accordingly, but the tenants would still pay a percentage of their income for rent. The rents would be budget-based, reflecting true operating costs, not the fictional "market."

Some housing aficionados might be shocked that I think rent should range between 15 and 30 percent of income. After all, many people without assistance pay 50 percent of income for rent. The Reagan administration implemented raising tenant contributions to 30 percent of their income. What's more, the Trump administration is suggesting 35 percent. In fact, having tenants pay such a huge percentage of income for rent makes daily living a struggle. Although 30 percent has been the recent norm, traditional New York State and City programs established income limits at 14 to 17 percent of income, depending on family size.

The Low-Income Housing Tax Credit

Much as I think that strong nonprofit organizations play a vital role in housing and community building, I still think that private-sector involvement and public housing are essential. The Low-Income Housing Tax Credit program, enacted in 1986, is an effective production tool providing significant equity, which reduces initial costs for government. The income limits are set at 60 percent of the area's median income. Rents are set at 30 percent of 60 percent of median income for the metropolitan area. (For example, if the median income was $80,000 for a family of four, rent would be $1,200 a month—30 percent of 60 percent.) Without Section 8, it is impossible to use the program for very low-income families. The program also excludes moderate- to middle-income tenants who are priced out of the market. Sometimes a building stays empty for months because it is hard to find a tenant within the narrow range of acceptable incomes. The New York Housing Conference and other organizations are recommending an amendment that would allow income averaging. The average income for a development would be 60 percent of median for the area. The amendment would certainly improve the socioeconomic mix for tax credit developments, and would make marketing easier.

I would also change the law so that income is checked only at initial occupancy, rather than recertifying every year. Recertification is expensive and a nuisance for the owner. The tenants hate it. Since the tenants remain in the building even if their incomes go up, recertification seems like a waste of time and money.

The tax credit program provides development fees for both for-profit developers and nonprofit development organizations. The developers form subsidiary or affiliated corporations that act as general partners with investors, known as limited partners. The investors get tax breaks, which have fluctuated in value over the years. Although the tensions can be significant, the investors and developers watch each other, often to the benefit of the housing.

I do not think the tax credit program will go away. There are too many organizations, lawyers, and accountants who lobby effectively to keep the program alive. Furthermore, government agencies like the program because it "leverages" other sources of funds. Multiple sources of financing are required for each project. Everyone "leverages" everybody else. And the private equity reduces the amount of direct government subsidy, if one excludes the tax revenue lost.

As corporate and other taxes go down, the credit will be much less valuable. At the time of this writing, banks are still investing, but the market is uncertain. However, alternative programs should be available, especially for nonprofit organizations. The suggestion by Greg Russ from Cambridge for an as-of-right tax credit fund at the U.S. Department of Treasury is an interesting idea for a substitute program. It would preclude the need for complicated applications and reviews and would be available for many more developers.

Nonprofit Models

Nonprofit organizations that provide permanently affordable housing should be able to obtain 100 percent financing to build or renovate developments. Operating subsidies should be available to bridge the difference between the cost of maintenance and what tenants can afford. All levels of government should value these organizations. Reasonable development fees should be available to sustain the missions of these groups, and they should be able to use cash flow from rents to cover community programs and administrative costs.

Sections 202 and 811

Section 202 of the Housing Act of 1959 allows 100 percent financing for housing for the elderly, and Section 811 provides similar financing for people with disabilities. Until recently, HUD provided loans and then grants to cover construction costs and fees, along with money to help the sponsor make ends meet in the first months of operation.

Tenants pay 30 percent of income for rent. HUD provides rental assistance payments to cover all the operating costs in excess of rents.

Both programs are still on the books, but there is no money for new buildings for the elderly. Existing projects can be upgraded, using loans or bonds, combined with tax credit investments. Buildings can be converted to assisted-living communities. This is important because many original tenants moved to these buildings when they were younger and remained until their eighties or nineties. They don't need to be in nursing homes, but they do need additional care.

Because so many people are living longer, the need to revive Section 202 is especially urgent. New environmental requirements and the high cost of land and construction had stalled development in recent years. The Section 202 and 811 programs need to be modernized and revived with significant new funding. Visiting a twenty-year-old 202 project is an uplifting, even inspiring experience, nothing like the sad feeling that comes from visiting many nursing homes.

Inclusionary Zoning

Many cities around the world require luxury developers to set aside apartments or provide funds for affordable housing. Some cities require the apartments to be included in the luxury buildings themselves. Others allow off-site developments to qualify for zoning bonuses or other incentives. There are many variations on the theme.

My own feeling is to let a thousand flowers bloom, as long as high-quality affordable housing is the result. In Malaysia, for example, luxury developers who build one thousand market-rate apartments are required to create new affordable buildings comprising three hundred apartments. This can be on the same site or elsewhere in the same city. In Kuala Lumpur in 2013 and in Penang in 2010 the building business was booming, and a lot of affordable housing was created using this method.

Zoning bonuses can be an effective way to bring resources to the table, especially in cycles in which market-rate development is profitable. Although inclusionary zoning should not be considered a panacea or a substitute for government support, it should be one of the tools available to create affordable housing.

Repairs and Upgrades

Buildings need constant maintenance, repair, and capital improvements. Often this cannot be accomplished by using rental income or reserves. New York City's 8A program provides low-interest loans for capital repairs. The program, though difficult to use, is a valuable resource.

The city also has provided funds over the years for rehabilitation with tenants in occupancy. Sometimes relocation is required, a difficult undertaking. The Community Preservation Corporation, a nonprofit bank, has financed the preservation of hundreds of thousands of apartments since its inception in 1974, often in conjunction with the city's participation loan program. This is a program that combines 1 percent city loans with commercial bank loans. It is a valuable program, especially for private developers.

Felice Michetti agrees with this approach. Because funds are scarce, she says, "it is important to make every dollar count." She demonstrated this back in 1979, when she was in charge of a neighborhood preservation initiative in the West Tremont section of the Bronx. People were predicting that this neighborhood would be the next place for fires and abandonment. Although some buildings were in terrible condition, no one was lending money to local property owners.

Michetti used her modest budget to blitz the neighborhood with information about city loans for boilers and new windows, specifically white-framed windows because they were more noticeable. Mass mailings were sent to owners, and flyers describing the program were distributed to local stores and community groups. Suddenly there were thirty buildings featuring white windows. They were conspicuous, and people started to ask about living in those developments. Then the banks came back, and the neighborhood remained intact. Good windows are also a great way to save on energy costs. Repairs saved the day for West Tremont.

Replicating New Settlement Apartments

The reason I wanted to write this book was to help people understand the exhilaration and the challenges faced by those who provide affordable housing. I thought it was important to discuss the sites in the Two Bridges urban renewal area and, even more important, to recommend replicating projects like New Settlement Apartments. Starting in 1990, by providing affordable housing to a deeply troubled area of New York City, it became possible to transform a large neighborhood. I believe that New Settlement Apartments could be a model for redeveloping other neighborhoods that have been neglected or suffered from disinvestment. And although the model must vary according to the needs of the locality, many features of the New Settlement example should be retained.

First, the development should be owned by a nonprofit organization committed to permanent affordability. The Housing Partnership Network, of which Settlement Housing Fund is a member, comprises seventy-five citywide or regional housing organizations from all over the United States. All have strong records of achievements. The founder, an energetic nonagenarian named Robert Whittlesey, describes the organization in his book *Social Housing Found*.[14] The groups are characterized by scale, professionalism, and a businesslike approach to development and ownership. They are all driven by a strong sense of mission—so much so that when I visited housing developed by some of the network's groups, I became uncharacteristically humble.

Second, a mixed-income population offers many advantages. At New Settlement, the mix was 30 percent formerly homeless, 40 percent low income, 20–25 percent moderate income, and 5–10 percent at the local market level. The mix could be adjusted for different neighborhoods. At New Settlement Apartments, now home to 1,082 families, the mix has worked well, especially because the formerly homeless families benefited from Section 8 subsidies.

Third, and perhaps most important, the nonprofit owner should be able to fund community programs as a line item in the rental operating budget.

14. Robert B. Whittlesey *Social Housing Found* (Bloomington, Ind.: Author-House, 2015).

Most government housing agencies don't allow this, but they should. From the beginning, New Settlement was able to set aside $578,000 a year for programs. The money was used to attract additional philanthropic and government support, resulting in award-winning programs and a transformation of the entire neighborhood. Thousands of young people enrolled in after-school programs, art programs, and community service programs, and thousands have gone to college using the resources offered by New Settlement's College Access Center.

Finally, the favorable financing for New Settlement Apartments should be replicated. There were no taxes and no debt service. The land was nearly free.

The cost of renovation was paid through a bond, repaid with revenue from Battery Park City. New Settlement Apartments had no repayment obligations. Without this financing, we wouldn't have been able to sustain these buildings as high-quality housing for over a quarter century. Today, Battery Park City has enough money to finance new affordable housing. It should do so.

A serious effort is underway to rescue Detroit, one of the most troubled cities in the nation. Perhaps some of the profits from the 2010 federal bailout of the auto companies could be siphoned off to develop a large-scale, mixed-income apartment complex with neighborhood amenities and community programs. When there is political will, creative people can often find new and innovative sources of financing.

As Maria Martinez, one of the original residents of New Settlement Apartments, said, "Can you imagine if there were developments like New Settlement Apartments all over New York? Everything would be so much better."

As for me, I wish we lived in a society in which everyone had a decent home, enough food, and health care, and young people had a right to a good education. With that basic start, it would be up to every individual to make the most of life. The jobs generated might even make up for the extra tax burden, as would indirect benefits like fewer jails and less illness.

I realize that we live in a political climate that is very different from the one in which the Two Bridges urban renewal area and New Settlement Apartments were built. The legislative landscape has been profoundly transformed, and few of the programs that created those two developments remain on the books.

Nevertheless, the need for clean, safe, attractive, and affordable housing is greater than ever, especially in a time of growing need and greater income disparity between the rich and the poor. Making affordable housing a reality is harder than ever. It requires enormous persistence, group efforts, and creative coalition building. It is also harder than ever to keep faith. But now more than ever, such efforts are needed.

I realize also that we live in a society that is deeply polarized and that widespread commitment to a progressive agenda is largely absent. Despite these formidable roadblocks, I ask myself why achieving such goals should be impossible.

Appendix
List of Federal, State, and Local Programs

Federal Housing Programs

Federal Housing Insurance: In 1934, during the Roosevelt administration, the height of the Great Depression, and the early days of the New Deal, the federal government established the Federal Housing Administration (FHA), which insures single- and multifamily mortgages. The 1934 law has been amended over the decades for specific purposes. The FHA Section 220 program insures multifamily buildings in urban renewal areas like Two Bridges in Lower Manhattan. The FHA Section 223(f) program insures refinancing of existing debt and was also used for a site in the Two Bridges area.

> **Public Housing:** Enacted in 1937 during Roosevelt's second term, the act permitted bonds backed by the federal government to be used to construct housing for low-income families that will be owned and managed by local authorities. Private entities were eligible to build apartment complexes and then turn over ownership to local authorities, using the method know as public housing turnkey developments.
>
> **Urban Renewal:** A program passed in 1954 under President Eisenhower as an amendment to the Housing Act of 1949, which had set a goal of providing a decent home for every American family. The 1949 act had referred to "slum clearance." The 1954 act originated the term "urban renewal," which could include both new construction and rehabilitation of existing buildings. Under this legislation, federal grants allowed the cost of buying land to

be subsidized, with the ultimate goal of eliminating slums and allowing development of various types of buildings, including but not limited to affordable housing. The federal government paid two-thirds of the cost of writing down the land, and in New York, the state and the local government each paid one-sixth. The program was eliminated in 1974 under President Nixon, and replaced by Community Development Block Grants to states and localities, based on need and an effort to assure that money went to wide array of communities around the country.

Section 202: This program was enacted in 1959 to provide low-interest loans to build housing for the elderly. In 1974 the program added operating subsidies and the loans carried higher interest rates. The program was amended in later years to provide grants instead of loans and then to allow refinancing of older projects.

Sections 235 and 236: The National Housing Act of 1968, passed during the Johnson administration as part of the president's War on Poverty, established the most ambitious housing goals in the nation's history. New programs included Section 235 interest-rate subsidies, resulting in 1 percent loans for home ownership, and Section 236 with 1 percent loans for rental housing plus deep subsidies for up to 40 percent of the apartments in a rental building.

Federal Tax-Deduction Programs: Through the efforts of senator Robert F. Kennedy before his death in 1968, the 1969 Tax Reform Act, included substantial automatic tax deductions for investors who provided money for new construction or substantial rehabilitation of buildings occupied by low- and moderate-income residents.

Section 8: Section 8 of the National Housing and Community Development Act of 1974 replaced most of the earlier housing programs. It provided money to owners of existing buildings and developers of new and substantially rehabilitated buildings to help cover the rent of eligible tenants. The Section 8 program stimulated the construction of one million low-income apartments that as of 2016 continue to receive these subsidies. More than two million families and individuals used Section 8 to find apartments in existing housing.

Low-Income Housing Tax Credit Program: As part of the Tax Reform Act of 1986, passed under President Reagan, tax deductions were replaced by a new system of Low-Income Housing Tax Credits. The most generous are awarded by states to developers selected competitively. Others are granted automatically to developers who use tax-exempt bond financing for their projects. In 2017, this is the federal government's only significant surviving housing program for new construction, rehabilitation, or preservation.

New Markets Tax Credits: The New Markets Tax Credit program was created in 2000 under President Clinton to provide tax incentives to lenders and investors who provide money for commercial and community projects in low-income areas. Allocations are given to intermediary groups that choose projects and work with all the parties involved. Many steps are involved, and the process is complicated.

New York State Housing Programs

Mitchell-Lama: Named for state senator MacNeil Mitchell and assemblyman Alfred Lama, this program, created in 1955 under governor W. Averell Harriman, provided tax exemption and long-term financing for middle-income apartments, pursuant to Article II of the Private Housing Finance Law. In some developments, federal subsidies like Section 8 and Section 236 were combined with Mitchell-Lama financing.

SONYMA (pronounced sunny-MAY): Under this program, the State of New York Mortgage Association, established in 1970, provides mortgage insurance for single-family homes and affordable multifamily housing.

New York State Enhanced Turnkey Program: This program, created through Article XVIII of the Private Housing Finance Law in 1989 under governor Mario Cuomo, provided permanent loans or grants for rental housing in which 30 percent of the apartments were reserved for formerly homeless families. The money came from a onetime state budget surplus. It was used for 35 Marcy Place, one of the New Settlement Apartments buildings added in 1993.

Member Items: Funds allocated to members of the state legislature to use for eligible local purposes.

New York City Programs

HD-9: In the 1970s New York City provided money in its budget to supplement money provided by the federal government for public housing and other kinds of affordable developments. Without HD-9, many developments in New York City would have been impossible to use. Federal cost limits were based on national averages, and therefore much too low to work in high-cost areas like New York City.

Urban Renewal: The city paid one-sixth of the grants needed to write down the cost of site acquisition.

Tax Exemption: For every affordable development, New York City real estate tax exemption is necessary to keep rents at levels that low- and moderate-income families can afford. Article XI of the Private Housing Finance Law provides tax exemption for up to forty years for projects in which a nonprofit organization is involved. In these cases exemption from sales and other taxes is also granted. For New Settlement Apartments in the Bronx, the J-51 program, available for rehabilitation of existing buildings, was used to provide tax abatement and tax exemption.

Article XII and XVI Bonds and Loans: Through Articles XII of the Private Housing Finance Law, the New York City Housing Development Corporation, the city's housing finance agency, issues bonds to finance affordable developments or provides mortgages using its own money. Federal and state money and equity from investors with tax credit allocations provide additional funds so that rents at these developments are affordable for specific income groups. The New York City Department of Housing Preservation and Development can also make loans pursuant to Section XVI, as it did for a "soft" second mortgage for Two Bridges Tower.

Bonds Repaid from Battery Park City Revenues: In 1986, thanks to the efforts of mayor Ed Koch and governor Mario Cuomo, the New York State Legislature authorized the New York City Housing Development Corporation to form a subsidiary, the Housing New York Corporation, that could enter into agreements with the Battery Park City Authority. The first agreement allowed the subsidiary to issue bonds, with the entire repayment coming from Battery Park revenues that weren't otherwise committed. The agreement allowed assisted developments to proceed without having responsibility for repaying debts. The renovation cost of New Settlement Apartments was financed through this program.

Resolution (Reso) A: Capital funding from allocation to borough presidents and City Council members as part of the annual city budget.

Acknowledgments

I am grateful to almost everyone I know, including one good friend, a former journalist who said, "Why would anyone want to read a book like this?"

My partner, Don Pfaff, who has written or edited over thirty scientific books, not only encouraged me, but greeted me every night by asking, "Well, did you write anything today?" My closest friend, Fredi Friedman, a literary icon, read part of the first draft and egged me on with love and support. My stepson, the writer Tom Barbash, helped me at all stages, and his sister, Ilisa Barbash, an academia author, also encouraged the work. My daughter, Donna Lee Lamberg-Bernstein, was very helpful. She hated the original title, *Hardly a Failure*, and saved my life with technical support again and again. When I told her brother Andy Bernstein, an international lawyer, that housing required money and smart people in charge, he said, "That's true about everything."

My colleagues at Settlement Housing Fund put up with me as I invaded the files and asked for technical support. Alexa Sewell, Kathy McAulay, Nicole Clare, Sheila Carpenter, Kofi Appram, Crystal Tatum, Kenyatta Turner, Valerie Mayo, Jack Doyle, and Megan Nolan were and remain the greatest.

My former work partner, Susan Cole, commented and responded when I needed good advice. Sarah Kolodny reminded me of experience during tenant selection at New Settlement Apartments.

Several professors at different universities read part or all of the manuscript, added valuable comments, and invited me to speak to students;

some even visited the sites. Thank you, Susan Fine, Nicholas Bloom, Alex Schwartz, Ingrid Ellen, Mark Willis, Todd Swanstrom.

Shirley Bresler, Mary McCormick, Lorin Silverman, Jeanne Dupont, Xenia Cox, Anne Lindgren, Victor Papa, Kerri Culhane, Elisa Espiritu, and Molly Garfinkel read a chapter or two and provided advice, even encouragement. Steve Swartz gave helpful advice at the start.

Constance Rosenblum, an author and experienced former *New York Times* Metro editor, was the star developmental editor. She was a great collaborator, helping to slash anything that seemed irrelevant, redundant, or awkward. I have the highest regard for Fred Nachbaur, director of Fordham University Press. He was encouraging, responsive, smart, and a great coach. How lucky I was to work with Connie and Fred. I appreciate Will Cerbone and Eric Newman as well. Nicholas Taylor was the conscientious copyeditor whose comments were insightful and meticulous.

Arin Gilbert was thankfully available for technical assistance.

Finally, thanks to everyone I interviewed. So many colleagues, tenants, and professionals gave their time so generously. My interviewees from the world of politics included the late Hon. Edward I. Koch and Hon. Richard Ravitch.

Among the Bronx tenants and neighbors were Cynthia Cummings, Maria Martinez, Emma Nunoz and her mother, Ramon Cepeda, Pedro Morales, Nancy Vandross, Emma, Jane Terry, Dana Smalls, Juana Diaz, Sheila Hines, Maggy Torres-Morales, and Adjoa Julie Abdul.

The Two Bridges tenants and former tenants I interviewed included Norman Lee, Aaron Gonzalez, Daisy Echevarria, Sheila Hart, Tanya Castro, Debbie Leung, Tamar Lopez, Trever Holland, and Helen Ong.

From the Two Bridges Neighborhood Council I interviewed Victor Papa, Kerri Culhane, Elisa Espititu, Wilson Soo, Francine Gorres, and July Yang.

Among the management experts I interviewed were former commissioner Felice Michetti, Natalie Weinthal, Ellener Tuitt, Barbara Cooper, Jamilah Colvert, Beverly Williams, Ana Lam, and Caesar Qing.

I also thank the Two Bridges developers I interviewed: Harold Grabino, Mike Melnick, Michael Rosenberg, Ron Moelis, Eben Ellerston, and Peter Gray.

Lastly, I thank the housing leaders interviewed for this book, among them Charles Edson, Frances Levenson, Denise Muha, Joseph Shuldiner, Stephen Norman, and Gregory Russ.

Index

ESE SELECT TITLES FROM EMPIRE STATE EDITIONS

Allen Jones with Mark Naison, *The Rat That Got Away: A Bronx Memoir*

Edward Rohs and Judith Estrine, *Raised by the Church: Growing up in New York City's Catholic Orphanages*

Janet Grossbach Mayer, *As Bad as They Say? Three Decades of Teaching in the Bronx*

William Seraile, *Angels of Mercy: White Women and the History of New York's Colored Orphan Asylum*

Andrew J. Sparberg, *From a Nickel to a Token: The Journey from Board of Transportation to MTA*

Gerard R. Wolfe, *The Synagogues of New York's Lower East Side: A Retrospective and Contemporary View, Second Edition.* Photographs by Jo Renée Fine and Norman Borden, Foreword by Joseph Berger

Howard Eugene Johnson with Wendy Johnson, *A Dancer in the Revolution: Stretch Johnson, Harlem Communist at the Cotton Club.* Foreword by Mark D. Naison

Joseph B. Raskin, *The Routes Not Taken: A Trip Through New York City's Unbuilt Subway System*

Phillip Deery, *Red Apple: Communism and McCarthyism in Cold War New York*

North Brother Island: The Last Unknown Place in New York City. Photographs by Christopher Payne, A History by Randall Mason, Essay by Robert Sullivan

Stephen Miller, *Walking New York: Reflections of American Writers from Walt Whitman to Teju Cole*

Tom Glynn, *Reading Publics: New York City's Public Libraries, 1754–1911*

Greg Donaldson, *The Ville: Cops and Kids in Urban America, Updated Edition.* With a new epilogue by the author, Foreword by Mark D. Naison

David Borkowski, *A Shot Story: From Juvie to Ph.D.*

R. Scott Hanson, *City of Gods: Religious Freedom, Immigration, and Pluralism in Flushing, Queens.* Foreword by Martin E. Marty

Dorothy Day and the Catholic Worker: The Miracle of Our Continuance. Edited, with an Introduction and Additional Text by Kate Hennessy, Photographs by Vivian Cherry, Text by Dorothy Day

Pamela Lewis, *Teaching While Black: A New Voice on Race and Education in New York City*

Mark Naison and Bob Gumbs, *Before the Fires: An Oral History of African American Life in the Bronx from the 1930s to the 1960s*

Robert Weldon Whalen, *Murder, Inc., and the Moral Life: Gangsters and Gangbusters in La Guardia's New York*

Joanne Witty and Henrik Krogius, *Brooklyn Bridge Park: A Dying Waterfront Transformed*

Sharon Egretta Sutton, *When Ivory Towers Were Black: A Story about Race in America's Cities and Universities*

Pamela Hanlon, *A Wordly Affair: New York, the United Nations, and the Story Behind Their Unlikely Bond*

Britt Haas, *Fighting Authoritarianism: American Youth Activism in the 1930s*

David J. Goodwin, *Left Bank of the Hudson: Jersey City and the Artists of 111 1st Street*. Foreword by DW Gibson

Nandini Bagchee, *Counter Institution: Activist Estates of the Lower East Side*

For a complete list, visit www.empirestateeditions.com.